Advance comments on
APOLOGIA:

"This is by any standard a very important book for all concerned with theological education and for all concerned with the articulation of the Gospel for our time. It is a powerful plea for a normative, as distinct from merely descriptive, approach to theological teaching."
— LESSLIE NEWBIGIN

"By reposing and exploring foundational issues, Apologia *provides a helpful stimulus for discussion and useful guide for consideration of reform in theological education."*
— JOHN H. WESTERHOFF III

"This is not only a helpful and interesting book, it is a study that is urgently needed. It speaks with sensitivity and integrity to matters that are crucial to the health of theology and theological education."
— RICHARD J. MOUW

"This is a pioneering dialogue about questions of international dimensions in theological education. Our North American churches urgently need to enter into this dialogue for the sake of effective ministry in post-modern global context."
— GERALD H. ANDERSON

"An apologia *calls for judgment. In this book Professor Stackhouse has passed a negative judgment on much of what passes for seminary education and ideology today. . . . This book demands an answer both from those who would find ways to implement its basic convictions and from those whose views of theological education are being rejected."*
— PHEME PERKINS

"Amid the welter of books recently published about seminary education, this book has the great virtue of reminding us that no discussion of theological education can avoid the question of the truth of Christian doctrine about such matters as sin and salvation, the authority of scripture, the Trinity, and christology. The book has the added virtue of placing this issue within our growing awareness that Christianity cannot be limited to the West."
— STANLEY HAUERWAS

APOLOGIA

CONTEXTUALIZATION, GLOBALIZATION, AND
MISSION IN THEOLOGICAL EDUCATION

by
Max L. Stackhouse

With Nantawan Boonprasat-Lewis, J. G. F. Collison,
Lamin Sanneh, Lee Harding,
Ilse von Loewenclau, and Robert W. Pazmiño
Foreword by Donald Shriver

WILLIAM B. EERDMANS PUBLISHING COMPANY
GRAND RAPIDS, MICHIGAN

Copyright © 1988 by Wm. B. Eerdmans Publishing Co.
255 Jefferson Ave. S.E., Grand Rapids, Mich. 49503

All rights reserved
Printed in the United States of America

This book has been funded by the Association of Theological Schools.

Library of Congress Cataloging-in-Publication Data

Stackhouse, Max L.
Apologia : contextualization, globalization,
and mission in theological education.
1. Theology. 2. Theology — Study and teaching.
I. Title.
BR118.S69   1988   230'.01   87-33080

ISBN 0-8028-0285-0

Contents

Foreword by Donald Shriver — ix

Part I: *A Dialogue*

One *An Introduction* — 3
  A Conversation Reported — 4
  Some Results and Implications — 7
  Early Objections Acknowledged — 11

Two *Our Context* — 15
  Liberal? — 16
  Modern? — 17
  Neo-orthodox? — 19
  Ecumenical? — 20
  Realist? — 23
  Biblical? — 26

Three *Texts and Contexts* — 29
  From Text to Context — 30
  The Context as Text — 33
  From Context to Text — 38

Four *Affirmations and Translations* — 43
  Minimalist Affirmations — 43
  So Long, Sola Scriptura — 50
  Translation Transforms — 53
  A General Pattern? — 56
  Where Are We? — 61

Part II: *Wider Discussions*

Five Consultations and Globalization 67
  On Community Engagement 68
  On Global Solidarity 73
  Toward Globalization 77
  Unresolved Issues 78

Six Praxis *and Solidarity* 84
  The Advocates of *Praxis* 85
  The Roots of *Praxis* 88
  Praxis Baptized 91
  Does *Praxis* Mean *Orthopraxis?* 95
  Is *Orthopraxis* True and Just? 98
  Praxis Requires *Theoria* 103

Seven Poesis *and Contextuality* 106
  Models of Contextualization 107
  On Reading Contexts 109
  The Science of Cultural Contexts 112
  Catholicity Forsaken? 114
  Doctrine as a Cultural-Linguistic System 119

Eight Theoria *and Phenomenology* 123
  The Loss of Integrity 123
  Toward Belief-Full Knowledge 127
  Dissatisfactions 129
  Schleiermacher Still? 132

Part III: *A Proposal*

Nine *Apologia* 139
  What Is Missing? 141
  Is Religion Really Important? 145
  Can Theology Judge Religions? 148
  Warranted Wisdom 152
  Grounded *Scientia* 156
  Cosmopolitan Apologetics 159

Ten *Orthodoxy?* 162
  What's at Stake? 163
  Four Doctrines 169
  A Review 182

Eleven *Praxiology?* 184
  The Foundations of *Praxis* 185
  Three Marks of Justice 202

Twelve	*Doxology*	209
	In Praise of Reason	210
	A Humble Confidence	214
	The Future of the Fields	217

Appendix 1
A Response to Apologia, *with Special Reference
to Problems of Text and Context*   223
  by Ilse von Loewenclau

Appendix 2
A Response to Apologia, *with Special Reference
to the Seminary as a Faith Community*   230
  by Robert W. Pazmiño

DEDICATED TO

those colleagues at Andover Newton Theological School who have tolerated with generosity of mind and spirit these incursions into "their fields" and who have been willing to sustain dialogue about the future of theological education

Foreword

Over a decade ago, I spent some weeks in a theological school in Kenya sharing with Methodist and Presbyterian ministers my perspectives on Christian ethics. At one point in the lectures I noted, with energy, the burden of Western culture that the early European missionaries to Africa carried with them. We all must beware, I said, that we do not confuse the gospel with our cultural baggage.

"That's all very well," responded some of my ministerial colleagues to this lesson of the day, "but we can never forget that the missionaries were the ones who brought us the News about Jesus." Be careful, they seemed to say, that in your repentance for the Westernizing earthen vessel of much missionary history, you do not minimize the religious treasure therein.

Thirteen years later, in the summer of 1986, I was present at a meeting of African theological educators called "The Future of Theological Education in Africa." At one particularly animated point in the discussion, individuals from opposite sides of the continent asked each other what *language* they should be using to instruct the next generation of church leaders in their respective countries. English or French? Both were the languages of colonialism. Swahili? It served East Africa better than West. Then the dean of the Kimbanguist Seminary in Zaire — associated with the Kimbanguist church, which is now five million strong in response to the "homegrown" African prophet Simon Kimbangu — rose and said, "Whatever language is best for continental communication in Africa, we must remember that the scholarly study of Christian theology begins with a knowledge of Hebrew and Greek."

Each of these incidents raised the question of the fleeting and the enduring themes of the Christian proclamation, the relation of something relative in each generation's understanding of this faith to something durable. In no small measure, theology and theological education are about this relationship.

For the exploration of this central issue, which encompasses the work of theological schools around the world, this is an important book. Unlike some books on education written by Americans, this one is more concerned to ask about the truth of what is taught rather than the methods of teaching it. Raised here, like a theme that weaves through every movement of a symphony, is the question that no educator can ignore: "What is true, and how can we be sure?"

As it happens, theological educators face a particular set of modern difficulties in answering this fundamental question for themselves. Like others in graduate professional schools, we are products of education in universities whose intellectual assumptions ironically render the concept "universal" more and more suspect. The subdisciplines of a university faculty may be quite confident of the truths that they know in their own respective specialties, but they are not confident of each other's knowledge. In today's world of "higher" education, the culture of specialization systematically undercuts claims that apply to all human thinking, acting, and being.

In such a culture, theologians have reason to feel out of place. From times ancient to modern, they have known that their subject is replete with universalistic claims. What would their adjectives for describing the Divine be without the occasional prefix *omni-*? The word *religio* means either "the sacred" or "what binds together." What if nothing can be identified as sacred for all humans? What if nothing can be said to bind all humans together? What if human history demonstrates that no human ever has the right to begin a sentence with "We all know that . . ."? It is common experience these days that there are few common experiences. So, for theologians who believe in a "good news" of universal human import disclosed in the person of Jesus, the question becomes this: "Would all efforts to speak of [a gospel] in the many contexts of the world be but an enormous exercise in cultural imperialism?" (see p. 119).

Though authored principally by Max L. Stackhouse, this book is nonetheless a collective product, and this is one of its important features for addressing the crisis of legitimacy in the theological discipline as such. Here, from beginning to end, are the results of a collegial dialogue among members of the oldest of the "denominational" seminaries in America—Andover Newton Theological School, founded in 1807 out of Congregationalist dissatisfaction with Harvard College as exclusive trainer of New England's nineteenth-century ministry. Specialized, scientifically defined learning was already on the march in that college, and as it became a university, it too would continue to train many of the faculty of this theological school. One result, in twentieth-century theological education, is that members of such a faculty have almost as much difficulty seeing themselves as inhabiting a similar frame of intellectual reference as do their cousins of the Yard. Inside our theological schools, the word "theologian" usually denotes a member of one of our subdisciplines. "Historians" are distinctly resistant to such a title, and even ethicists shy away from it. What ties a theological faculty together intellectually, anyway?

As the new seminaries of the nineteenth century veered off into their own institutional independence, some educators inside and outside the seminaries assumed that theology was thus claiming for itself a newly defined status as a special area of knowledge alongside other specialties. Except for a few faculty imbued with the German university ethos of the time, such an assumption was little warranted. Andover Newton was born, like so many of these early nineteenth-century seminaries (including the one where I now work), from the second great evangelical "awakening," and those early Andover Newton professors knew that the ministry and the churches of the Christian faith consisted of a certain intimate blend of faith, knowledge, behavior, and worship. The coherence of these things was to compose the stuff of theological education. Universities were steadily swearing off responsibility for introducing their students to any such existential combination. Specialized knowledge was their calling, and most particularly all those forms of knowledge that could pass muster under the truth criteria of the empirical sciences.

Nothing in eight hundred years of theological thought interests the authors of this book more than the question about whether theology can still be called a "science" in a sense integrally related to other uses of this word in the modern university. Above all, they want to identify some positive core of Christian faith and some positive intellectual methods associated with that core which, together, make up the rationale, the warrant, the *apologia* of the theological project itself. In this respect, the book is not so much about education as it is about theology. And the authors put forth this hypothesis about the historical circumstance that warrants just such a book:

> The reputed decline of the influence of religion, and indeed of theology, in the modern world may well be due to the fact that theological education began to think of itself, and to allow the world to think of it, as utterly beyond the range of "warrant" for its "wisdom," and without a "ground" for its *scientia*. It allowed itself, for a time, to become trapped in the protest against all universalistic criteria. The nominal, the immediate, the direct, the subjective, the existential, the historically variant, the pietistic, and the particular became the focus, and we are today reaping the whirlwind in the form of a number of highly sophisticated contextualisms. . . . Nevertheless, it is beginning to dawn on theologians today, as it did on theological faculties of the past centuries, that nearly all if not all the enduring contributions have been made by those who have attempted to instruct the church and the world about what would and could count as warranted wisdom and grounded *scientia*. At their best, these were linked with profound piety, sensitive to contextual realities, and dedicated to a mission of global reach. (pp. 158-59)

Later on the authors express this idea more bluntly: "There is little reason to have a theological school that is self-consciously Christian and dedicated to contextualization, globalization, and mission if its wisdom is not genuinely warranted, or if the chief tenets of this religion are not grounded in a *scientia* defensible in public discourse, or if it makes no great deal of difference whether or not one believes its purported truth rightly in disparate times and places" (p. 166).

Being "always . . . prepared to make a defense to any one who calls you to account for the hope that is in you . . . with gentleness and reverence" (1 Pet. 3:15) has long been the project of that branch of theology called apologetics. This book is a serious call for more attention, by entire theological faculties, to this ancient intellectual vocation. And the call is for a rethinking of the grounds and meanings of the Christian faith in a world-historical context quite different from the one in which Christianity was born and the one by which it was transmitted to its adherents in this century. The writers of this volume make a good case for believing that the task ahead for Christian theologians is an appropriation of the faith that will constitute a third great intellectual achievement on a par with what Jews and Christians did between the fourth century before Christ and the fourth century after, and what Western intellectuals did between the high Middle Ages and the mid-nineteenth century to construct modern scientific-technological culture. On the wings of this periodization, the sweep of the book is momentous. Inside theology, these authors claim, there is a need for a "scientific revolution" in a sense similar to that of Thomas Kuhn: a new paradigm for understanding God, for speaking about God to all kinds of people in all kinds of conditions, and for combining true speech with the full orb of true Christian discipleship.

Most of the parties to theological dispute inside today's churches are represented on one page or another of this book. Some will feel that they are inadequately represented, and they will want to register protests with those who wrote these pages. My own hope is that, especially if they are members of theological faculties, these protestors will turn to dialogue with their immediate colleagues on these matters. Most of the favorite, disputable questions among members of those faculties are up for notice here: the claims of the fundamentalist and the scriptural literalist are here for questioning, as are those of the liberal, the liberationist, and the charismatic. If I read it rightly, the aim of the book is to put a fence around all these major parties long enough to compel them to hear and address each other's favorite questions: What is the authority of the Bible? What is our most fundamental image of the God of Jesus? Is any doctrine essential to the Christian life? Is personal behavior informed by, or does it merely express, the content of faith? Is engaging in the struggle for justice for society's victims incidental to, correlative with, or the essence of following Jesus in our time? What are the signs of the presence of a Spirit who is truly Holy? Is there any formulation of the faith that is at once contextually rooted, globally plausible, and capable of undergirding the Christian movement with a proper, nonimperialistic sense of mission?

With unrelenting passion for analysis that opens the way to at least the beginning of synthesis, this work means to be a matrix in which all these questions get posed to each other, in the conviction that the connections between the questions can be named, made explicit, rendered into a theology about theologies. No small intention for a book, to say the least. But the intention is on the target of a widely sensed need among theological educators today: that Christians now and in the century to come may learn to feel, think, speak, and behave toward all their earthly neighbors with an integrity that combines confidence with humility, local pertinence with universal meaning, and religious particularity with respect for the universal in other religions.

My own sensitivity to this yearning among my colleagues in the United States and Canada was considerably enhanced over the past six years by my participation in a study of the Association of Theological Schools called "The Globalization of Theological Education." Among our colleagues from other countries who read the report submitted to ATS on this subject was an African theologian who rightly detected the keynote of the report and commented, "Enlargement of love is possible only where there is enlargement of acquaintance." Many thoughtful appreciators and critics of religion these days are haunted by the suspicion that much religion is too narrow in concept and consequence to serve the interests of an increasingly close-knit global human society. Religion should serve to broaden human acquaintances, or it should lose the plausibility of its claim to speak about universality. For this broadening — of thought, relationship, and action — the parties to religious dispute may need each other. Within the Christian community alone, it may be high time for liberals and liberationists, fundamentalists and spiritualists, personalists and revolutionaries to talk together into the night on questions as basic as these: How do Christians know that one question — or one answer — is better than another? If some truth alleged by Christians is closer to God's truth than another, what are the criteria by which anyone might decide? If any party to a theological discussion, including the agnostic and the atheist, were to change his or her mind about some point in the discussion, what would constitute a good, right, and true reason for doing so?

I like this book for posing these questions. But what I like best of all is that such questions are posed here by and to colleagues spread around the world of theological education. At the beginning, not only do we come upon the members of a Protestant theological faculty searching together for the core of theology, practice, and pedagogy that holds them together. We also hear their conversation with four consultants invited from cultures about whom Andover's Puritan forebears knew very little. These "outside" voices participate intimately in the discourse that follows, which searches for a form of theological truth and learning that might be "contextually alert, globally concerned, and mission-oriented" (p. 26). Again, the point of the book is to invite all the current parties in today's theological debates into a partnership of inquiry. Without doubt some of these potential partners will respond to the book with a certain indignation: "You have not taken with true seriousness the claims you ascribe to the likes of us." But even this response will be one measure of the importance of this book to theological educators in general. What if these pages could be a catalyst of talk among theologians whose differences have been so fundamental that they have stopped talking to each other about fundamentals?

The book gives them new, urgent reason to do so. The most

effectively catalytic part of the book, for me, is Chapter 12 and the two appendices that follow. This final chapter concludes a section of four chapters advancing positive proposals for a method, a doctrine, a practice, and a liturgical witness expressive of a truly plausible theological *apologia*. In a time of much analysis and timorous suggestions for reform of education, this last section is an act of considerable courage and humility. It seeks to practice what the first two-thirds of the book has called for—a theory of Christian thought mated to appropriate educational forms. Near the beginning of this chapter is an admirable summation of the book's central positive argument: "Theological education rests on the assumption that humans can speak with some measure of reasonable confidence about what is ultimately mysterious, that in some degree it is possible to point to, if not fully grasp, the *logos* of God" (p. 211). The chapter then goes on to fortify confidence (at least in this theological educator) that theological faculty members have much to teach each other for their modern, collective reappropriation of "the truth and justice of God" (p. 209).

Here are intriguing illustrations of how historians might help biblical scholars walk the line between the revelationism of fundamentalists and the relativism of agnostics. Every subdiscipline of the past, present, and future theological curriculum rightly has to do with questions of biblical authority, historical accuracy, theological consistency, and practical relevance. No one in such a faculty has a right to ignore a basic question—part normative and part empirical—like, "Which spirit is really Holy?" For example, in any seminary today "the biblical scholar and the church historian may want to risk asking what [a particular text] reveals about contemporary spiritualities, doctrines, preachings, and teachings that may be of quite ephemeral import, and to point out the dangers of taking everything purportedly sacred as valuable" (p. 218). In thus addressing questions of central intellectual importance for all their disciplines, theological scholars would be involved in "testing the adequacy of what they do, in confidence and humility, by showing how it aids in clarifying God's truth and justice in new and wider contexts" than their original academic training may have equipped them to face (p. 219).

These new and wider contexts of a religiously diverse, globally human world are crucial dimensions of this requisite "testing." As a theologian from South India commented recently in relation to our 1986 ATS Globalization Report, "As far as I know, the North American faculty live by the motto 'Publish or perish.' I am looking forward to a time when they will begin to live by the slogan 'Be cross-cultural or perish.' "

Consistent with such hope, this book ends with two appendices, one by a biblical scholar from the German Democratic Republic, the other by an evangelical theologian who speaks as a member of the Hispanic-American community. Each has read the book, and brings his or her own perspectives and criticisms to bear upon it, and these responses make a fair beginning to other books that need to be written. That such responses are included in *this* book adds to its integrity. It is a book that begins in dialogue and ends with the same. It starts more conversations than it finishes. It is not afraid to ask Christians to converse with partners as old as Abraham and Sarah, as remote as Hindus, and as hard to envision as our neighbors of a century hence. It encourages me to pursue my own profession as theologian with many new partners around the world. With sufficient enlargement of acquaintance, could *we* make a contribution to that enlargement of love that this vexed humanity so sorely needs for its own survival into another century? I know of no higher aspiration for any profession, including that of theologians.

Donald W. Shriver, Jr.
President, Union Theological Seminary, New York

PART I

A Dialogue

CHAPTER 1

An Introduction

There is always much talk in theological schools. Professors, seminarians, and clergy generally are a loquacious bunch. To be sure, it is not always the case that this talk is sustained, deep, or engaged with the most significant issues that confront faith and morals, human understanding, the church, or the world. And yet, this talk is potentially important, for ideas are the only innately valuable and inherently powerful resource that the church, its pastors, and its theologians have. Few theological talkers are rich or of influential status; fewer have, or aspire to, political authority or military power; and fewer still have those striking personalities or stunning talents that destine them for fame and fortune. Nor can we say that the power of faith, of hope, or of love is more pronounced in centers of theological education than it is in nursing homes, among revolutionary cadres, or between newlyweds.

What we do in theological education is talk. We teach and we discuss; we preach and we analyze; we read and we write; we think and we criticize. Words are our medium; talk is our method; ideas are our *raison d'être*. The question is whether any of them are worth anything. That is, do they point to, touch upon, grasp, convey, suggest, evoke, identify, or invite recognition of that which is ultimately true? And, if so, is that truth just — that is, does it provide reliable guidance for human community in a way that lifts up the oppressed, casts down pretense, honors good, constrains evil, and provides a vision for the righteous and compassionate ordering of the common life?

It is obvious that seminaries are not the only places where

theological education takes place. It occurs in university departments of religion, in churches, wherever encounter between religions takes place, whenever religious figures or groups attempt to influence public policy, and in the quietness of the study where people attempt to discern the ultimate foundations of meaning and morality. Yet, examining the nature, character, and future of theological education by focusing on the seminary has certain merits. A seminary has no other reason to exist.

The single resource we have is of inestimable importance in the lives of individuals and the destinies of societies. Individuals may be consumed by greed, lust for power, or desire for honor, but these are fragile foundations for living. Unconstrained, they bring emptiness and death. All sensitive people seek a vision beyond these, and even those driven by greed, lust, or desire try to manipulate ideas to "prove" that they have a "right" to what they obtain. Civilizations may appear to be driven by wealth, violence, authority, status, and renown, but over time they are never better than the metaphysical-moral visions that give them rootage and guidance. Such visions are inevitably produced and distorted, actualized, or dissipated by religious institutions and leadership; and these are never better than the quality of the ideas encountered, examined, shared, adopted, propagated, and taken as normative for life. For at least a century, a large number of educators thought that theology was not important for, and perhaps even an impediment to, serious learning and a sound social order. But today academia seems rudderless, and the society is beset by a metaphysical-moral disease, and much of it can be traced to the relative triviality of ideas in and about theological education.

A CONVERSATION REPORTED

This is a study — an interpretive report, really — of the substance, cluster of issues, presuppositions, and contradictions that appeared in a specific time and place where talk approximated a genuine dialogue about important ideas, a relatively serious if episodic and often uneven conversation about theological education. Such a dialogue is not unique, but it is sufficiently rare that it has seemed useful to record it, to examine it, and to attempt to extend it. Part I in particular recounts the key issues debated recently at Andover Newton Theological School. To be sure, much of this report is one person's perspective on what occurred, and surely contains all the limitations which that involves; and yet, the dialogue had a broader base. International consultants joined the faculty at ANTS in a series of meetings, discussions, and retreats in which dialogue about that which theological teachers do in common was the primary focus. We had a series of presentations by heads of departments and several panel discussions on "excellence." We debated some of the best current literature on the state of theology and the future of theological education (Part II). We talked about our priorities in a context increasingly aware of and committed to the world church, and we did it in a way that was intentionally designed to reach well beyond our own enclave.

It is hard to say exactly when this conversation began. It may well have begun in 1982, when we celebrated our 175th anniversary as a seminary. During the celebration we were challenged by a series of speakers to reclaim leadership in charting new directions for theological education that the old Andover theologians had developed for their era in the nineteenth century. It was after delivering such a challenge that Robert Lynn of the Lilly Foundation and of the "Auburn Study" of the history of theological education prompted us to apply for the grant, awarded subsequently through the Basic Issues Research Program of the Association of Theological Schools, which made this study possible. Another part of our discussion began when we revived the neglected Adoniram Judson Chair of Missions, reactivated the "Society of Inquiry" (which founded the American missionary movement at this seminary in 1910), hosted a celebration of the formation of the American Board of Commissioners for Foreign Missions, and were challenged to think again about theology's responsibilities to the wider world.

Our conversation took a fresh turn when newly elected president George Peck took as the theme of his inaugural address the vision of a "transpositional theology." The term, taken from the work of Choan-Seng Song, one of Asia's leading theologians, implies the need for a new clarity about the primal meanings of the faith, stripped of merely Western cultural accoutrements, and a willingness to risk the "transposition" of it into new contexts.[1] Shortly thereafter, Peck appointed both a committee to develop a new framework for a pending curriculum revision and a committee to work on questions of international dimensions of theological education with some overlapping membership. It was clear from the start that he also intended a new attentiveness to the Third World in the midst of North American society. Religious education

---

1. See Song, *Third-Eye Theology: Theology in Formation in Asian Settings* (Maryknoll, N.Y.: Orbis Books, 1979); and *The Compassionate God* (Maryknoll, N.Y.: Orbis Books, 1982).

specialist Maria Harris was chair of the first committee; Max Stackhouse, having recently returned from Asia and having just completed a comparative study of several religions and societies as they influence human rights, was chair of the latter.[2] Certainly the work of both committees was intensified by the new dean of our faculty, Orlando Costas — a Hispanic evangelical in background, a United Church of Christ missionary in the Caribbean and Central America, and a dynamo of commitment to ministry among the disadvantaged peoples of the world. A "manifesto" of his on these matters was early delivered to the ANTS faculty, and is considered in Chapter 3.

But in a less immediate sense, much of what began to coalesce under the stimulus of these intentional conversations had already been in place. We were, in a sense, ripe for them. In 1973, ANTS had established a "fraternal" relationship with the United Theological College of Bangalore, South India; and in 1981, a similar relationship had been established with Das Sprachenkonvikt, an independent seminary of the United Protestant Church (Evangelische Kirche der Union) in East Berlin.[3] In addition, ANTS has recently taken steps to establish a similar relationship with the Evangelical (Baptist) Seminary in Nicaragua. Professors and students have begun to be involved in exchanges, although political and language considerations have made the exchanges with Das Sprachenkonvikt and Nicaragua less frequent. Further, ANTS also became a sponsor of an international seminar held each year at Mansfield College, Oxford University, which a number of our students and faculty have attended.

The present study was designed to draw upon the insights of international leaders. Thanks to the ATS grant, we were able to include Dr. Nantawan Boonprasat-Lewis, former Buddhist and subsequently dean of the theological faculty at Payap College, Thailand; Dr. J. G. F. Collison, until recently the director of graduate studies at United Theological College, India, who represented what Christian dialogue with a Hindu context might entail;* and Dr. Lamin Sanneh, noted scholar on the history of missions, originally from a Muslim background in Gambia and now professor at the World Religions Center, Harvard University. In addition, Rev. Lee

---

2. For an example of our cooperative work, see the *Bangalore Theological Forum*, the special collaborative issue on the Sermon on the Mount, Jan.-Mar. 1985.

3. See my *Creeds, Society, and Human Rights: A Study in Three Cultures* (Grand Rapids: Eerdmans, 1984).

*Frank died of a heart attack in Bangalore, India, on January 2, 1986. The loss of this friend and scholar is deeply felt.

Harding, one of the outstanding graduates of ANTS who has been a successful pastor for several years, is presently completing a doctoral program at Boston College on closely related topics. He became a valuable participant in our dialogue. Another important participant was Dr. Ilse von Loewenclau, an Old Testament scholar, recently rector of Das Sprachenkonvikt, involved in questions of what theological education might mean in a Marxist-Leninist society. Because of some delays in visa arrangements, Dr. von Loewenclau was only able to join Hispanic Christian educator Robert Pazmiño, a new member of the ANTS faculty, and social ethicist Donald Shriver of Union Theological Seminary in writing comments on this discussion as it neared completion. (See the Foreword and the Appendices.)

In all these dialogues, three themes constantly reappear: "contextualization," "globalization," and "mission." What does it mean to engage in theological education when it appears to be the case that every statement we make and every response to it is contextually shaped? What does it mean to engage in theological education at a time when the world is shrinking and new voices are entering the dialogue? What is the mission of the church, and especially of its academic wing, the seminary, in a "post-modern" global context?

Part II of this study moves beyond our own discussions to an examination of some of the most significant works that have appeared on these questions in recent decades. These studies make it clear that the ANTS discussions reflect a wider quest for adequate foundations in contemporary theological education. At the same time, these studies reveal the fragility of our present situation, for in them we see some of the best minds in the leadership of modern theological education compounding certain problems while creatively drawing our attention to other key issues. Their work tellingly shows that today some widely held interpretations of contextualization, globalization, and mission are freighted with epistemological, metaphysical, moral, social, and historical assumptions that appear to compromise, covertly or overtly, the notion that theological education can be carried forth with intellectual integrity and faithfulness. We found ourselves indebted to them and simultaneously in sharp debate with parts of what they propose, for finally they offer little guidance to the substance or directions of normative theological and ethical discourse.

SOME RESULTS AND IMPLICATIONS

In one respect, many of the practical results of these efforts are neither dramatic nor totally innovative. A revised curriculum was unanimously adopted, one that contains more required exposure to contextual, global, and missiological studies than any previous curriculum in our history, or in any other curriculum that we know of. Nevertheless, in curriculum revisions, it seems almost self-evident that one of Christianity's ancient doctrines has special application: God's creation of the world *ex nihilo* surely implies that we humans do not create *de novo*. Everything that we create is built upon the foundations that have been established well before we arrive on the scene, engage in dialogue, and attempt to do anything new. Not only are the personalities of faculty members rather definitively formed by the time we engage in dialogue, but our disciplines, our styles, our divisions of labor, our limitations of time and energy, and our agendas regarding "the most important things" are fairly well defined. When these factors are coupled with the inevitable element of "horse-trading" between departments, we see how much present possibilities are limited by pre-existing conditions. Curricular reconstruction always takes place within quite narrow limits and serves only as a potential basis for further change in the future.

Nevertheless, within limits, it is possible to identify critical issues, priorities, and questions — if less often definitive answers — around which debates ought to be centered and which are fateful for the present and the future. These debates are the substance of this study. While this study does not represent a consensus but rather a response to several matters that became increasingly clear in the course of discussion, and a proposal about how they might be addressed, we can state the results in this way: Modern theological education, perhaps especially in ecumenically oriented seminaries, is in a severe crisis even where it is carried out with some "success." The situation is programmed for greater disarray and intensified conflict. The grounds on which it is presently conducted are shaky. What we need is a fresh appropriation of the grounding for theological education.

For reasons that shall become clear in the subsequent chapters, it emerged that the decisive question is one of criteria. Are there any criteria that can be reliably known and that can allow us to identify what it might be, in the various contexts of our shrinking globe, that is worth heeding or sharing? And do these criteria, should they become visible to us, have anything intrinsically to do with the knowledge of a true and just God? We know that various religious concerns are psychologically, historically, politically, and socially influential, but such knowledge tells us only that psychologists, historians, politicians, and social theorists have to take account of religion as a significant variable in nontheological research and practice. We also know that every religion establishes a creed, a cultus, and a code by which it judges whether or not beliefs, practices, and behaviors are acceptable to it, but this knowledge tells us nothing about whether these standards are in fact true or just or godly. The phenomenology of religious matters can be studied and taught, and hence is proper to education. But *theological* education is ultimately based upon something else. It is based upon the presupposition that there are, in the final analysis, some reliable criteria whereby we can know and talk about what is and what is not divine, true, and just. If there are no such criteria, or if we could not know them even if they did exist, or if they cannot be discussed in reasonable discourse even where they are intuited, theological education is a pretense — at worst, the rationalization, or ideologization, of privileged insight or group interest; at best, the poetry of personal or communal imaginings. Both rationalized interests and poetic dreams have been of tremendous importance in religious movements and in the formation of popular piety. But neither requires theological education, and serious theology suspects both of idolatry.

The question of criteria is a question that, as we shall see in Part III, demands a fresh turn to *apologia*. We use the Greek term rather than the English because the common usage today seems to have something defensive or excusing about it, but the classical theological meanings of the Greek term can be understood to entail several things: (1) a willingness to enter into the thought forms of those who do not always share the faith assumptions or worldviews that we hold when we enter into dialogue, (2) a willingness to attempt an account of that which we hold most dear in the face of skepticism, doubt, or suspicion, (3) a willingness to hear and evaluate on their merits any alternative perspectives that are opposed to our own, and (4) a willingness to refute unsound objections to a defensible theological perspective. To be sure, all such efforts involve the presumptions that it is possible to transcend our own biases in some measure, and that we can have some prospect of knowing something reliable about God, truth, and justice in sufficient degree to recognize it in views held by others, and to preach it and teach it with humble confidence once it is discovered.

A serious *apologia* would have significant implications for contextualization, globalization, and mission. The very word "contextualization," for example, implies that something that is recognized in one context to be transcontextual in significance and validity is properly to be introduced into a secondary context and, in a process of reception and indigenization, become adopted and adapted as a part of the fabric of life in this new locale. An *apologia* would surely be necessary in making the case that what derives from, or is discovered in, or is revealed to one context is indeed of broader significance and therefore should be recognized as authentic by other contexts. If no serious *apologia* is made, or if a serious case cannot be made, the spread of everything thought to be transcontextual is nothing more than adulteration of culture or cultural imperialism. Contextualization involves the recognition that many aspects of what humans believe, think, and do are contextually shaped, but that some matters not initially found in many particular contexts may properly be introduced to them.

"Contextualization," thus, stands in the sharpest tension with "contextualism," with which it is frequently confused. As we shall see, contextualism is the view that anything we can say, believe, think, or claim is, and must be, understood as a reflection of the context in which it is found, and that anything we say, believe, think, or claim must be directly pertinent to the needs of the context. Otherwise, it is judged to be "abstract."

One of the key problems, of course, is that it is very difficult to know what people mean by the word "context." How big is it? How long does one last? What are its main marks? How does one know when one sees one?[4] In this regard, "globalization" suggests that a world process is taking place that relates all local and immediate contexts of whatever description to new common realities. Thus every specific context has to be interpreted in terms of the growing reality of global interdependence. In the eighteenth century, Wesley engendered the slogan "The world is my parish." In the nineteenth century, Troeltsch engendered another: "History is our epoch." Today we must say "Global history is our context."

It is likely that modern theological education has to discern those things that are merely contextual in the narrow, limited, and parochial sense, and those things that are translocal, perennial, and transcultural in a new way, so that the latter can be properly transposed into new places and times. And it may be that awareness of cross-cultural realities is the necessary context of theological education (indeed, of all learning) today. If so, the sense of mission is also modified. It will have to be based on those things that can be shown to be universally true and just; and this requires, among other things, a warranted general theory of the relation of religion to societies and cultures, and of theology to philosophy and the

---

4. See Max L. Stackhouse, "Contextualization and Theological Education," *Theological Education*, vol. 23, no. 1, pp. 67-84.

world religions. Mission that lives by pious zeal for "our" truth alone is tempted to become merely the private preference of sectarian enclaves or the imperialistic fanaticism of fundamentalists. It simply will not suffice.

EARLY OBJECTIONS ACKNOWLEDGED

We should note at the outset that a number of our faculty members and consultants are committed to a more decidedly "contextualist" approach to theology, to education, to metaphysics, epistemology, and ethics than *apologia* implies. A number would agree with Douglas Meeks's recent statement that "in Europe and the United States there is a search for the integrating meta-theological unity of theory itself, which, in my view, threatens to make theology utterly illusory."[5] Indeed, some seem to be convinced that the cutting edge of theological education is to be found through a rapid departure from normative questions of criteria, through negation of all abstractions about truth or justice, metaphysics, and morality, and through an intense engagement with particular and immediate contexts where God is present among the poor, the oppressed, the neglected, the sick, and the despised. Nothing in this study can be construed as opposing direct encounter with or commitment to engagement in such contexts. Indeed, it is one of the proper tests of, at least, an adequate Christian theology. But several accents in this study will challenge the current conventional presumption that such engagement is best served by theologies that pretend to avoid systematic thinking, abstract concepts, and general theory. Indeed, this study will at many points focus on the fact that direct involvement and identification with such peoples and contexts inevitably drives us to context-transcending questions, because the dynamics of particular contexts always involve "abstract" issues of truth and justice, "abstract" metaphysical-moral visions of varying merit that present themselves, and "theoretical" epistemological questions by which we can say (even if seldom with more than relative certainty) "this is of God." Indeed, such accents themselves require an *apologia*.

Those who object to setting the course in this direction are not alone. Indeed, a number of serious objections to anything smacking of apologetics have been launched in recent theological history. For example, the great "neo-orthodox" theologian Karl Barth

---

5. *The Future of the Methodist Theological Traditions,* ed. Douglas Meeks (Nashville: Abingdon Press, 1985), p. 23.

refused to make any apology for the faith, because he thought that faith had nothing to do with the forms of reason, the worldviews, and the non-Christian religions, sciences, or philosophies that one who engages in apologetics would have to embrace to make the case. Dogmatic proclamation is the proper form of Christian discourse. Thus, *apologia* ought not be undertaken for the sake of the gospel. However, any number of studies have appeared to show how much Barth's view of the gospel depended on religious, scientific, metaphysical, moral, and epistemological foundations that were simply unstated and not always reliable.

Wilfred Cantwell Smith, the noted comparative religionist, also argued that apologetics is not to be undertaken. But his reasons were different. He held that what each faith believes to be true, just, and godly is less important than the fundamental commonality of faith itself. Any effort to compromise what anyone else holds by faith rests on an unwarranted presumption that we have access to some transcultural standards by which we can, without bias, evaluate someone else's quality of faith. What we should do instead is recognize that faith takes many forms and has many expressions, and that the common phenomenon of faith is what all share. However, to suggest that we do share faith and to judge that all faithing is of equal value demands appeal to a particular transcultural standard that many do not think is true.

Today, one can find no small supply of authors who accent a radical historicism, authors who hold that all or nearly all of what has heretofore gone on in theological education is so intertwined with the political-social-racial-sexual-economic patterns of domination that we need "a whole new way" of thinking about theology. In the more striking examples of this approach, however, we find little but sophomoric and stereotyped echoes of the nineteenth-century debates between Enlightenment rationalists and libertine romanticists.[6]

We are aware that some claiming to represent the Third World suspect that apologetics might be dysfunctional. It might be a premature burden on the imaginative new efforts being made by peoples emerging from colonialism as they rediscover and reassert their own traditions and feelings. However, other voices from the Third World argue that those who are not Westerners are *not* opposed to reasonable discourse, appeals to universal principles of justice,

---

6. See, for an example, the Mud Flower Collective, *God's Fierce Whimsy: Christian Feminism and Theological Education,* ed. Carter Heyward (New York: Pilgrim Press, 1985).

careful thought, or common canons of logic in regard to basic criteria. Indeed, Third World scholars criticize one another when they do not meet these standards, and they offer the sharpest criticisms of Western theology precisely at those points where it has not offered an *apologia* for its claims but simply presumes that its own contextually or culturally conditioned insights are self-evident and universal.[7] On such grounds, some find it to be condescending or paternalistic if theologians do not hold Asian or African or Latin American (or black or female) students, authors, or ecclesiastical leaders to common human standards of evidence, reasonability, and coherence when they make unwarranted or incredible claims.[8]

And finally, we must recognize that some fear any turn to apologetics because it has recently been associated with a stream of theology that only quite conservative theologians are now pursuing. On this point, however, we see no reason to abandon this term to one wing of the church any more than we allow that stream to take full possession of such terms as "evangelism" and "mission." Nevertheless, we acknowledge at the outset that we confront powerful arguments which claim that *apologia* is (a) confessionally wrong, (b) impossible, (c) anticontextual, inappropriate to our modern needs, (d) arrogant, (e) dysfunctional, or (f) constrictive.

Given such weighty criticisms, it might be considered wise to abandon this project before we go further, but that would be premature. Part of the reason for the current crisis in theological education may well be that precisely these current arguments are at least partially in error and lead to injustice. Surely, what we have to do is to make the case for what we hold to be true and just theologically as well as we can, in part by dialogical encounter with these objections. And then we need to invite others to evaluate its adequacy — not on the basis of some predetermined objection to apologetics in principle, but on the basis of whether what we find in this effort commends itself to others in some measure, and whether the present debates in and about theological education do not demand that we recover, and recast for the future, with new horizons and accents, one of the central responsibilities of theolog-

---

7. See the *Report of the International Consultation of Theological Education,* ed. M. Abel (Madras: Gurukul Lutheran Theological College, 1984).

8. From consultations in the fall of 1984 of the ANTS International Committee with a group of international doctoral candidates in the Boston area. We are especially grateful to Thomas Tangeraj of Tamil Nadu Theological College, Madurai, India; Keun Soo Hong of the Korean Presbyterian Church, Seoul, Korea; Luis Rivera of the Evangelical Seminary of Puerto Rico; and Natan Setiabudi of the Reformed Church of Bandung, Indonesia.

ical education as a quite specific link between the church and academia and society that gives theological schools a special vocation. In fact, any attempt to "make the case" for a theological position, whether supportive or critical of the positions taken in this volume, is already at the brink of *apologia*. Whether or not we have begun to establish a credible case will have to be tested by others, and that is the core reason for extending this dialogue to those beyond our own circles.

If what follows, then, is persuasive, we can expect others to adopt, adapt, and improve on what they find here. If it is not persuasive in the sense that it does not point convincingly to that which accords with the truth and justice of God, then we expect to hear persuasive refutation, and to alter our views ourselves. Otherwise, it will not have been a genuine dialogue.

CHAPTER 2

Our Context

Theological education in seminaries prepares leaders for the churches. That is not all it does, but that is what it is designed for. The question is always what the leadership and the churches should be thinking, the presumption being that thought will influence actions. And this question is always at least partially shaped by a fundamental perception of what the context is in which leaders will work. Today, the horizon of our perception of context is expanding. Theological education is in the midst of a series of efforts to redefine its focus. It is beset by a rather vague discomfort, a sense that what we and others do is really not so bad, but that it also does not have an overwhelming and fully compelling focus. One could, of course, echo grand phrases for this condition. It could be called a "sickness unto death," a "vacuous nullity," a "pompous pretense." But such phrases suggest that the present discomfort of theology is terminal, which is too severe a judgment. The situation may be curable if carefully diagnosed and given a rehabilitative regimen. On the one hand, what happens in theological education seems too narrow, too self-satisfied, too geared to the maintenance of unimaginative ministries, and too cafeteria-like; on the other hand, it seems so diffuse, without governing vision, purpose, intensity, or center. The various parts do not integrate into a compelling vision of ministry, of the role of religion in civilization, of the place of Christianity among the world's religions, or of the relationship of theology as a "science" either to Christian piety and action or to the nontheological sciences. Frequently we are tempted to put the most favorable light on this situation by calling it "pluralism" and "openness." We less often state what is clearly the case: much of it lacks integrity, and some of it is simply confused. That is the case partly because the most common terms of self-description are confusing.

LIBERAL?

We should, perhaps, acknowledge that this condition is most pronounced in the ecumenically oriented Protestant seminaries in the West, those which, for the most part, have the highest prestige and the highest academic standards in theological education. They are usually tagged "liberal" by others. It is not at all clear what the word "liberal" means today. Clearly, the situation in these seminaries is distinct from those in many Roman Catholic seminaries, where a rather firm episcopal and sometimes papal guidance enforces adherence to authorized doctrines of faith and morals. The recent international debates about Hans Küng and Charles Curran also represent a situation quite distinct from that in the seminaries referred to here. Even more removed are those debates currently being waged in fundamentalist seminaries (today frequently reported in the press), where trustees, administrations, and whole faculties become embroiled in summary dismissals for the teaching of "modernist" doctrines. The situation also differs from that of many seminaries in the Third World, where missionaries established systems of education based, essentially, on the export of European university models of learning on one side, and on confessionally fixed prescriptions of what could and could not be taught in seminaries on the other. Such seminaries cannot be called "liberal." Nevertheless, the term "liberal" is ambiguous.

If by "liberal" is meant the use of higher biblical criticism, a recognition of the resources of the social sciences, an appreciation of the modern ecumenical movements and bodies, a willingness to encounter — with respect — philosophy, science, and the world religions, and a theological orientation that presses believers and the churches toward the democratization of political, economic, and social life, then ecumenically oriented seminaries and many departments of theology are on the whole "liberal." If by "liberal" is meant an unqualified reliance on humanist or naturalistic frames of reference to interpret all theological principles, a distrust of all that is implied in terms such as "conversion," "evangelism," "eternal verities," "doctrine," "authority," and "piety," or a decided commitment to socialism as the wave of the future, then these centers of theological study are not obviously "liberal."

What such schools are today experiencing is not brand new.

Symposia on the question began to appear in the literature over two decades ago. It is as if the theological community recognized that the ideational capital that informed the structure of theological educational institutions in the nineteenth century was being used up. Structures were coasting without the inner coherence that seemed to have informed the earlier pattern, yet no call to the past could suffice.

MODERN?

Earl Thompson documented the roots of the "liberal" seminaries in a 1968 article called "The Andover Liberals as Theological Educators." These forebears saw several tasks as constitutive for theological education.

> [They] sought to establish and explicate the notion of the finality and universality of Christianity . . . [and] they endeavored to harmonize Christian Truth with all ostensibly conflicting truths. Third . . . they revised and enlarged the traditional curriculum to accommodate new methodologies and materials from disciplines of the scientific study of history, natural science, and social science. Fourth, they directed much of the missionary zeal . . . into channels of educational reconstruction. Fifth, they attempted to stay abreast of and to exploit new teaching methods emanating from centers of university education. . . . Sixth, they thought of themselves as waging a critical battle for the liberation of theological education from arbitrary . . . denominational interference and restrictions [which limited both ecumenical cooperation and academic freedom].[1]

Since working out such patterns, most seminaries have added several other accents. Emphases on religion and society or Christian social ethics, which grew out of the Social Gospel movement, were institutionalized in the 1920s and augmented again in the 1960s under the influence of both thirty years of "Christian Realism" and the civil rights movement of Martin Luther King, Jr. Requirements for clinical pastoral education were introduced in the 1930s, but were more fully institutionalized only in the 1970s. Also, in the last two decades, substantive changes have been brought about by the influx of women into our faculties and student bodies — a third area where most educators in these centers believe that truth and justice has been served.

Other post-World War II developments have seriously al-

---

1. Thompson, "The Andover Liberals as Theological Educators," *Andover Newton Quarterly*, Mar. 1968, pp. 204-6.

tered the sociocultural and intellectual milieu within which theological education takes place. Certainly massive urbanization and technologization have had and continue to have a tremendous impact around the world. These changes were stimulated in large part by impulses growing out of previous Protestant traditions, although many recent manifestations of these developments seem to have escaped conscious theological guidance, and some see them as manifestly anti-theological, even demonic, in character. Many Christians as well as many critics of Christianity cite the dangers of ecological disruption and the threats of nuclear destruction as evidence that the "Western Project" — the modern synthesis of Protestant and Enlightenment thought that promoted a scientific, technological, and capitalist-economic dominion of the earth — must come to an end. Such dominion, it is held, is the cause of modern sin, the wages of which are the threat of nuclear and ecological death.[2]

Internationally, however, industrialization, democratization, urbanization, mechanization, computerization, militarization, and the development of a world-capitalist system are producing the same dramatic social changes that once radically disrupted traditional cultures in the West. Governments right, left, and center, oppositions of multiple stripes, business leaders, technocrats, and labor organizers both condemn these developments and eagerly introduce them at every opportunity. All over the world the introduction of these Western-induced developments is producing unique new situations in multiple contexts. Not everyone agrees with what Arend van Leeuwen argued a generation ago: that these developments ought to be warmly embraced as the way in which God is indirectly pushing and prodding us to become a new interdependent global community in which local ontocracies and magic are banished and the often hidden presuppositions of Christianity are finding their way in non-Western and non-Christian settings.[3] In fact, whether the truly prophetic stance in our time is to endorse or to resist these developments induces all sorts of intense reactions among friends within faculties and in the churches, and between churches on different continents. Indeed, theological stances are frequently evaluated as much by whether they seem to enhance or oppose these developments as by any other single criterion.

---

2. See, for example, Gibson Winter, *Liberating Creation: Foundations of Religious Social Ethics* (New York: Crossroad, 1981).
3. Van Leeuwen, *Christianity in World History* (New York: Scribner's, 1964).

NEO-ORTHODOX?

A second factor affecting theological education is the tremendous impact that "neo-orthodox" theology has had. Much has been and much could be said about this movement. Virtually no one in contemporary theological education has been untouched by at least parts of it. In this discussion, however, we want to accent only one dimension of it as it bears on our particular questions. It may be that the most remarkable thing about "neo-orthodoxy" and "crisis theology," as influenced by existentialism in general, is that they challenged the validity of the liberal agenda of theological education as it had developed out of the nineteenth century. In fact, neo-orthodoxy declared the legacy of that period bankrupt, and turned again to theology as dogma and confession. At the same time, however, we must note what Robin Lovin has shown about this movement: it has proven to have little capacity to build or sustain guidelines for intellectual or social-ethical life.[4] The reason is simple: the great Continental neo-orthodox theologians shouted down the earlier attempts by theology to engage world-religious, philosophical, and social-scientific modes of thought. Despite all the profound insight and obvious genius of figures such as Karl Barth and Dietrich Bonhoeffer, the simultaneous influence and intellectual-institutional impotence of neo-orthodoxy has had consequences for educational and ecclesiastical organizations that purport to be directly relevant to social life at home and abroad.

This movement focused attention on Christian confessional theology in a new way, tending to deny the possibilities for dialogical encounter with science, technology, world religions, and social or psychological analysis, and it did so precisely during the years that these were being more fully incorporated in seminary curricula and gaining strength in society at large. The ancient question of Tertullian — "What has Jerusalem to do with Athens?" — was revived. The basic structures formed by the "modernizing" liberals and by the acceptance of modern civilization thus were carrying a theological message that was opposed to these very structures. The result was an inevitable dissonance, one that tempted theologians into a new form of sectarian and confessionalist opposition to everything in sociocultural and secular intellectual life while in fact they lived comfortably with both the culture and the standards of "secular" academia. Many theologians found themselves plunged into

---

4. Lovin, *Christian Faith and Public Choices: The Social Ethics of Barth, Brunner, and Bonhoeffer* (Philadelphia: Fortress Press, 1984).

a schizoid existence. They were scholars in academia and dogmaticians in faith. The connecting links were difficult to find or, if asserted, difficult to defend. Theological education became an exercise in programmed alienation; a new version of a "two-kingdom theory" was widely adopted.

Still a third development affecting modern theological education was the rise of university departments of religion, which both removed (as had been the case in Germany in the nineteenth century) scholarly studies in the theological fields from the life of the churches and, in substantial measure, removed the study of religious matters from the processes of preparation for religious leadership. In that new environment, however, anthropological, critical, and phenomenological orientations to religion became predominant. More often than not, religious beliefs were seen as a manifestation of some other force in the human psyche or human culture that caused the rise and fall, the shape and character of all particular religions and theologies. This had the effect of relativizing all claims that any religion might wish to make about the truth or justice of its understandings, doctrines, or practices. A priority was put on those forms of learning that were acutely critical, even skeptical, about all claims of truth or justice. The former was treated as an unprovable perspective, the latter as a "value" that some people held. Ironically, this development comported well with one aspect of Protestant thought revived by some branches of neo-orthodoxy — namely, the idea that what Christianity was about could not and should not be defended in public discourse. It could be seen only through the eyes of faith, and then proclaimed. A decision, not an argument, was required. In the university world, this simply confirmed the suspicion that what theologians thought and taught, what churches confessed and believed was unwarranted and unconfirmable opinion, not a verifiable claim to something true and just. Religion was like an inside joke: you either got it or you didn't.

ECUMENICAL?

But perhaps the most dramatic development affecting theological education — and the one least consciously taken into theological educational planning in part because none of the several developments just discussed would lead one to anticipate it — is the new global awareness that has begun to deprovincialize all that we have to think about. Not only do the new electronic media bring the whole world into immediate presence, but daily encounters bring us new bursts of interest in missiology, prompted especially by the rise of evangelical groups, a new awareness of people belonging to the world's religions, and a growing body of information about international problems of hunger and human rights. These signal to believers the altered world context in which theological education will have to take place in the future. These developments indicate that all contemporary theology must recognize that we live in a global society, one inevitably bound together in a technological, economic, and political, as well as religious, web of interdependence. Not only does the very idea of one universal God, of a "theology" based on a valid knowledge of that universal reality demand attention to the largest possible vision of reality, but our very context demands genuinely ecumenical orientations in faith and ethics. We do not know quite what to make of all this, and only a few have begun to wrestle with what may be entailed.[5]

For one thing, our new global context seems to demand a familiarity with a new range of subcultural contexts where mission and ministry must be developed in new directions. But how that is to be done is a decisive question. If it is not to be simply a multiplication of serial parochialisms, we may have to work at a new level of generality. Our governing concepts and categories, forged by our parochial histories and memories, may be quite incapacitating for ministry to people whose life and work also are dominated by new international structures and increasingly complex societies. Parochial "Western," "white," "male" perspectives will certainly have to be deprovincialized. And just as certainly, minorities, women, and Third World peoples will — if they hope to be effective in ministry in the next generation — have to encounter global issues in a new way as they move out of the ghetto subcultures, the domestic roles, and the localistic environments to which they have been confined. And they will have to have, and help develop, frameworks of greater amplitude to interpret these issues than their previous experience allowed them to develop. Certainly their friends and relatives who begin to study economics, or engineering, or management, or politics, or agriculture, or comparative cultures are not going to be interested in a ministry based on sub-

---

5. Two of the best studies of this sort, one from an "ecumenical" perspective and one from an "evangelical" perspective, are these: Roger Shinn, *Forced Options: Social Decisions for the Twenty-First Century* (San Francisco: Harper & Row, 1982); and Charles H. Kraft, *Christianity in Culture: A Study in Dynamic Biblical Theologizing in Cross-Cultural Perspective* (Maryknoll, N.Y.: Orbis Books, 1979). A third fine study is that by Kosuke Koyama, *Mount Fuji and Mount Sinai* (London: SCM Press, 1984).

cultural particularism alone. In brief, engagement in the particular subcontexts of tomorrow may require steps toward a clearer "general" or "unified" theory for belief and ethics in a global context. Few in contemporary theological education are equipped to meet these demands. *Apologia* thus might well demand a warranted "general systems theory" of global reach, for that is what, at its best and in its most creative moments, theological education has provided to faith, to religious leadership, to the neglected and oppressed, and to civilizations over the centuries.

Certainly, many of the people to whom all our students will minister in the twenty-first century are people who also live in the midst of globally linked professions and institutions. Education, science, technology, law, business, corporate life, labor, finance, medicine, industry, and politics are all global in reach. And it simply is not clear that we are preparing the next generation of church leadership to preach to and teach, to pastor and organize the people in ways that will allow them to grasp what is happening to the world from a theologically informed perspective. That means, of course, that people will get their primary categories for interpreting the realities of life from nontheological sources, and will determine their policies for these arenas of life on nontheological grounds — while "religion" will be increasingly confined to the relativities of personal idiosyncrasy, to useful techniques for psychic stabilization or interpersonal relationships, or to little conventicles of the faithful in a new, alienated diaspora. In fact, some leading sociologists say that this situation already exists.[6]

The problems of our present context are compounded by the fact that each of our various specialized fields of study has developed — since the older "liberal" agenda set the tone of modern theological education — its own technically specialized tools of understanding and interpretation that are seldom related either to the common task of theological education or to the problems of the world church. To put it another way, the corollary of the new awareness of globalization is the new awareness of radical contextualism, a situation in which each region of the world, each discipline, each field of human endeavor, each local situation, each group and each subgroup, and finally each individual becomes sovereign in itself. Theological conversation and theological education become less and less a dialogue about the most important questions and more and

---

6. Robert Bellah et al., *Habits of the Heart: Individualism and Commitment in American Life* (Berkeley and Los Angeles: University of California Press, 1985).

more a power struggle about who is to be allowed to speak. In general, we can say that the ecumenically oriented churches and seminaries have been among those most sensitive to the enormous variety of contexts, but in an odd way it is precisely this sensitivity that has exacerbated the current discomfort in theological education. Although it may be a valid temporary step on the road to a new universality, what that sensitivity has wrought is a kind of sensitivity to pluralism that is tempted to become a moral, spiritual, cultural, subcultural, and intellectual relativism. Everyone and every caucus is presumed to have its own way of viewing reality, and each is viewed as equally valid.

REALIST?

This development raises in dramatic form the question of whether we have any coherent and governing message that we can discuss in terms of its truth and its justice that ought to be at least encountered everywhere by everyone, in all the contexts of the world. And whereas it was once thought that each field within theology would contribute to the clarification of an integrated larger vision, it turns out that each discipline has become focused on itself. The problem could be stated this way: precisely where there is greatest openness to global concerns and the multiplicity of contexts, each new perspective is taken as another discreet reality with its own time, place, sense of reality, meaning system, and agenda. The result is less the breaking of barriers or the broadening of horizons than the uncritical celebration of an infinite number of differences. In short, we find ourselves living amidst and unwittingly fomenting a new polytheism in which each person, group, discipline, society, or culture projects its own peculiar religious message onto a cosmic screen without clarifying either what might be of universal significance or what can be energetically articulated, organized, and celebrated by all.

Most theological students and many faculty members today are decided nominalists. That is what is produced by modern romanticism, by those religions and churches which demand that everything meet the test of pertinence to personal "experience," and by disciplinary specialization wherein each academic field develops its own purely empirical methods. The nominalists, it will be remembered, argued that all humans could really know was their own experience, and that on the basis of some apparently common features of particular experiences, those who had control of a culture could give names to — could "nominalize" — some general phenomena to organize them for the sake of what would make sense to their own experience. How humans name things, of course, is of considerable consequence, for those who name things in an arbitrary world control it. In late medieval and early Reformation discussions, this view was contrasted with "realism" — a term that has undergone considerable transformation since then. In modern secular usage, "realism" (as distinct from "Christian Realism" as advocated, for example, by Reinhold Niebuhr) has become almost a substitute term for nominalism. Modern realism, which is really classical nominalism, presumes that all truth comes from the focus on empirical facts rationally explicated, technologically utilized to control reality, and arbitrarily valued or disvalued according to preferences or interests. Such a view is thought to be in contrast to mythic, visionary, impractical, abstract, or transcendental speculations about "truth" or "justice."

In the classical sense, however, the realists, in contrast to the nominalists, argued that when we spoke of things like God, or God's truth and justice, or Christ's presence, or "the gospel," or the power of the Holy Spirit, we were speaking (always inadequately) of real, universal phenomena that not everyone experienced in the same way, but to which we were normatively subject in our thought and actions. Such things could be distorted by the way we represented them, but they could not be technologically manipulated to meet our needs, interests, or preferences. These phenomena could be known to be universally valid by the deeper reaches of reason and revelation, which in the final analysis were not viewed as incompatible with one another. Knowledge of them was, in principle, accessible to all people, in all cultures, in all conditions of life. Thus, when these phenomena were transposed into new contexts and indigenized there, they brought about a transformation that stimulated those newly aware of them to reclaim and transform their indigenous culture and religion into ones that reflected a new level of universal human understanding and global historical participation. In the process, the new communities also found their own quite particular and idiosyncratic insights refined. The dross could be, in some measure, separated from the gold. That which was of wider significance could be brought into the wider discussion, and that which was purely local could be appreciated for what it was, but not thought to be more than it was. Thus, new syntheses were developed, ones that also served to deprovincialize the perspectives of those who brought the new message, for their treasure always was carried in earthen vessels. This is a perspective made vivid to us by the new, revisionist historical work of Lamin Sanneh, as we will see in Chapter 4.

It may well be due to processes such as the ones Sanneh identifies historically that Christianity has never been fully satisfied with either an exclusively nominalist or an exclusively realist answer. The very idea of a sovereign, living God who is present in a very particular Jesus Christ seems to demand both realist and nominalist elements. As we will see, this set of issues will tend to crop up again and again; it is the simplest way of stating one of the core questions with which we shall have to wrestle anew. But the crisis of our context is that the "realist" side of this theological logic is being obscured.

It may well be that seminaries are victims of a mistranslation of Scripture. The text does *not* read, "Where two or three are gathered, they form a committee." But committee work is the way in which a great number of things get done in theological education. Indeed, that is how, in our context, the issues just surveyed were raised and dealt with at ANTS. The Curriculum Revision Committee identified an "almost universal corporate desire to widen our perspective to one of world concern," a desire that is intensifying; a need to clarify our common understanding of what our theology of education is, or can be; and a recognition that, for many students, basic courses in religious, cultural, and civilizational history, philosophy, and ethics are likely to be required, since seminaries can no longer count on college graduates having any substantive exposure to these subjects.

The central features of this committee's work that are of ongoing importance for this study involve two recommendations:

A. "That the school articulate its theology of education and reformulate its statement of purpose [in its catalog]. That it further develop such articulation in the light of 'transpositional theology' . . . [in part through the ATS research represented by this study]." In this connection, the committee also recommended the following:

1. Encouraging cross-cultural experience by expanding [faculty and] student exchange programs.
2. Supporting opportunities for students to learn and use modern languages.
3. Relating each discipline specifically to a theology of mission.
4. Representing international perspectives in course bibliographies.
5. Devoting special class sessions to international issues.

B. "That the faculty as a whole take responsibility for the content of the core curriculum." This deceptively simple sentence encompasses a number of very critical issues. Among other things, it means that each department must show that what it offers contributes to the emerging sense of theological education that is contextually alert, globally concerned, and mission-oriented. In short, *apologia* is required of each professor.[7]

BIBLICAL?

One major difficulty also emerged from this committee's work. That is the "problem of the biblical fields." The mention of this should in no way be taken as a reflection on the quality or integrity of the scholars we have in Old Testament and New Testament studies, for they are widely recognized both within the school and in the wider scholarly community as individuals of very high standard — indeed, several are of international repute. The "problem" is that many of the difficulties that theological education has appear most acutely in this area.

Protestant seminaries take their point of departure, at least in theory, from the Bible. While current theological education tends to focus, like this chapter, on "the context," context is not taken as the basic authority. Protestant ordinations have few vows, but one is almost always present: the candidate for ministry must assent to the Bible as "source and norm of faith and morals."

Yet, nowhere else is the historical-critical method more fully developed, nowhere else is the subdivision of an area of scholarship more refined, nowhere else is the difficulty of interdisciplinary conversation more pronounced, and nowhere else is the concern for *apologia,* globalization, and mission less accented by many leaders of a scholarly guild. To be sure, fundamentalist authors can be found who are deeply concerned with apologetics and mission of a sort, but no ecumenically oriented evangelical, Protestant, or Roman Catholic believes that the methods fundamentalists use can be defended. For the most part, it appears that radical contextualism has become a predominant assumption of a number of historical-critical methods, and these methods have been deeply interwoven with phenomenological and existential, decidedly nominalist, or historicist understandings of what might be meaningful. That is to say that a number of the scholars in biblical studies who have developed the contemporary study of the Bible as it is most often carried out in ecumenically oriented seminaries operate on the presumption that each scriptural text is so deeply shaped by

---

7. Maria Harris, "Report of the Curriculum Revision Committee," Spring 1984.

the context in which it was written that it can be understood only in terms of those contexts and the literary forms those contexts generated. Others argue that we have to interpret the texts through the understanding of contexts, but that the interpretation of contexts themselves is determined by our present context. Thus, what we must do is choose our present context, and then read the contexts and texts of Scripture in these terms so that we can find a way to make Scripture speak to our context. If that is the case, it is difficult to see in what sense Scripture can be "source and norm."[8]

Theological education — if it is to render anything that is worthy of contextualization, globalization, and mission — demands that we reconsider the possibility that at least some texts, however much they are influenced by their context, have context-transcending elements of potentially universal importance, and that this is why we can take them as source and norm, defend their validity in public discourse, and utilize them to critically assess current contexts. But the case has to be made in today's context for this possibility. Contemporary biblical scholarship has so contextualized the texts that the very idea that texts can judge contexts is methodologically doubted. Further, those contexts are understood to be very far removed from those in and by which we today interpret those same Scriptures. They are also removed from what the great framers of the theological traditions in the past — such as Augustine, Thomas, the Reformers — or the liberal, Social Gospel, neo-orthodox, or liberation theologians have had to say. Only the specialist can give us any guidance about what the texts might have meant — let alone what, if anything, they might mean. Thus, only they have access to what is most decisive to know, and what they know is viewed to be inapplicable beyond either the texts' contexts or their own contexts.

While laboring in this vineyard has sometimes produced heady wines, and while no other religious tradition has subjected its own Scriptures to such intense critical analysis, the fruit of this labor has not been applied to consequential questions of the nature of biblical authority, the ways in which the biblical message might be of perennial and transcontextual import, or the question of whether there is anything universally true or just in the Bible. Some branches of biblical scholarship, in fact, have turned almost entirely to the study of the contexts in which the Scriptures were formed or re-

---

8. See, for example, Elisabeth Schüssler Fiorenza, *In Memory of Her: A Feminist Theological Reconstruction of Christian Origins* (New York: Crossroad, 1983).

ceived—the history of Israel, the redaction processes, the thought world or social world of the Greco-Roman context of the New Testament, and so on. Thus, the normative and thematic significance of the biblical message, which many of the other disciplines in the seminary presume (in different ways), has practically disappeared from the discussion in scholarly biblical literature, even if creative teachers want very badly to show the authority, importance, and theological-practical utility of biblical studies for worship, spiritual development, ethical witness, mission, and the ministry of the faithful in the world.

The problem of "text and context" turns out to be a critical issue, and in our study at ANTS we discovered that we would have to spend more time working on it. In fact, it turned out to be the decisive issue in discussions with our international consultants, for they relied on the same texts as we did, spoke to us from different contexts than we knew, and pressed us toward transcontextual thinking. As we shall see, they did not do so in the same ways or even in fully compatible ways. Nevertheless, their contributions are valuable, and it is to these that we now turn.

CHAPTER 3

Texts and Contexts

It is characteristic of ecumenically oriented Protestant circles to take up each substantive question of current interest in terms of Scripture, and the ways in which the "Word of God" found in and behind the words of the Bible addresses these issues. Such a method has become more complicated in view of modern understandings of both text and context, as we saw during an all-faculty ATS retreat on the subject of contextualization, globalization, and mission in theological education. Major papers were presented by Nantawan Boonprasat-Lewis, J. G. F. Collison, and Lamin Sanneh. In addition, Dean Orlando Costas, representing accents from both the Radical Reformation tradition from the sixteenth century and more recent encounters with Latin American liberation theology, offered a lengthy sermon to the ANTS faculty and its consultants that turned out to be a manifesto on mission, ministry, and theological education. His views were based on a particular understanding of the relation of the biblical text to the modern context which differed from that of our international consultants and from that of our own biblical scholars. In the next two chapters we will summarize the substance of several discussions of these materials and the "problem of the biblical fields" as identified in the last chapter. In quite different ways, each of these participants represents key perspectives on contextualization, globalization, and mission. Each also allows us to see, in a direct and dialogical setting, certain promising and certain perilous dimensions to the characteristic ways in which we all tend to relate text and context.

 Reviewing these contributions in this chapter and the next

one will allow us to gain from their insights, and to identify difficulties in the ways in which we Protestants ordinarily work. The attempt is consistently made to exhume basic presuppositions from the wealth of material each contributor has provided. The guiding question is "What would one have to believe to hold this view as valid?"

FROM TEXT TO CONTEXT

We begin our review of this material by summarizing several themes in Dean Costas's manifesto.[1] Seminaries prepare women and men for the ordained ministry. They also do other things, and they do some of them rather well, but preparation for ministry is the genius of theological education. And mission is, as it has always been, the core of ministry. Mission — in the sense of bringing the gospel and its liberating message to the dispossessed, the marginalized, and the oppressed — is what God put the church on earth to do. Costas draws his text from Acts 11-13, regarding the church in Antioch. There, a new leadership, gripped by the Holy Spirit, dared to cross cultural barriers in order to evangelize Gentiles as well as Jews. Costas sees in this particular text the universal pattern for what the church should be and do. The church in Antioch generated a wide variety of leaders in the service of the missionary churches that established the model for evangelism and missionary church planting. If the ministry of the church is faithful to its source and norm, it has, and must have, a charismatic and mission-oriented foundation. Ministers are resources that the Spirit gives to the church to enable it to participate in mission, and ministers are instruments of the Spirit who enable the church to grow in its missionary service. Those who are drawn by the Spirit into the church via the ministry are themselves not only baptized and confirmed in the Word but nurtured into a new style of life and called to missionary activity. Thus, the fruit of mission and ministry is belief and practice on new foundations — a new *theoria* and a new *praxis,* as it were; a combination of dynamic beliefs and actions under the leadership of the Spirit that is sustained by the sacrificial sharing of material resources in, by, and beyond the missionary congregation.

---

1. Costas, "Mission, Ministry, and Theological Education in the Last Quarter of the Twentieth Century," address delivered at the ATS Retreat, 15-16 Mar. 1985. See also his *Christ outside the Gate: Mission beyond Christendom* (Maryknoll, N.Y.: Orbis Books, 1984), which the members of the ATS research team also used to interpret his remarks.

In this context, some are called to special tasks in the mission of God. This vocation has an internal dimension — a passionate desire to be at the exclusive service of the gospel — and an external dimension — the public recognition and confirmation by the community of faith that God has set one apart for a special task. Among the ways to prepare for this vocation, besides prayer and nurture in the church, is formal theological education. This program of study is ordinarily understood to involve academic study of biblical, theological, and historical materials and the gaining of practical insights and skills considered essential by theologians and ecclesiastical leaders for competence in ministry.

This model, however, is not without its difficulties, says Costas. For one thing, it is not always the case that academic theologians and ecclesiastical leaders are themselves deeply involved in mission or ministry among the people in ways that clearly manifest the vitality of the Spirit. For another, we live in a meritocratic and professionalized society, and patterns of status, honor, teaching, and learning have been adopted almost uncritically by theological education. The standards and processes of present academic programs cannot guarantee the effective shaping of ministers. The focus is academic and professional, not spirit-filled or practical formation.

To remedy this situation, Christian theological educators need to remember that the most dramatic experiences of church expansion in history, and today in other parts of the world, have occurred when clergy were formed by neither the virtues of academia nor the privileged skills of the modern professions, but by the power of the Spirit in the context of ministry and mission. It was the Spirit who anointed Jesus for the fulfillment of his messianic ministry with special emphasis on the poor, the oppressed, and the dispossessed; it was the Spirit who was the force that brought him back from the dead; it is the Spirit who fills the church with the presence of the risen Christ; and it is the Spirit who makes it possible for Christ to be found among the prisoners, the sick, the hungry, and the naked — these are God's "little ones," and it is they who constitute the fundamental historical reference point by which we are to judge the integrity of the church in the empirical sense. Only from this sociohistorical vantage point, which can be read only from a pneumatological perspective, can the church and its leadership discern the priorities of its mission in a given period and setting.

These, says Costas, are the foundations upon which we can determine the agenda of theological education here and now. First, theological institutions need to equip the student to help the church address the challenge of a world wherein the vast majority do not have the least notion of what the Christian faith is all about, and where billions lie beyond the reach of local congregations and the witness of individual Christians. Second, theological institutions should prepare dedicated people to lead the church in its ministry to, with, and among the "sinned-against"—the victims, the vulnerable, the poor, the oppressed, and the powerless—bringing the promise of liberation, justice, and God's Kingdom to them in word and deed. And third, theological education must prepare the called leadership of tomorrow to promote Christian unity and human solidarity. The present fragmentation of the church is a stumbling block to those who do not have a saving knowledge of the gospel, and it is an impediment to effective witness against the classism, racism, sexism, ideologism, and militarization that divide and threaten our world. These matters are seldom directly addressed by those who take the professional and academic patterns of our context to be supreme. In brief, the mission of theological education is the spiritual formation of women and men in ministry for the *praxis* of mission in the world.

Costas's views have been extensively discussed at ANTS and in the wider theological community. In 1987 he undertook a world tour lecturing on missiology in similar terms, and was warmly received on three continents. Many, evidently, embrace the move from a particular text about a specific context to an agenda that appears to be universally applicable. The connection between the particular text, the universally applicable patterns discernible in it, and the multiple contexts where this pattern is to be lived out is the Holy Spirit. The Spirit is what forms the church, shapes the leadership, breaks the barriers between peoples, and calls to mission. Those who are grasped by the Spirit will immediately and spontaneously adopt this orientation; others may resist it by taking recourse to "professionalism" or "academic meritocracy." In such a view, theological education is above all an instrument of the church; it is, indeed, instrumental in nature, and not an end in itself. It exists to provide the servants of the Holy Spirit with the knowledge and skills to be effective in carrying out their missions.

It may be that a number of those engaged in theological education at ANTS or around the world are simply not grasped by the Holy Spirit, or do not properly understand Scripture. Whatever the reasons, it soon became clear that some people in our dialogues were not fully convinced by Costas. If we are to take the dramatic growth of a religious movement as the mark of the Holy Spirit, we should have to turn to the missionary efforts of the Buddhists or the expansion of Islam to find the world's premier examples. Even within Christian understandings, not all historians of either the early church or modern missions read the expansion of the Christian church as Costas does. And those who professionally study the development of doctrine ask how we are to know that this missiological discernment of the Holy Spirit is more valid than that of, say, the enthusiastic "tongues" and "healings" of Pentecostal churches, or Thomas Müntzer's proposals during the Peasant Wars of the Reformation period, or William James's understanding of "religious experience," or Paul Tillich's views of the Spirit in the third volume of his *Systematics*?

These objections do not, of course, refute Costas. He may in fact be correct even if he has not presented his argument convincingly. However, the objections compel him, and compel us all, to press the questions one level deeper. The debate over Costas's contribution demands that we overtly raise the questions of whether the Holy Spirit as reported in this text works the same way in all contexts, whether we can reliably discern that Spirit when it is at hand (and, if so, by what criteria), whether that model can and must be our guide in Christian mission, whether it drives the church in the directions Costas identifies, and whether we can make these directions the basis of theological education. And, if we think that all this is the case, how might we argue for such a view in the face of skepticism about it within and beyond the community of dialogue?

Several colleagues doubted these views on the grounds previously mentioned, and also because they felt that theological education is, in fact, an end in itself, and that the churches would be well advised to make themselves vibrant centers of theological education and stop doing a lot of the rather trivial things they do. Further, several Christian feminists in our dialogues differed with Costas more vocally precisely because they saw other texts and other ways of understanding contexts as more decisive for theological education today.

THE CONTEXT AS TEXT

Throughout the course of our dialogues, the most persistent and articulate advocate of a more radical contextual approach was Nantawan Boonprasat-Lewis. Her earlier studies with Gibson Winter and Richard Shaull, her appreciation for the methods of Gabrielle

Dietrich and Letty Russell, her research and teaching in Thailand, her work on Asian theology and ethics while a visiting professor here at ANTS, and her involvement with feminist perspectives in contemporary church and society — all these have led her to press vigorously for recognition of the contextuality of all theological education.

To grasp Boonprasat-Lewis's point of view, we need to draw both from the paper she prepared for the all-faculty ATS retreat[2] and from a series of comments that she made in small group discussions. She argues that contextual thinking is nothing new in Christianity, although it has been obscured time and again by those who want to establish fixed dogma prematurely and impose it on new contexts. Indeed, she reports that many students in Third World seminaries have little interest in studying the contexts in which they work. They have been taught by missionaries to prefer a fixed doctrine and an absolutist understanding of Scripture, and often use these to isolate themselves from the social and cultural questions that surround them. In reaction against that approach, and with an appreciative nod to the work of Gabrielle Dietrich (the German expatriate, socialist, and feminist thinker who has worked in South Asia for many years), Boonprasat-Lewis argues that the contextual character of Christian thought, after years and even centuries of neglect, was rediscovered only by biblical scholars of the nineteenth century who adopted historical-critical research methods and recognized that texts could be fully understood only when they were seen in terms of their *Sitz im Leben*. Since then, it has become increasingly clear that not only biblical texts but doctrines, dogmas, and indeed "whatever we do, whatever we write and say, emerges from a context, *and has to do with a specific environment*" (italics added). It is this last phrase that is most decisive, for it can be read in two ways, depending on whether we mentally supply the word "only" or the word "also" in the middle of it. In either case, of course, to fail to engage directly in contextual analysis is to become subservient to texts, doctrines, or dogmas produced by someone else's context, for we will be unable to tell whether what is said is only or also contextual.

To be sure, much of the biblical research of the nineteenth century focused only on the "textual contexts" of ideas, symbols, religious beliefs, festivals, cultic traditions, and the like, and omitted the most important structures and dynamics of societal life; but

---

2. Boonprasat-Lewis, "Some Motifs in Contextual Thinking," address delivered at the ATS Retreat, 15-16 Mar. 1985.

already the die was cast. Wider social, anthropological, and historical perspectives were gradually taken into account, and as a consequence, modern contextual analysis has developed an appreciation for the pervasive and often decisive influence of economic and power relations — an influence Marx and others had begun to argue during the same time period in which biblical scholarship was developing its historical-critical methods.

Theologically, Boonprasat-Lewis's contribution can be said to emphasize less pneumatically guided mission — an emphasis we saw more clearly in Costas (but which feminists preceived as but a license for aggressive domination) — than incarnational presence. Among the presuppositions that appeared again and again in our discussions was the claim, stated in several ways, that the gospel of Jesus Christ is above all the good news that the divine reality which brings hope and justice, love and peace, and which was once thought to be far off and removed — sovereign, distant, abstract, legalistic, and forbidding — has entered into life and history and can now be recognized in the midst of community, culture, and liberating movement. The divine and eternal has taken the risk of the secular and the temporal in order to "become" salvation through human fulfillment and not simply to "be" above and beyond our human worlds of meaning, suffering, joy, and relationship. The transcendent has become embodied, subject to contextual conditioning, yet pervading the contexts of life and thereby infusing them with new possibilities. Such a view is in striking contrast both to the Buddhism of Boonprasat-Lewis's background and to the "missionary Christianity" as it continues to be propagated in many parts of her homeland by men claiming to speak for the Holy Spirit.

With references to the work of Richard Shaull, she speaks of "what God is doing *in* the world." Thus, all theology is to be encounter with, inquiry into, reflection upon, participation in, and active response to the concrete struggles of humans in contexts that are always specific and particular. Theology is descriptive, empirical, and indicative, and not prescriptive, speculative, or imperative. The subject matter of theological education, therefore, is everything that is really going on in the world that saves humanity, for what is going on in such contexts is, at some level, fundamentally shaped by God's active incarnate presence in history, however conditioned, "un-sacred," "non-eternal," and "unspiritual" that activity may appear to be.

In several of our ATS team discussions, Boonprasat-Lewis recognized that some forms of contextual understanding might well be understood to be "merely nominalist" — that is, merely descriptive of the settings and factualities of historical existence, merely particular without universal import, and merely anomic or ethically relativistic without normative content. Further, a good bit of "what is going on in the world" is oppressive, arrogant, and destructive. Contextual analysis, unable to establish criteria by which to discern contexts ethically, is always tempted to become contextual*ism,* which is but a baptized form of journalistic sociology. But Christian contextualism, she argues, has a "referential aspect." It is always seeking to penetrate the mere eventfulness of the contexts of our lifeworlds to the dynamic authority behind and within. It does not take things at face value, but sees them in the context of the larger fabric of society, history, suffering, and redemption from evil. Thus, genuinely theological approaches to contextual thought will attempt to discern the *content* of "word," "faith," "love," and "salvation" within specific settings, a content that presses the contextualist theologian to see the connective tissues by which each particular context or event is related to larger and more comprehensive processes and structures that in turn are connected with human life everywhere and always.

Also, drawing on the writings of Letty Russell, Boonprasat-Lewis argues that putting universality and contextuality in a polar or oppositional relationship betrays a contextual*ism* and thus a false understanding of Christian contextual thinking.[3] In the gospel message of Incarnation, she says, "universality and contextuality are joined together.... The universal proclamation of hope for all humanity is at the same time the concrete, situation-variable proclamation that the blind see, the lame walk, the prisoners are set free." What is universal about such quite specific, local, diverse, immediate, and situation-determined events is that they carry on and manifest the one story of God's involvement with human salvation. Each is a concrete, anthropologically focused chapter in the universal story that has its meaning unveiled in the particular Christ who, as God incarnate, was crucified for us and with us, and who is risen so that we may have hope.

Closely related, in her view, is the fact that if we take any particular context as the point of departure for Christian contextual reflection, response, and action, and press through to the deepest levels of contextual analysis, we will soon recognize that every context is related to every other context. We will be opened to intercontextual communication, and ultimately to the theological question

---

3. See Russell, "Universality and Contextuality," *Ecumencial Review* 23 (1979): 23-26.

of who God is as the one in whom all contexts cohere. Thus, serious contextual analysis involves not only critical interpretation of particular situations but inevitably invites the idea of globalization. It opens up a search for meaningful ways to actualize human hope universally.

Boonprasat-Lewis knows that, in ethical theory, the most frequent charge against contextual thinking is that it leads to ethical relativism or anomic particularity. Nevertheless, she thinks that a Christian contextuality must focus on people in their situations, and not on "abstract" ideas, concepts, or theories. And when we focus on people, especially those on the bottom edge of society, we find that people orient their lives in terms of the future, in terms of the real prospects for hope, and in terms of those forces and dynamics in the context that can bring salvation from whatever it is in the immediate environment that represses or suppresses viable hopes. In other words, justice is foundational to human hope. Justice is the goal of Christian contextual theology, and liberating people's hopes for justice from below is the process by which justice becomes incarnate in particular contexts, as a manifestation of God's real presence in the global context.

In one sense, this view simply insists that social ethics — insofar as social ethics involves analysis of the ethos, engagement with the social dynamics of hope and justice, and historical activity to make these more fully manifest in concrete communities — not only is a part of the Christian life, but is the fundamental core of what the gospel, and thus theological education, Incarnationally understood, is ultimately all about. Insofar as biblical studies, doctrinal and historical theology, evangelism and missiology, and church management and counseling neglect this, as they do in most of theological education, they simply have missed the point.

Boonprasat-Lewis represents a view that is compatible with the perspective presented by Costas in regard to concern for the people, and for justice and liberation. But her viewpoint differs from his at at least one major point. We should not, in the understanding of contextuality she presents, try to derive general "realist" principles — whether patterns, beliefs, dynamics, or functions — from Scripture and then gear up to contextualize them by bringing them to contexts where they are not already present. Rather, we should plunge into the realities of the contexts as they exist, as did God in Jesus Christ, and allow whatever provisional patterns, beliefs, dynamics, or functions are concretely pertinent to the context to arise out of the quest of hopeful people for justice and salvation. What we learn from Scripture is that this approach is possible.

Text is an epiphenomenal expression of God's presence in life's contexts, and the Christian text, the Bible, is authoritative because it genuinely expresses, and thus its expressions reflect, the contextual presence of God in social history.

Not everyone agreed with Boonprasat-Lewis. For one thing, her theories depend upon a view of the Incarnation that overlooks the reality of the Ascension. That is another way of saying that transcendence and otherness are as much a part of the gospel as imminence and presence, and that certain "abstract" texts may well contain elements of hope, justice, and salvation that are *not* present in most contexts and that need to be brought to them through contextualization. But it is clear that her view of "Christian contextuality" rests on an assumption that a metaphysical event of universal importance (the Incarnation) has taken place and that it is Christian insight about that event which makes it possible to be simultaneously contextual and global in perspective. This view, however, ends up having a very low estimate of the importance of text. Text is something one may investigate in order to penetrate through it to what is really important — context.

FROM CONTEXT TO TEXT

It would be possible, at this point, to show how a number of leading thinkers have developed perspectives close to that of Boonprasat-Lewis. But perhaps it is more fruitful for our immediate purposes to look briefly at the work of Old Testament scholar Carole Fontaine to see how some of these motifs appear in a field of study ordinarily thought to be quite removed from the missiology of Costas or the contextual ethics of Boonprasat-Lewis — a field that is commonly text-oriented without remainder, but that in fact manifests the strides taken by those forms of historical and biblical studies centrally concerned about *Sitz im Leben*. Fontaine draws on several contextual and intercontextual methodologies (especially current semiotic theory) in her treatment of wisdom literature as a way of discerning new meanings in the texts of Scripture.[4] She charts how "traditional sayings" give linguistic expression to the operational categories or worldview of a particular culture, and simultaneously serve to consolidate or create meaningful order in the midst of chaotic or potentially disruptive inter- or intra-societal

---

4. Fontaine, *Traditional Sayings in the Old Testament: A Contextual Study* (Sheffield: Almond Press, 1982).

conflict. Once a text becomes refined and codified in several contexts, it becomes capable of shaping still others.

Drawing on a wide range of anthropological research into the nature and role of "folk wisdom" around the world, Fontaine demonstrates that contextual analysis of this genre of literature allows us to distinguish the content, structure, and use of wisdom sayings at various levels of particular societies, and to recognize deeper common human parallels that transcend any particular time or space. The sayings almost surely derive from highly specific circumstances, and are treasured because someone gave "poetic" expression to a creative way of perceiving and responding to a characteristic problem that humans experience. To be sure, these sayings are often collected, systematized, or stylized by elite sages who utilize them as resources for pedagogy or the legitimation of governing regimes. But more important, says Fontaine, are the contextual ways in which these sayings are employed in daily life to respond to life's ambiguities and to maximize *shalom* in everyday existence. It is through such means, she suggests, that a kind of populist, predogmatic theology at the grass roots comes into existence and gives enduring integrity to particular communities. Emerging from the small insights drawn from shrewd observation and openness to experience, Wisdom represents the honing of inchoate presuppositions into formulated patterns of thought of such art and general validity that they can become flexible tools by which solidarity, evaluative judgment, guidelines for "active duty," and the social construction of meaning can be implemented across life settings without need of "appeal to creation or special revelation to legitimate its existence."[5]

Here is a much more "nominalist" approach to the understanding of how we can and should learn to apprehend text from context. Social and historical causation are seen as determinative for religious meanings, and the latter refer less to any metaphysical-moral vision than to a combination of practical cleverness and popular art. But this approach is not simply nominalist, for it presupposes a particular kind of epistemological universalism in its treatment of these materials. The study of context as the source, setting, location, and arena for the employment of Wisdom texts presumes that modern scholarship has access to certain general categories of understanding by which we can identify, interpret, and explain common processes cross-culturally. It assumes, in short,

---

5. Fontaine, *Traditional Sayings in the Old Testament*, p. 104.

that these texts fit into a much larger logic that is decisive for the formation, use, and meaning of all texts.

It may well be that some folklorists have simply imposed categories from their own environments onto the understanding of folk wisdom. But Fontaine presumes, as do most serious comparative and historical scholars who focus on contextual analysis, that it is possible to identify structural features common to the content of both biblical and nonbiblical texts, to the social functions these texts perform in highly divergent contexts, and to the artistic-linguistic forms these expressions take over time and space. Fontaine presumes, as did the Wisdom authors of the Old Testament, that Wisdom sayings were grasping something that should be propagated beyond the context of origin. Fontaine agrees, when questioned, that her argument implies that the depths of Wisdom are the pre-Christian manifestations of the *logos* as it is built into the logic of creation, history, and human communication — available to all who could see, respond, and act with discernment. Further, the cross-cultural modes of contextual analysis used to explicate the meanings of the biblical texts imply that categories of human understanding extrinsic to the Scriptures and most generally applicable for the analysis of particular contexts are the ones that we ought to use to discern the most profound meanings of scriptural texts. No "special doctrines," such as "Holy Spirit" or "Incarnation," are necessary for anyone to understand the deepest levels of scriptural text.

In this view, we get at the meaning of the texts through the analysis of context, but the text-producing context is recognized as expressing something potentially context-transcending when it is interpreted in terms of the most universal categories of human understanding that we can gain by cross-historical and cross-cultural analysis.[6] Thus, the contextual study of text drives us to intercontextual, global, and practical engagement on human terms. At certain points, Fontaine's argument converges with that of Costas, but it also drives us to anthropological (rather than missiological) categories of a universalistic sort that allow us to put both specific text and specific context in a larger logic of understanding. At certain points, Fontaine's argument also converges with aspects of Boonprasat-Lewis's, and yet it is more easily distinguished from

---

6. Here Fontaine follows views of modern anthropologists and folklorists who have been deeply influenced by both the social theories of Emile Durkheim and the linguistic theories of the French structuralists. More recent interests have taken her, like these streams of thought, toward "deconstructionism."

the ideological forms of contemporary contextual*ism*. Yet Fontaine differs from both Costas and Boonprasat-Lewis because she is manifestly suspicious of universalistic metaphysical-moral or theological presuppositions while maintaining that some social processes and epistemic functions are universal.

Fontaine's concerns are not overtly about the implications of the interaction of text and context for modern theological education. But the implications, if we but extrapolate a bit, are manifold. And, because of the difference just noted, these implications diverge from primary emphases of both Costas and Boonprasat-Lewis. Fontaine's arguments suggest that the purpose of theological education is to provide a scholarly environment wherein, in its study of both texts and contexts, it is possible above all to develop the categories whereby both can be understood in terms of their social-historical meaning and community-forming power. A seminary is first of all a school, and all that it does must be of broadest and deepest intellectual — that is, academic — worth. And that means a certain decided commitment to examine, wrestle with, and test all abstractions and categories — theological ideas and metaphysical-moral theories — that claim to grasp common, perennial, and ubiquitous features of human understanding and human existence. This we do to enhance wisdom in community wherever it appears, under whatever religious label.

In drawing out these implications of Fontaine's work, we also have uncovered several major points of contention within our ATS team and very likely within theological education elsewhere. Shall the texts that we take to be authoritative for us be taken in the realist sense as source and norm for our work in multiple contexts? If so, which texts, since not all of them point to the context? Shall participation in the contexts of life be taken as the source and norm of our work, since we have a confidence, expressed compellingly in some texts, that God is contextually present in at least some parts of life and history? If so, which contexts? Does the interaction of text and context require the development and utilization of extra-textual and extra-contextual scientific categories to guide all that we do and think in theological education? If so, which categories, since scientists do not agree on these matters? In short, if such matters are to be treated as theological matters and taught in theological education as true, by what criteria do we — can we — recognize and respond to the wisdom of God wherever it appears?

In addition, we need to inquire further about the relationship of justice to such questions. Are there normative kinds of meaning and normative forms of community that are superior to others? If so, how would we know on such grounds as these? If not, then isn't our choice of texts or of contexts arbitrary or accidental (i.e., determined by such factors as gender and the religion or culture into which we are born)? Clearly, these questions shall have to be pursued further.

CHAPTER 4

Affirmations and Translations

Two members of the ATS team tended to take up the questions of text and context in ways quite distinct from those thus far presented. As a New Testament scholar who was delightfully sardonic about any view of text that smacked of evangelical proof-texting, and as a Third World theologian (a South Indian who also had experience teaching in Kenya) who was openly contemptuous of those who speak constantly of contextualization but never do a careful contextual analysis or even contextualize anything, and as a biblical scholar who thinks that one of the chief contributions of the biblical witness is that it breaks the romantic quest for communitarian solidarity, J. G. F. Collison — "Frank" to all in name and style — wrote a major paper for our common research. In a parallel paper, Lamin Sanneh, a former Muslim from Gambia and a noted historian of religions and missions in Africa, focused on the role that the translation of Scriptures has played in social and cultural contexts. Reviewing the materials and the concerns introduced by these participants in our study may allow us to extend the boundaries of the whole effort, bring fresh accents into the mix of discussion, clarify even further some of the critical issues, and draw Part I of this whole effort to a close.

MINIMALIST AFFIRMATIONS

Collison begins his paper[1] by noting that in India, Africa, and the United States, there is a fairly strong undercurrent of dissatisfac-

---

1. Collison, "Mission, the Word, and the Spirit," paper presented at the ATS Retreat, May 1985.

tion among faculty and church leadership about theological education in its present state. This stems in part from the fact that the pastors produced by it do not seem to be leading the church into the fulfillment of its mission. Collison also notes that he, as a participant in the process of preparing men and women for ministry, is not unlike a number of others involved in teaching. That is, he often feels almost overwhelmed by the constantly changing "shoreless seascape" of his own discipline. To be sure, he not only has managed to keep up with and to contribute to the manifold insights of "the field," but in a somewhat desultory fashion magisterially has decided what is appropriate to pass on to students as "knowledge." He doubts that he or others who teach have integrated their reflections on these matters into a coherent, general idea of what ought to be taught and how it ought to be taught, whether we are speaking of texts or contexts.

However, as he reflects on theological education around the world, it appears to him that the key factor is not, in the first instance, text or context. Rather, it is the church. That is the decisive center of meaning and the decisive center of both pastoral and social formation. Indeed, the text is the church's text, and the context is always the church's context. Only if we know what the church is are we likely to have a clear grasp of the vocation of theological education, and it is very clear from the Indian context that if Christianity becomes but another religious community like the Sikhs, the Muslims, the Parsees, the Hindu castes, and the neo-Buddhists, it is lost.

By posing the question of the nature of the church, Collison does not intend to define any single ecclesiastical organization or appeal to fixed marks (such as "where the Word is rightly preached and the sacraments are rightly performed"). Rather, we might better understand the church as a movement, one which, like a river, takes many forms as it passes through many landscapes. But unlike a river, it has a purpose that can be identified in terms of focus. In this regard, the church is an organized company of the committed in motion toward some end. Even here Collison avoids over-definition and definiteness. By using the image of "focus," he does not mean to bring everything into a prescribed uniformity. The idea of "focus" concedes that there are many rays of insight, but it also implies that these converge at closely related points so as to illuminate the basic structure of existence. This conjunction must surely be the fundamental purpose of that movement which we call the church, and thus the focus for theological education.

It serves little, Collison argues, to say that "the gospel" or "the Spirit" or "Scripture" or "Incarnation" is the focus of the church, for the questions of "which gospel?" "whose Spirit?" "what parts of Scripture?" and "Incarnation how understood?" become real, persistent, and controversial. Whenever someone in our faculty or team discussions attempted to appeal to one or another of these terms, Collison cited biblical materials to show that some contrary perspective on gospel, Spirit, Incarnation, or Scripture is at least as valid as the one to which the appeal was made. Indeed, one of the major results of modern scholarship, he argued, is the finding that it is not possible to show that the Christian Scriptures possess qualities which make them unique or which allow us to use the Scriptures deductively. Further, Collison asserts, "every effort to find some evident common quality possessed by . . . [the books of] the Canon, which would render them immeasurably superior to other sources . . . has been in vain." Whatever else modern biblical studies have taught us, we know that there are no simple answers to these questions. It is no wonder that such terms as "the Gospel," "the Spirit," "Incarnation," and "Scripture" simply do not project a clear image, and that seminary students and pastors — indeed, theological educators — who appeal constantly to them lack integration, lack focus.

Collison doubts whether any careful analysis of text, given the present state of biblical studies, or any "scientific" approach to contextuality, given the present state of social epistemology, can render the focus now lacking. Instead, we must depend upon certain core "faith affirmations" as the governing guidance system of the movement. These are not doctrines or dogmas, not provable or final. They are suggestive, hypothetical, and provisional articulations, congruent at the most general level with what many of the saints and martyrs of the movement's tradition have also held, and they faithfully portray a viable construal of the actual human predicament. There are three core affirmations:

1. That humankind, in its natural state as we know it, is alienated from God;
2. That all the ills of humankind, personal or social, derive from this alienation; and
3. That in Jesus Christ we have been given the wherewithal to "remove" this alienation and to "cure" humankind of its ills.

Collison holds that to assert much more than this "minimalistic" core would force us to rely on formulations that are now known to be contextually conditioned. We cannot deny what we now know to be the case: namely, that even Scripture as we have it is a collection of contextually derived records of those moments when the individuals involved in them felt that alienation was overcome. We can find little else that holds Scripture together, for all of its expressions of this experience are culturally conditioned — even when this experience of overcoming alienation from God alienates those who undergo it from their own cultures and contexts. In this connection, argues Collison, it is not always a bad thing to be alienated from our cultural contexts. Sometimes it is precisely these contexts that alienate us from God. Indeed, the church can in some ways be understood as that collection of people who are alienated from their contexts for the sake of God and who re-enter the alienating contexts to transform them. Thus, we can hardly use Scripture deductively. We perhaps can use it "evocatively," to promote that kind of alienation *from* our contexts that empowers us to overcome alienation *within* our contexts by transforming our contexts.

Collison also suggests that life in the world today is pervaded by five major dimensions of alienation that ought to be overcome: the fragmentation of humankind into regional, ideological, or communal power blocs; the exploitation of some sectors of humanity by other dominant groups; religious, ideological, and cultural imperialism; the elevation of humanity over other parts of creation; and the exaltation of the self-sufficiency of the individual over social responsibilities. In different places and at different times, one or another form of worldly alienation is likely to be dominant. But in every place and every time, the church is a company of the committed — though usually not the only one — which finds its identity in the overcoming of alienation. What is distinctive about the church is that it makes contextually influenced affirmations about its own sin (while everyone else tries to obscure or deny their sin) and its own faith (which it believes but cannot prove). The church bases its sense of ethical action in the world on reconciliation with God. It is inductively apparent that some in that company draw their motivations and ways of speaking about this sin, faith, and reconciliation from nonbiblical religious and cultural contexts, but that does not make any difference.

Accordingly, theological education will have two points of integration. One will focus on the clarification of the very minimal, common affirmations of the faith community through the evocative use of Scripture, creeds, and confessions. The purpose of these is to induce a reconciled relationship with God. The other point of integration will focus on the overcoming of the particular forms of alienation that are at hand in all the manifold conditions in which people find themselves. The latter will have to be done in concert with non-Christians, and it is finally the critical test of the adequacy of the former, even if the former is, for Christians, the necessary provisional guide in the midst of the latter.

The implications for theological education are clear: each program of instruction, each department, and each instructor or course will be judged according to a standard of excellence based on how well it evokes the fundamental "faith affirmations" in one or another form, and how well it gives focus and energy to the decisive movements that overcome alienation in time and space. These, in turn, depend in the final analysis on reconciliation with God.

Collison is candid about the fact that his view is influenced in good measure by several factors: by his own life in the midst of the turmoils and opportunities of a religiously pluralistic, economically dichotomous, and self-consciously renascent Third World society; perhaps by his own personality and life choices in the midst of and in dialogue with a predominantly Hindu context; and by the fact that much of the legacy of missionary theology and education is stodgy, deductive, mechanical, and dull — something that needs to be shattered and revitalized by a new, simple, yet dynamic movement of affirmation and reconciliation. He is also candid about the fact that he has been to a number of conferences of "Third World theologians" dominated by internationally known figures who speak for the peoples of the Third World but have increasingly lost contact with those people — representing instead tiny minorities of radical elites who are paid to induce guilt among Western "liberals" who seem to love to wallow in it.

But Collison's view suggests something more than simply the accidents of his background. He demands a rigorous honesty about what can be said theologically, and he warns against overstatements by *both* older, Western-based styles of theology *and* the newer emerging theologies of the Third World. He claims that faith affirmations — if guarded, intellectually rigorous, properly modest, and evocative of a new relationship with God — are in fact the most vibrant ways of grasping the crises of human existence in history and guiding the movements that can transform life. Those centers of theological education that hope to become related to the new contexts where alienation is being overcome, to the emerging global awareness, and to a vital redefinition of mission must open themselves in new ways to the simple things going on in people's lives all over the world, even if it means the sacrifice of all those treasured "standards" of canon, doctrine, and polity that presently dominate the international conventions of theological studies, conservative or liberal, classical or radical.

In dealing with Collison's perspective, as with all others treated in these pages, we shall attempt to clarify the position by asking what one would have to believe — metaphysically, morally, and epistemologically — in order to hold this view. Collison presupposes a distinction between the materiality of historical existence and a transmaterial realm of the divine. But he also thinks this dualism can be overcome. Or, to put it another way, he assumes a realm of physical alienation that takes its social form in civilizational oppression and can be overcome by inspired ethical action, and a metaphysical alienation that may be evocatively overcome and take social form in the church. But the connection point, the necessary "focus," is essentially "confessional" and existential. That is, we believe these things and take them as focal points for us because they agree with our faith and experience.

To some partners in our dialogues, such a position seemed to imply that there is no reason for holding such views except that they are *ours.* It would thus seem to be the case that any other affirmation that a group, movement, or religion confesses or experiences is equally valid for them. And if that follows, then surely it also follows that in concrete situations — when each group is attempting to contextualize its existentially derived confession by ethical action, to overcome the alienations it perceives — conflict is inevitable, and the overcoming of alienation is unlikely. Unless, of course, what Collison has identified in terms of the "minimalistic" confession and his "five dimensions of alienation" is universally the case and not simply one perspective on the human situation.

Clearly, what Collison has brought to our attention is a perspective on the human condition, one that many Christians might well share. But part of the problem is that just these points are of considerable dispute around the world where Christians are attempting to contextually globalize such insights and conduct missions on comparable bases. Indeed, the earthly alienations that Christians confront at home and abroad, in and beyond the churches, have surely been brought about on the basis of someone's faith and experience, and evocatively legitimated by deeply held alternative confessions. Thus the alienations we face may be based on precisely the kind of metaphysical, moral, and epistemological grounds Collison uses. That is one of our problems: our metaphysical-moral affirmations are not supported by our epistemology, and hence become nothing more than affirmations. How could these faith affirmations and this analysis of our social situation be contextualized or globalized or carried out in mission without the temptation of an imperialistic impulse to make *our* experience normative?

Collison responded to these objections by focusing, as had Costas, on the Spirit. But members of our faculty reminded him that what he said about appeals to Christ, the Scriptures, or the gospel is equally applicable to appeals to the Spirit. There is the Holy Spirit, of which there are many interpretations, and there are many spirits — of cultures, of peoples, of religions, and of movements in history, or "spirit of the times." The question again becomes one of criteria. Are there any principles of discernment whereby we can say which Spirit is Holy? It is possible to argue, of course, that the critical criterion is the overcoming of alienation, and to claim that this is a criterion that we can empirically verify and name the Holy Spirit. Is it not the case that when we look around in the world we find alienation on all sides? And is it not the case that people so treasure the overcoming of this alienation and the "spiritual impulses" that give impetus to the movements against alienation that they call them "holy"?

In Collison's arguments we meet a particularly compelling, modern, empiricist, and pluralistic form of "nominalism" in epistemology wedded to a hypothetical affirmation of a metaphysical-moral sort. But that is part of the problem of what we have found in modern theological education generally. What some call alienation is what others identify as the natural (or the holy) structure of existence, as Collison knows when he confronts, for example, the caste structure in India. Some trans-empirical, meta-physical, and meta-historical standard is inevitably used to interpret the empirical data at hand. And when we ask what that standard might be, how it has been previously discerned, and how it is grounded, so that we might learn how to discern it today, we find ourselves driven back to the unavoidable fact that doctrines, ecclesiologies, and indeed the Scriptures themselves were developed precisely to demark and delimit where (as Costas might claim) the power of the Spirit can be found, and what (as Boonprasat-Lewis might argue) God is doing in the world, and how (as Fontaine might suggest) wisdom is functioning to prevent chaos and form community.

Despite these rather stiff objections to some of his formulations, it is clear that Collison has reinforced motifs that we have already seen in other terms: that theological education is first and foremost for the mission of the church; that faith affirmations have to be made; that a minimalistic, provisional statement of the core may be all that we can, at present, affirm with intellectual integrity.

Even that core must be stated as an existentially based confession about the need for human reconciliation with God, and not quite as a claim about God's nature, truth, or justice.

SO LONG, SOLA SCRIPTURA

Collison presents a perspective that is of considerable import for at least two further reasons. On the one hand, he represents a position that can be found among many Western New Testament scholars today. And on the other hand, he represents a Third World suspicion about the way Western Christians have used Scripture. Let's look at each of these.

The careful and advanced use of higher critical scholarship appears to have led many students of the Bible to be not only sharply skeptical of the ways in which the church most frequently uses Scripture, but dubious of the ways in which the post–New Testament church has built up doctrinal and ecclesiastical systems that seem to stultify as much as guard, cultivate, or release that life-transforming dynamic, expressed in sometimes highly contradictory ways, in the writings of the early church. Thus, while some faculty members want the introductory biblical courses to be foundational for that which is subsequently developed in courses on church history, theology, ethics, ministry, and pastoral care, it often turns out that those engaging in the more advanced forms of biblical studies find little in them to provide the foundations desired.

When Martin Luther stamped Protestantism with the principle of *sola scriptura,* it was presumed that the Bible could provide criteria by which to judge the adequacy of tradition, doctrine, morals, church practice, and the cure of souls. Today, biblical scholars who have taken this touchstone of Protestant understanding most seriously thrust the questions back at contemporary systematicians, ethicists, and pastors to sort out the meanings of what they have historically discovered, with all its plurality, variety, and lack of clear cohesion. To state the point sharply, the Protestant tendency to rely on Scripture as the decisive source and norm of faith is increasingly difficult to maintain unless one turns to extra-canonical theories of inspiration or authority. In this regard, we may well be at the end of the Protestant era. At least the questions that could have been posed to Collison on this front are those that also emerged in discussions with biblical scholars Charles Carlston and William Robinson.

When Carlston made his presentation to a faculty forum on academic excellence, for example, he stressed the difficulty of dealing with the range of contemporary scholarly approaches to biblical materials — textual criticism, literary relationships, thematic developments, history of the tradition, and the newer perspectives derived from competing schools of social theory, structuralism, feminism, and the like — let alone all the various ways that denominations and preachers use Scripture.[2] It is all well and good for some modern biblical critics to say with Markus Barth that "without theology one cannot understand a single book of the New Testament." But that only raises the question "Which theology?" Do we best understand the New Testament by using a theology of revelation or one of the newer "empirical theologies" of the twentieth century, the hermeneutics of Gadamer or of the deconstructionists? And why should we choose one over another of these if the New Testament itself does not supply the criteria whereby we can assess their relative adequacy?

Carlston concluded with an emphasis that Collison also approves. We really have only three options, Carlston said: to "juggle at once" several things, which stretches the competence of every instructor and limits the sense of focus that can be conveyed to students; "admit that much of the New Testament world is strange to us and that we must find a hermeneutic to make that strange world relevant" — an option which suggests that the meaning of Scripture depends on our present construction or discovery of a hermeneutic; or to "give up teaching the New Testament as sacred Scripture," simply working professionally as any historian of the ancient world might, "and get on with the really significant work" of undoing the damage the present U.S. administration is doing to the country and the world. Carlston pursues all of these options and hopes for a convergence of focus.

In a subsequent presentation on text and context,[3] Bill Robinson claimed that the chief tasks of the New Testament scholar are (a) simply to be stubborn and to build the case for the probable meanings of the words in their original context, and (b) to translate, with the understanding that translation is necessary because of cultural distance and possible because of the limited but significant cross-historical accessibility of meanings. All else is the job of theologians and ethicists. They are to tie the knots and show whether

---

2. Carlston, "Academic Excellence and Scripture," lecture presented to the ANTS faculty, 1 Feb. 1985.
3. Robinson, "Biblical Studies and Theology Today," lecture notes from a graduate faculty colloquium jointly sponsored by Boston College and Andover Newton, Mar. 1985.

those meanings and translations have any significance for today, and if so what that significance might be.

Thus, what Collison has done is propose a way to integrate the variety that Carlston notes and to provide a vision for theologians and ethicists in which New Testament scholars like Robinson can be stubborn and exercise their linguistic skills in translation. And if one wanted a historical warrant for doing it this way, we might point out that Luther never really spoke of *sola scriptura* without also speaking of *sola gratia* and *sola fidei,* and that only *gratia* and *fidei* allow us to make any sense of *scriptura.* Of course, if we take this route, we would have to acknowledge that the contributions of biblical scholars to theological education have less to do with their scholarship in the usual sense than with their faith and graciousness.

Collison also represents a view that is also frequently found among Third World theologians who suspect that much of what passes for the authority of Scripture in the West is in fact a rather parochial set of traditions about its meanings derived from "Judeo-Christian culture" as it developed in the West. Protestantism may have protested the Roman Catholic subordination of text to magisterial authority, but unwittingly subordinated the text to the presuppositions of Euro-American culture instead. That phrasing is important, for "culture" is the noun, and "Judeo-Christian" and "Euro-American" are only adjectival. It is simply not clear, in the view of Collison and others, why the orthodoxies and orthopraxies of the West (said to be based in Scripture, but frequently projected into Scripture by the West) should be normative for those who confess that "in Jesus Christ we [all humanity] have been given the wherewithal to overcome alienation and cure all human ills," when Western culture presents distinct forms of alienation and ills, and many who want to confess Jesus Christ find themselves alienated and ill-treated by the increasing accoutrements of Western culture only modestly moderated by Judeo-Christian influence. Those Christians in non-Western parts of the world who have nothing particularly Hebraic or Greek or Roman or European or Slavic or American in their background—why can't they express reconciliation with God in their own terms and give it new articulation in fresh faith-affirmations and new expression in dynamic movements as their situation requires? As Christ overcomes the alienations of Hindu, Buddhist, Confucian, and Taoist cultures, these cultures will find quite different things in Scripture than those the West has found in it.

TRANSLATION TRANSFORMS

The questions of the relationship of mission to cultural imperialism and the implications for both the globalization of Christianity and a deeper understanding of the relation of text and context constitute the primary focus of the recent work of Lamin Sanneh.[4] Like Costas, Sanneh is committed to mission; like Boonprasat-Lewis, he is deeply concerned about contextualization and the actualities of conditions and processes in local situations; like Fontaine, he is versed in the logic of folk wisdom; like Collison, he demands a rigorous intellectual honesty about what can and cannot be said with relative security; and like Carlston and Robinson, he uses historical-critical methods and leaves some questions to the systematicians and ethicists.

The reason for these accents, however, rests on different grounds than any view we have thus far examined. The center of Sanneh's research has focused on the intellectual, cultural, and religious implications of scriptural translation as they have actually worked themselves out in cultural history—particularly as modern social, political, and religious developments in Africa have been influenced by the often unintended effects of missionary activity during the last century and a half. As we will see, not only does his work directly address the question of cultural imperialism and have direct implications for the understanding of text and context, but it introduces a way of working at this question that suggests indirect contributions to both the study of biblical texts and the theological-ethical analysis of context that can be derived from the study of church history and comparative religion.

Sanneh argues in the paper he presented that the prevailing view of Christian missions—both in modern Western intellectual circles and among some Third World nationalists who have struggled to overthrow foreign domination—is that missions is an anti-vernacular, anti-indigenous cultural manifestation of Western territorial expansion, motivated by both the desire to impose the cultural values of the West on other peoples and the desire to legitimate commercial and military exploitation. He accepts without argument the rather obvious fact that many, perhaps even the majority, of missionaries had elements of these motives lurking in their minds,

---

4. Sanneh, "The Contextual Repercussions of Translation: Christian Missions in Africa," paper presented at the ATS Retreat, 15 Mar. 1985. See also his *West African Christianity: The Religious Impact* (London: C. Hurst & Co., 1983); and *Translating the Message: The Missionary Impact on Culture* (Maryknoll, N.Y.: Orbis Books, 1988).

consciously or preconsciously, and that, at times, missions served just these imperial purposes. But Sanneh's research shows that other dynamics, even if the more neglected and less obvious ones, are quite probably more remarkable and socially consequential. Those dynamics are based in the fact that translation is the indispensable basis of mission. To convey its message, every mission must learn the language, the idioms, the values, and the meaning system of the culture into which it moves so that the message it brings can be clearly understood in the vernacular of the people. And to do that, the bearers of the message from the outside are utterly dependent on those who know the culture from the inside.

Sanneh documents what anthropologists, cultural historians, and comparative religionists have known for a long time but have failed to recognize as being of decisive significance: the attempts at conversion by preaching and teaching from "the text" require translating the text into the meaning systems already present in the context. And this entails precisely those dynamics that can be shown "to have stimulated a much wider cultural process which, among other things, achieved the inevitable marginalization of the missionary as a Western cultural agent, . . . [and] changed the missionary into an agent for the local assimilation of the religion."

The dynamics seem to have worked in several phases. One of them occurs during the attempt by outsiders to understand the local language. Where languages are not written, at least, that demands peaceful and trusting rapport with local experts. And the deeper one goes into the understanding of a language, specifically for purposes of translation, the more unavoidable becomes the knowledge of etymology, roots, and variations of usage and form. This in turn requires inquiry into variant dialects and the encounter with neighboring languages and culture in an atmosphere of peace rather than conflict. In short, it was in such atmospheres that missionaries, aided by local experts, investigated and documented the various aspects of language structure and usage. The result, says Sanneh, was "an amazing wealth of detail . . . , grammars, dictionaries, vocabularies, primers, commentaries, collections of proverbs, idioms, myths and folk-lore. For the first time we had a meticulous inventory of local cultures produced by the most exacting standards of scientific inquiry" — although it was not always prosecuted with equally detached brilliance, and there are awful specimens of incompetence.

This dynamic is related to another one. By viewing indigenous languages as the medium for conveying Christian views of God, missionaries had to come to very difficult decisions about what ideas and terms for God might be possible to use. Drawing examples from a series of efforts to find appropriate indigenous words for God, Sanneh shows that every effort to impose terms or neologisms from Greek, Latin, or Germanic linguistic roots failed, and that sooner or later the translators of Scripture used a term for God (*Tui'qua,* or *Tsui//goab,* or *uTikxo,* or *uKulunkulu,* to use some examples from African languages cited) that was already in use for the One who made all things, who is in heaven, and who is relevant to life in time and space. The adoption of such cultural terms for the transmission of the Christian faith not only "unyoked the religion from its Western carriage and . . . [linked] its destiny to the vernacular context," but also entailed a theological transformation that was quite unexpected. Such usage suggests that knowledge of the one true God was already present among the people before the Christians arrived. In a sense, it meant that the "Spirit of God" had already gone into the context before the bearers of "the text" or "the text" itself arrived, and had generated reliable knowledge, named with sufficient accuracy, that the highest truth of the imported text could be articulated in terms already at hand without betrayal of the message and the truth behind the text.

To be sure, the encounter of Scripture and indigenous language also brought processes of refinement to traditional conceptions. What was thought to be "our" high deity was connected by indigenous peoples with the God of peoples and times far beyond the range of the known world. And the fact that this God was now recognized to be a God of universal truth, justice, and peace, Sanneh notes,

> [brought a] renewed sense of purpose and commitment, something akin to the experience of a *rite de passage.* The old vessel of the vernacular was revitalized from transmitting the new spirit of Christianity, and those imbibing from it would find themselves pushed into new fields of experience. Translation gave the old vistas a fresh elevation and the promise of new life . . . ; the converts were roused by the renewed vision of truth that struck home with compelling authority, in language at once familiar and uncompromising. . . . The old landscape, meticulously restored by the detailed linguistic investigation and reconstruction . . . , began to stir with vitality as local converts marched to the tune and rhythm of Zion.

These dynamics were related to still others. On the basis of the critical collection, study, and preservation of cultural and linguistic traditions, and through the linking of the vernacular to a new sense of universal meaning, the cultures about to be inundated with all sorts of pressures for "modernization" were made self-conscious about their identity and significance. The new Christians, now possessing the Holy Scriptures in their own vernacular, perceived an unsettling gap between the promises of that Scripture and the motives and intentions of many a missionary. Attempts to circumvent the promises and principles of Scripture on the part of the missionaries or their cultural allies from abroad were construed as unacceptable interference. "It is from such objections," Sanneh states, "that the sentiment for cultural nationalism sprang. By a somewhat circuitous route mission may be said to have spawned the seeds of self-confidence from which in due season the robust strains of selfhood appeared."

A great number of contextual questions remained unsolved, to be sure. How this new synthesis of imported and indigenous faith was to assess local customs and practices was and has been a matter of considerable dispute. Some demanded celibacy; some approved polygamy. Some denounced witchcraft; some adopted "Christian incantations" to serve ends once served by witchcraft. Some made Holy Communion the center of tribal solidarity; some denied the authority of Communion as an authentic mark of faithful practice. But everywhere, it seems, an "inevitable incipient cultural nationalism" was generated by the translation of the biblical texts into the vernacular, a development in which converts intentionally alienated themselves from some aspects of their traditional cultural practices, but did so on the basis of a new vision of a reintegrated culture, the terms of which were at once universalistic and particular. This reintegration would eventually "set itself against continued foreign domination." The anti-colonial movements of the modern Third World surely owe as much to missions as to any other single force, and rooted in this is the fact that previously ignored peoples are presently contributing to world science, politics, and theology. In other words, Sanneh concludes, missionary efforts through the medium of translation led in a different direction than did colonialism. It is the former, not the latter, that has induced the most vibrant forms of a kind of contextualization that links indigenous cultures to a new global consciousness that touches on universality, and thereby claims before the world the right to resist colonialism, even if this new consciousness is still expressed in diverse and sometimes parochial ways.

A GENERAL PATTERN?

In several discussions, Sanneh stimulated the ANTS faculty to compare and contrast the pattern just sketched to developments in other periods of history and in other regions. Faculty members who had studied or taught abroad pointed out that similar patterns occurred in modern missions in the Pacific Islands, in India, and in Latin America. Historians pointed out that parallels can be found in the roles that the Septuagint and the Vulgate played in early Western Christianity and that Wycliffe, Tyndale, and Luther — as translators — have played in modern European culture. Indeed, William Holladay, a member of the translation committee of the Revised Standard Version of the Bible, pointed out that the process of translation is not always so dramatic as these great single moments, but is a proper, necessary, and ongoing task of the church in every culture. And very often the cultural use of language leads the translator rather than the other way around.

Black members of the faculty pointed out that direct parallels can be seen in the history of the American slaves. Some slaveholders may well have wanted to "Christianize" slaves to make them good, obedient workers. But, as professor of preaching Eddie O'Neal pointed out, when black Americans appropriated the meanings of the Scriptures into their own idioms — in this case, less linguistic and cultural than spiritual, ethical, and subcultural — the seeds were sewn to challenge and overthrow the distortions of the biblical message and promise that at first accompanied the missionizing efforts. Similarly, some feminist members of the faculty saw parallels in the attempts of some modern ecumenical Christians to translate the Scriptures in ways that are sex-inclusive and not dominated by male imagery. Obviously, the decisive question here is whether the Spirit of God has already moved and is moving amid the contemporary movements among Christian women who are trying to identify the transcendent elements of their religious experiences in ways that allow comparable namings of the divine, and the indigenization and contextualization of the Christian message in these new terms. If that is possible — as attempted by the new "Inclusive Language Lectionary," for example — fresh extensions of the human understanding of the truly universal God are not only possible but required of the contemporary church, even if some of the current experimental formulations are finally not accepted.

These patterns contrast with what has occurred in some other major world religions that have also known missionary expansion. Sanneh is most familiar with Islam, and uses it as an example. He contends that the Islamic view of the Koran makes the problem of translation and contextualization extremely difficult. The idea of the "uncreated" character of the words of the Koran, and the notion that the words of this scripture are the very thoughts of Allah and thus are not to be translated into some tongue foreign to the way these words were dictated to the Prophet — these conceptions limit the capacity of this religion to contextualize in ways that other religions have. An entirely different relationship of text and context tends to be established, one that in modern Western Christianity is clearly heterodox, if not heretical, and is called "fundamentalist." To be sure, numerous contextual interpretations of Islam can be found, but something in the constitutional structure of this tradition mitigates against the dynamics that have been so crucial for Christian history. Indeed, the structure of Islam contrasts with the constitutional structure of Christianity, argues Sanneh, in that the primitive church itself "in straddling the Jewish-Gentile worlds was born in a cross-cultural milieu, with translation as its birthmark." By contrast, insofar as Islam attempts to globalize its vision, it inevitably tends to bear in it an Arabic cultural hegemony that is more difficult to distinguish from political, military, and economic expansion. Scholars investigating the still infant field of comparative missiology are still debating the degree to which this phenomenon is present in other missionizing religions.

The implications of Sanneh's presentations for theological education are striking. More than any other voice we have heard thus far, his critical-historical analysis suggests a quite overtly "realist" understanding of the truth and justice of God. Something stands behind both text and context. Indeed, where these converge in historical life, truth and justice are clarified by the dynamics of encounter. Fresh apprehensions of meanings behind the text and within the depths of culture are grasped, and peoples are thereby equipped to become participants in the world historical process in ways that more nearly reflect the universal truth and justice of God. Seminary students must therefore be given the opportunity to catch a sufficient glimpse of that universal truth and justice as it lives in texts and contexts so that they will be prompted to seek their fuller meaning by engaging the text with the multiple contexts of the world and the contexts with the text.

In the process, these students must recognize that some of the truth and justice of God has already arrived in the multiple contexts of life before they have, and that all the rich meanings of the text are not yet manifest. Students must, therefore, be equipped to discern the meanings of the texts and the contexts in all their nuances. That entails their being willing to subject themselves to the wisdom of those patterns of meaning already present in the contexts, and their developing a competence in the skills of translation so that what they bring into contexts most adequately empowers various peoples to renew their worlds, to become agents in the indigenization of the message on their own terms, and to distinguish the cultural accoutrements that are of less than universal import from those that link them to the universal truth and justice of God.

However, critical questions can also be posed to Sanneh. Among these, three seem to be the most important. One is historical and comparative in character, another is philosophical in nature, and a third is social and ethical in import.

The historical and comparative question is this: Has Sanneh identified something that is in fact distinctively Christian, or has he identified sociocultural dynamics that can occur, have occurred, and do occur among some non-Christian missionary movements as well? A recent survey of research into the comparative analysis of missions on a cross-cultural basis suggests that Mahayana Buddhism as it manifested a missionary impulse from India to China brought with it the universalistic, speculative wisdom of Hinduism in a way that produced what some call the "Indianization of China." And it has also been shown that this wisdom was transformed in its reception by a process that has been called the "Sinicization of Indian Buddhism." A process of translation occurred there also — one that, like those to which Sanneh refers, produced dictionaries, collections of folk wisdom, poems, books of regulations, and so forth, which "modified and transformed aspects of the Buddhist message so that it could graft onto, and in some ways revitalize, dimensions of the indigenous folk religions and of the Confucianism and Taoism of that land." Here too, apparently, a message — which was generated out of what at least was held to be a "salvific metaphysical-moral vision understood to be of universal import for all humanity" — sprung adherents loose from their countries and cultures of origin, took them into foreign missions, demanded contextual dependency, was altered in the process of reception, and generated new directions of piety and practice that were subsequently mediated also to new lands — in this case, Korea and Japan, among others. At each point along the way, it seems to have done very much what Sanneh documents with regard, especially, to Africa.[5]

In this connection, one might also refer to something that

---

5. See Max L. Stackhouse, "Missions/Missionary Activity," in vol. 9 of the *Encyclopedia of Religion,* ed. Mircea Eliade et al. (New York: Macmillan, 1987), pp. 563, 566.

Collison mentioned with regard to India. There, the Christian missionary impulse followed several of these same dynamic patterns, but it also seems to have stimulated less a conversion of the majority of Hindus than the internal renewal of the indigenous and dominant religious orientation through the "Hindu Renaissance." That intellectual, cultural, and social movement has turned out to have, at the hands of such leaders as Gandhi, results quite comparable to those that Christian missions have had in Africa, but in clearly Hindu terms.[6] And it is possible to suggest that Marxism, as a modern form of "secular religion," is today being exported to a number of environments where it seems to be received in terms other than those of its exporters and serves to revitalize and give new identity to the indigenous cultures, prompting them to new ranges of participation in universal world history and to new confidence in their abilities to assert their own cultural traditions in new and refined ways and to overthrow foreign domination. The question that these observations raise is this: Can it be said that the truth and justice of God are present in these movements as well as in those prompted by Christian missions? Or have we merely identified a general set of sociohistorical dynamics that operate with equal potency wherever any profound and universalistic metaphysical-moral vision comes into contact with traditions that may have latent universalistic elements, but whose universalistic elements are somehow constrained by temporarily dominant and merely localistic loyalties, themes, and practices?

Such questions point directly to the philosophical question, one that we have already met in a variety of forms: What is the relationship of the descriptive analysis of the processes of contextualization, globalization, and mission to the normative analysis of the truth and justice of God? It is surely the latter which are the central issues in theological education. It may be that we can identify the dynamics of cultural encounter, and derive a subtle and well-documented understanding of the dynamics of civilizational transformation. But such a historical analysis does not clearly answer the criteriological question about what, if anything, is a real, reliable, and universal guide to the truth and justice of God even if it does render a compelling account of the "natural law" of translation, missionary activity, and the encounter of texts and contexts. The unanswered questions remain metaphysical, moral, and epis-

---

6. See David Kopf, *British Orientalism and the Bengal Renaissance: The Dynamics of Indian Modernization, 1773-1835* (Berkeley and Los Angeles: University of California Press, 1969).

temological in character. And they are directly related to questions of whether there is any scholarly or "scientific" coherence in the way we deal with these matters as we attempt to educate people for leadership with regard to that which we believe to be a true and just foundation for contextualization, globalization, and mission.

The third question that we can pose to Sanneh, and to all the others mentioned in the last two chapters, is this: Is it not the case that, for all the talk of contextual awareness, there is a notable absence of any concrete analysis of the actual fabrics of community life or the governing values woven into them that define, sustain, guide, and enhance the quality of life? Most of the discussion of text and context and of alienation and indigenization seems to lack institutional body. Where, for example, is the analysis of actual economic, legal, familial, political, technological, medical, or educational structures? To be sure, linguistic and ecclesiastical structures are alluded to periodically, but how these are related to those patterns of life that are found everywhere and are indispensable to the maintaining of a society is hardly mentioned.

Of course, it could be argued that linguistic and religious institutions are the core of every civilization, and that the values built into them determine the shape and development of every other aspect of social life. But such an argument would demand two presuppositions that are not, at present, clear to all. On the one hand, it would presuppose that ideas are in large measure determinative for institutional development, and that the variations in social-historical patterns are due to the divergent values that are built into our various cultures. This is a presumption that today is widely disputed in the social sciences and especially among those who have argued most vigorously against all "idealisms" that underestimate the influence of contextuality on ideas. And on the other hand, this argument would presume that we can assess these various ideas and values cross-culturally, altering them when they lead to oppression, exploitation, cultural imperialism, or alienation. But to make such evaluations would demand a clarity about the cross-cultural standards of right and wrong, good and evil, and truth and justice that none of the methods or perspectives under discussion provide.

WHERE ARE WE?

The contributions of the several participants in the dialogue summarized in these four chapters are enormous. Each presupposes that there is a "faith" that we hold as Christians which guides us in our quests for God's truth and justice (and each would be judged as more or less "faithful" by all the others). Yet, what remains is the question of criteria and of warrants for the criteria proposed. It is unclear whether it is possible to develop any criteria for judgment at the metaphysical, ethical, or social levels. All the contributors seem to agree that humans can, in some measure, understand several texts from differing social and historical contexts, and understand some aspects of the texts in terms of widely valid patterns in multiple contexts. And all would agree that faith affirmations are necessary and that all of Christian ministry involves participation in the ever-new translation of faith into new contexts in processes that evoke new readings of texts and new learnings from new contexts. Further, each of our partners in dialogue presumes a metaphysical or an ethical or an epistemological normative universality, but each avoids speaking of it in normative and universalistic terms. Often, it is only in the negative that these universalistic and normative motifs appear. The arguments against alienation, exploitation, colonialism, and cultural imperialism point indirectly to some normative ethical view of what it means to be human and to live in community everywhere, and affirmations about the power of the Holy Spirit, the Incarnation in Jesus Christ, and the truth and justice of God point to metaphysical-moral symbols familiar to and rich in meaning for Christians. But none of us has yet identified, developed, or made a case for the normative and universal theological-ethical grounds by which these principles and symbols ought to be taken seriously in contexts where they are not already assumed to be valid. Yet they are not self-evident historically, cross-culturally, or epistemologically, nor are their meanings clear to church members, seminary students, or theological educators.

Costas invites us to liberating engagement, Boonprasat-Lewis calls for the analysis of the sociopolitical context, Collison's perspective demands overcoming alienation in the service of a faith affirmation, and Sanneh points out the reciprocal cultural influences that make faiths more universalistic in content. And everyone engaged in dialogue with such perspectives finds them suggestive, important, and promising. All of them use, as do most members of most theological faculties, conceptual tools from the modern linguistic, psychological, sociological, anthropological, and historical sciences, as well as from contemporary philosophies of history. All hint that these are pertinent to ethical judgments, social reality, and theological education generally. But the relationship of these sciences — which are essentially descriptive, analytical, and material—to theology and ethics—which are inevitably evocative, constructive, and finally normative—is not spelled out. Nor are matters settled about the possible relationships of universals and particulars, "realism" and "nominalism," reliable knowledge and preferred confession. If such rich insights as we have thus far encountered are to be taken as central foci of theological education, and if theological education is to be regarded as a reliable guide to the most universally true and just perspective that humans can develop under God—a guide indispensable to life in all contexts of the globe and not merely the socialization of religious leaders into our preferred worldviews—then we will have to become more secure than theological educators are at present about the grounds on which we work.

To help us gain focus on these questions, we turn to those with major, representative, current perspectives outside our own dialogues who have worked on these questions. That is the substance of Part II.

PART II

Wider Discussions

CHAPTER 5

Consultations and Globalization

No conversation in theological, church, or educational circles begins *de novo*. Scholarship presupposes that study of "sources" is necessary before judgments and proposals are made, and in the history of faith the word "original" has most often been connected to the word "sin." The most creative developments involve building on the foundations of those who have gone before, drawing fresh insights from those who are refining, extending, and augmenting the resources of the past for the present, and wrestling with the views of those who point toward the future.

Most of the key questions that surfaced in the dialogue reported in the previous chapters have been addressed by contemporary authors over the past quarter of a century, and continue to be dealt with. In this section of this study, we turn to selected, though in many ways widely representative, discussions of contextual, global, and missiological issues in theological education. Some of the important materials are derived from ecumenical consultations surveyed in this chapter. Other important materials (such as those in Chapters 6, 7, and 8) can be found in several books dealing with matters central to current debates. All will be discussed in terms of the ways in which their various perspectives have been perceived and evaluated by our ATS study team and by members of our faculty who have discussed them with us. Thus, our purpose in reviewing these resources is less to present the full intentions of the authors than to assess whether these views can and do contribute to the resolution of the decisive questions facing theological education.

ON COMMUNITY ENGAGEMENT

One of the first consultations taking up the question of new directions in theological education — as it grew aware of the need for new emphases in global and missiological thinking — was the Division of Overseas Ministry Assembly, sponsored by the National Council of Churches in November 1968. It was an international consultation of Third World seminary deans, presidents, principals, and other professors. Discussion centered on two papers. One was delivered by Howard Schomer, then president of Chicago Theological Seminary, and subsequently the World Issues secretary of the United Church Board for World Ministries. The second was given by M. M. Thomas, then director of the Christian Institute for the Study of Religion and Society in Bangalore, India, and a man deeply involved in the leadership of the World Council of Churches. Both have been visiting professors at ANTS in the last decade.

Schomer is in some ways an exemplary product of the great "liberal" tradition that the old Andover faculty had inaugurated in this land. He is a self-conscious heir of the ecumenically oriented free-church tradition, of the grand tradition of "liberal education," and of the Social Gospel. Schomer began his presentation[1] by reflecting on the history of the development of the term "seminary." It comes from the old Latin word meaning "a protected plot of ground for the growth of seedlings." By the time of its adoption into Renaissance English, it meant "a school for the formation of . . . persons for a particular trade." Its modern use, however, really dates back to the Council of Trent (1563), where the term was applied to those advanced centers of theological education for priests who were given a specific mission — in that case, reconverting Protestants to Catholicism. Schomer noted that the first theological seminaries were mission- and task-oriented, although it cannot be said that they were notably successful at achieving their stated purpose. Indirectly, however, the idea had its consequences for Protestants: they began to form seminaries.

William Ames, the most influential Puritan divine of the seventeenth century, elaborated the basic Protestant conception of the new centers of theological education in a way that included previous meanings. Clearly, a theological school should involve nurture and formation of that which is yet tender; surely it also should

---

1. Schomer, "How a Modern Seminary May Discover the Reality of the Inner Life," paper presented at the Division of Overseas Ministry Assembly, Nov. 1968.

involve the upgrading of learning and educational excellence. And the purpose of these is that souls may be conquered through the artful use of the mind for the true church. But nurture and learning for mission are to be sought with three emphases. The study of theology should be composed of "doctrine, method and practice," Ames wrote. "Theology is finally, truly and usefully learned not when it settles down in the stomach of the intellect . . . ; but when it is carried over into the springs of action . . . in the innermost center of the heart." And from thence it motivates and guides the formation and the reformation of civilizations.[2]

In contrast to what took place in the dogmatically oriented theological faculties in the universities of his day, Ames argued, the study of theology should be more fruitfully compared to the study of medicine and law. That is, it is preparation for salvific and prudential action among the people and in society. In Ames's view, as in Schomer's, theological education involves getting first principles of doctrine straight, but that is only the beginning. More important, it also involves studying the methods by which these principles can be planted in life, incarnated in personal habits and social practice. It is in habit and practice that the spirituality to which principles point comes alive and provides the prospect for a vital "inner life" for a modern seminary community, the heart of both the church and the world.

Rather sadly, pointed out Schomer, these promising directions were disrupted in the nineteenth century by the impact of denominational rivalry. Esoteric formulations, often masking nontheological disputes, became the marks of "in-group" and "out-group" dynamics. Ecclesiastical bodies tightened their control over their seminaries and protectively removed the seminaries from the disturbing influences of worldly engagement. Liberal arts, theologies that were not ecclesiastically confined, modernist waves of thought, political movements that were alive on the national and international horizons, as well as social changes occurring in the cities under the impact of industrialization — these were all neglected in favor of the formation of a convinced corps of energetic true-believers who would be good promoters of one or another particular branch of the church. In fact, it was this model of the seminary that the missionary movements, also lively at the time, exported to what we now call the Third World, movements that were often confusingly at odds with one another abroad, and that often trap-

---

2. See M. Nethenus et al., *William Ames*, trans. Douglas Horton, Harvard Divinity School Library, 1965.

ped many "new Christians" in denominationalist dogmatisms irrelevant to their contexts. (It now becomes clear why the "independence from ecclesiastical control" of the old Andover Liberals [p. 17] was so important.)

Schomer then turned to the more recent developments whereby those constrictions had been loosened. He spoke of the rise of departments of religion in the universities where the study of religion had become less "theological" and more "scientific" in the anthropological, psychological, and sociological senses. This development paralleled the increase of "professionalism" in seminary self-understanding, particularly the adoption of the idea that ministers — like social workers, psychiatric counselors, probation officers, and community organizers (if no longer quite like lawyers or physicians, as Ames had held) — are members of a "helping profession." Here Schomer echoed motifs identified by H. Richard Niebuhr in his influential study of the previous decade,[3] and by Charles Fielding's contemporary study along these lines for the (then) American Association of Theological Schools.[4]

In addition, Schomer spoke of the influx of students who grew up under the influence of World War II, Hiroshima, Nagasaki, the Cold War, and the rise of McCarthyism and Birchism. For them, theology, as it was taught, seemed to supply little meaning. Yet, Schomer noted, new programs in field education, such as required participation in local "block organizations" among the disadvantaged, brought many students from numbness to action and spiritual renewal. Those were the days of direct involvement, the recovery of practical mission that prompted many to march in Selma, to learn to pray in the midst of struggle, to renew the empty spirit by reflection in the midst of social mobilization for change. In this part of his discussion Schomer anticipated what is today called "praxis-based education," one of the most powerful influences in contemporary thinking about theological education. He argued that it is through existential participation in the ethical and social crises of the day that a new and vibrant spirituality is born.

Schomer took Ames as his point of departure and, like Ames, wanted students to get "the *principles* straight — the Doctrine clear," but his focus on method and practice had, by the end of his reflections, eclipsed his concern with theology itself. The shift that his paper exemplifies, as a paradigm of many current shifts, seems to

---

3. Niebuhr, *The Purpose of the Church and Its Ministry* (New York: Harper & Row, 1956).
4. Fielding, *Education for Ministry* (Dayton, Ohio: AATS, 1966).

be rooted in three operative assumptions. First, the *basic* first principles are already clear. They have to be taught, of course, but recognizing their truth and justice intellectually is not a major problem for reasonable, concerned, and open-minded people. Second, the real problem is making these principles effective in life — a task made difficult by ecclesiastical self-interest and narrow, confessional dogmatism, which confuses a formulation about first principles with the principles themselves and thus both obscures the principles and fractures the body of Christ. That difficulty can be overcome by recognizing what many in ecumenical circles have taken as their slogan: "Service unites; doctrine divides." Schomer's cosmopolitan activism represents a pronounced shift in the understanding of what theological education is. It is nurture of those clear, true, and just convictions that drive leaders into ethical action. Thus — third — the relative worth of convictions is proportional to their social and ethical potency. Practical theology, not systematic or dogmatic or biblical or creedal theology, is the queen of the theological sciences. "By their fruits ye shall know them."

The second major voice in this conference was that of M. M. Thomas.[5] He too is concerned with practical action, but he roots his concern more self-consciously in doctrine — or rather, a doctrine, Christology. As a representative of that remarkable generation of Third World, ecumenically oriented leaders who find in the emphatic Christocentric accents of neo-orthodoxy echoes of classic, patristic Christianity's confrontation with the paganism and learning, sometimes chaos and sometimes tyranny of the Roman Empire, he finds the confessional basis for a new interpretation of world history. It is one that challenges the pretenses of Western cultural colonialism and the pietism of evangelical Christianity as exported by missionaries to the Third World. Thus, Thomas began his presentation with an exposition of what "two-natures Christology" implies:

> Christian spirituality is the experience of a double presence in Jesus Christ — the presence of God and the presence of the world. . . . We cannot talk of the presence of God without a deep concern for the world; and in reverse, we cannot truly understand and experience the world without acknowledging the presence and work of God in relation to the world. No doubt, there are other kinds of spirituality. . . . [In] Eastern Spirituality, if you move nearer to God

---

5. Thomas, "The Relationships of the Inner Life of the Seminary to Its Role as Servant of Society. . . ," paper presented at the Division of Overseas Ministry Assembly, Nov. 1968.

you will go further away from the world. And in opposition, secularism seeks to know and experience the world . . . without recognition of God.

Thomas connected this motif to theological accents current in the ecumenical movement at that time (particularly as articulated by Albert van den Heuvel,[6] Willem Visser 't Hooft,[7] and the East Asian Christian Conference[8]). Thomas argued that the formation of a link between God and the world in the event of Jesus Christ is the paradigm of all living theology, for it is this event that points to the central reality of history with its new beginnings and eschatological promise. "In the events of our time," seen Christologically, "is the substance of true theology." Particularly for those in Asia, Africa, and Latin America, the overthrowing of colonial rule and the formation of new nations are the substance of theology. These events which redeem from oppression, which make concrete the aspirations for community, which overcome imperialism and division — these are the "Christ events" of the present. Understood in terms of the decisive event of the past, they portend a new future.

Participation in nation-building thus becomes a form of obedience to Christ.[9] It demands the overcoming of pietistic withdrawal from the events of the age, encounter with the new forms of rational discourse as we find them in the modern natural and social sciences, and concern for the "human communities" within which the Christian churches find themselves. However, this invigorating participation needs a contemporary spirituality, one that remembers the core of the past and points to the kernel of the future. Thomas sees eucharistic worship as the one focal point where the "self-offering of Jesus Christ . . . is offered to God, and received back as New Creation" again and again. That, he argued, is the locus where true "theological fellowship" becomes concrete in a genuine community. That is the parabolic act which embodies the Christ who has come, and which anticipates the full humanization of peoples and nations that is yet to come as it empowers us to discern, and respond to, the historical demands of the moment.

Schomer's accent on involved engagement for social change

---

6. Van den Heuvel, "Address to the Convention on Religious Education in Chicago," World Council of Churches, 1965.
7. Visser 't Hooft, *None Other Gods* (New York: Harper & Row, 1937).
8. East Asian Christian Conference, "Christian Community within the Human Community," published reports, 1965.
9. In these accents, Thomas articulates themes more fully stated in P. D. Devanandan and M. M. Thomas, *Christian Participation in Nation Building* (Bangalore: Christian Institute for the Study of Religion and Society, 1960).

and Thomas's emphasis on sacramentally centered "humanization" through participation, modernization, and nation-building anticipated a series of more recent developments. The contemporary horizon of theological education has been substantively altered by placing practical theologies at the center of seminary education. In contrast to subsequent developments, however, the views of these two leaders as recently as two decades ago presumed that the basic foundations of Christian theology are relatively clear, that Christian teaching and sacrament give reliable knowledge about what is true and just, right and good, in the midst of history. The chief problem seemed to be one of making those general principles come alive in action.

ON GLOBAL SOLIDARITY

A second major international consultation — the U.S./Canadian Consultation on "globalization" and theological education held in Toronto in July 1981 — resulted in a substantial report that includes major addresses, summaries of discussions and findings, and valuable references to bibliography and organizations that focus on international theological education.[10] The consultation was jointly sponsored by the ATS and the Programme on Theological Education (PTE) of the World Council of Churches; the report contains brief summaries and numerous references to other similar consultations held around the world — from the Philippines, to Brazil, to Switzerland, to East Europe, to Great Britain — as well as short papers summarizing emerging perspectives on women in theological education and the efforts of major Protestant denominations to develop global and international emphases in their seminaries. This consultation paid special attention to the relationships of minority peoples in North America to global issues, and to new movements from the Third World for this context. Samuel Proctor, of the Abyssinian Baptist Church in Harlem, set the tone for the gathering in his keynote address, and José Miguez Bonino of the Instituto Superior Evangelico de Estudios Teologicos in Argentina, a noted leader in Latin American liberation theology, delivered a major plenary address that also identified key issues decisive for the proceedings and the results.

Proctor takes as his point of departure the question of what

---

10. A. Sapsezian, S. Amirtham, and F. Ross Kinsler, *Global Solidarity in Theological Education* (Geneva: World Council of Churches, 1981).

we might mean by the "world community."[11] By 1981, many in theological education spoke of "community-building" as a centerpoint for education and action. Also, many had become aware that most of the time our sense of community is too small. We live today in an age striding toward a "global community." What are the theological requirements needed to bring about such a community, to anticipate it most creatively in theological education?

Of course, Proctor argues, we all have some notion of community by virtue of the smaller communities to which we belong, and everyone belongs to some national community. Further, there are "extra-national" communities such as those of musicians, tennis players, financiers, and so forth, as well as those kinds of community that, for example, Catholics, Communists, or black people seem to feel in the face of dominant cultures that are suspicious of them. But the key question is whether, beyond these embryonic forms of community that seldom embrace very much of our total identities, there is a basis for "broader, deeper and more durable community that embraces our common destiny . . . , affirms our common humanity, . . . [and] recognizes our possibilities as persons who have freedom . . . , and hear the voice of God." We should recognize, says Proctor, that the idea of a global community is not the same as the Kingdom of God, but "any complete discussion of a global community will lead to the threshold of the Kingdom of God, the regnancy of God in the hearts of all."[12]

Proctor sets forth three tests as decisive for movement toward such a community. First, the community must be broad; it must overcome our parochial or trivial identifications of who we are and of what the critical communities of identity are to be. Second, the community must be deep; it must ask if our care and stated concern actually reach out to see that children are fed, education is available, the sick are cared for, the elderly are comfortable, the oppressed are freed, and the rules governing deviant behavior are fair and consistently applied. And third, the community must be durable; it cannot base its existence on the outcome of one or another ephemeral issue. It must, in other words, take the long view of history. While it is important to gather a movement around, say, recent U.S. policies damaging to black Americans, the only community that will be durable in the long run is one that also takes into its purview the plight of those of color in Southern Africa,

---

11. Proctor, "Theological Requirements for Global Community," in *Global Solidarity in Theological Education*, pp. 15-21.
12. Proctor, "Theological Requirements for Global Community," pp. 16-17.

literacy programs in other parts of the world, and environmental protection everywhere. We do not characterize those who gather for some purpose or other as a community unless "they have other interests and values in common that last far beyond the span of one lifetime."[13]

To have a community that is broad, deep, and durable, we have to have a vision of its culmination. That vision generates an enthusiasm and leads to a common endeavor which rests on "a foundation of moral and spiritual values, a view of the world and of history that affirms such goals, . . . and celebrations that keep such a vision alive." Commitment to these things is not instinctive. "It has to be cultivated and theological education must have a key role as an agent of this enterprise."[14] Ultimately, that vision must rest in a profound knowledge of God. But today we are besieged by indifference toward ideas about God, childish and anthropomorphic views of God, and uses of God concepts that seem to do little more than make the Pentagon feel at home in the world.

In the face of these narrow, shallow, and temporary views, theological education should embark on that high adventure manifest in the Prophets, who knew that the true God is a God of justice; in Ruth and Jonah, who knew that God was for all peoples; and in Jesus, who knew that God sets moral integrity above religious particularism and spiritual devotion above power and riches. Such an adventure demands intellectual integrity and moral courage: "God does not need weak and intellectually fraudulent defenses. God does not need the curtain of fear drawn on questions about his person or his works."[15] Such an adventure also requires an understanding of the human that transcends our narrow cultural biases. Present anthropologies do little to challenge racism, nationalism, and social divisions. And a key clue to such an anthropology, Proctor argues, is to be found in ethics, in what is generally valid in universal human morality. Ethics as the science that bridges universality and particularity is the core of practical theology in a day of "global community."

José Miguez Bonino is less inclined to speak in terms of ethical questions. He believes that these matters, and all matters of justice, are for the Christian first of all *theological* and *pastoral* ques-

---

13. Proctor, "Theological Requirements for Global Community," p. 17.
14. Proctor, "Theological Requirements for Global Community," p. 17.
15. Proctor, "Theological Requirements for Global Community," p. 19.

tions.[16] It would be a mistake to try to move toward globalization by relegating the decisive issues to the ethics division of any seminary. "The battle for global solidarity in theological education is fought and won or lost in the teaching of the Bible, in the teaching of Church history, of Systematic Theology, of Pastoral Theology. If it is not fought at that level, all that we add in terms of other more fancy things will not help very much."[17] It may well be important, for example, to have an ethics course in economic justice — but are the students who take such a course prepared to deal with the "soul care" of those in the congregation who are involved in industrial complexes, corporations, and world banking (or those who are damaged by decisions they make)? Surely students need to be prepared to deal with people in terms of nurturing spiritual health in the face of what they do every day.

Just as important might be exegesis and interpretation of the book of Acts. There, using all the historical-critical methods, one could deal with the question of gospel and empire, the Lukan view of church history and the history of mission. And such a study could fruitfully be carried out by raising the questions of church and peoplehood, theology of history, and missions in our time. Or the decisive theological and pastoral issues could be raised in systematics. For example, in speaking of God's omnipresence, we ought to deal with the fact that God is surely and particularly present with other people in other ways than those known to us. Then we can begin to establish a sense of the root solidarity.

Such matters are of critical import, says Miguez Bonino, because today there seems to be much less general awareness of the world than there was even a decade or two ago. Seminarians and laity seem focused on their local and immediate situations. Certainly few pastors seem prepared or able to lead their people to any global sensitivity without engaging in a rather sentimental or idealistic appeal to "care" (which evaporates when hard issues have to be faced), or without becoming cynical and ideological when they try to deal with the "hard issues" without pastoral sensitivity. Thus, Miguez Bonino takes the issues of Schomer and Thomas, as well as of Proctor, as the centerpoint of the whole of theological edu-

---

16. Miguez Bonino, "Global Solidarity and the Theological Curriculum," in *Global Solidarity in Theological Education,* pp. 22-25.
17. Miguez Bonino, "Global Solidarity and the Theological Curriculum," p. 22. However, Miguez Bonino has focused on specifically ethical matters in a major subsequent publication: *Toward a Christian Political Ethics* (Philadelphia: Fortress Press, 1983).

cation and pastoral training, and he puts them in the context of a theoretical and practical "theology of history."

TOWARD GLOBALIZATION

Yet a third consultation was held by a commission sponsored by the ATS. The results were summarized in the so-called Shriver Report of 1984,[18] which has as its focus the development of guidelines intended to inform those theological schools that move toward "internationalization" or "globalization" in their programs. Seen in the light of the kinds of debates previously recounted, these efforts attempt to draw on the insights of international consultants in a quest for some clarity about how global-contextual problems can be addressed in today's renovation of theological education, and how to do so in a time when a new ecumenical, "catholic," and missiological awareness is being called for.

Here the presentation and summary of these materials are shaped by the debates about them at "Convocation '84: Bi-National Forum on Issues in Theological Education," held in Chicago on October 9-10, 1984. The "Shriver Report" was required background reading. Max L. Stackhouse chaired the section on the globalization of theological education with Robert Schreiter (see Chapter 7). On five points there seems to be considerable consensus, although each point entails an agenda for further work:

1. Whatever the seminary develops as a program must be of significance for humankind. That is, it may not be consciously or preconsciously limited in implication to some segment of humanity — in terms of race, class, culture, or gender. Meeting this criterion demands, of course, some basic agreement about theological anthropology that is more comprehensive than the divisions which we experience on these grounds. At present, we do not have a common understanding of theological anthropology that we present clearly and cogently to the next generation of leaders.

2. Whatever we do should induce global perspectives without colonialism or imperialism. This does not mean that particular insights generated out of, or discovered in, one cultural context are

---

18. D. W. Shriver, Jr., et al., "Committee on Internationalization of Theological Education," ATS, 1984. See also D. S. Schuller, "Globalization in Theological Education: Summary and Analysis of Survey Data," ATS, 1984; J. C. Hough and J. B. Cobb, *The Education of Practical Theologians* (Chico, Calif.: Scholars Press, 1986); and the entire issue of *Theological Education* 23 (Autumn 1986).

relevant only to that context. Some things that are discovered in particular contexts are indeed of universal significance. However, we do need to clearly establish the criteria that we use to assess which things are of particular import and which are of general import.

3. Whatever we do should be related to the quest for the visible unity of the church. That is, we should make every effort to relate the efforts in seminary education to the denominational and ecumenical organizations already in existence. This demands a certain familiarity with the core confessions, beliefs, practices, and polities of the major families of Christian tradition, their roots and reasons for being.

4. Whatever we do must be alert to other developments of global significance — science, technology, transnational corporations, international politics, military policy, and the discovery of common patterns of linguistic structure, social institutions, and ethical elements in all religions and cultures. These global developments are bringing disruptive change to particular contexts where Christians live and yet seem to provide common bases for global interaction and exchange. By what principles are we to know when to resist the disruptions, for the sake of protecting particular traditions, and when to embrace the transformations they effect as harbingers of a wider human solidarity?

5. Whatever we do must prepare students to practice ministry with excellence. Among the key implications of this criterion is the demand that the pastor be, above all, the "theologian in residence" among the people of God, able to preach, teach, counsel, lead worship, and organize in such a way that the people can themselves become theologians and ministers in the world.

UNRESOLVED ISSUES

Thus far we have discovered in dialogue that theological education is presently experiencing a loss of metaphysical-moral vision (Chapter 1), a simultaneous sense of living in a world of increased complexity and interdependence (Chapter 2), new difficulties in understanding the relationship of text and context (Chapter 3), and new perceptions of the nature and functions of missions in multiple contexts (Chapter 4). We have also reviewed (in this chapter) the agenda of some of the representative, ecumenically oriented consultations that have, in recent years, proposed new directions for theological education in regard to globalization and mission. In all of these, we note a certain disenchantment with inherited relationships of theory and practice in modern seminaries, a resolution to be more internationally alert and less imperialistic, and an insecurity about the criteria that should guide our more inclusive thought and our more relevant efforts.

However, even the remarkable achievement of consensus on, by, and about the "Shriver Report" did not resolve all problems. When the report was finally adopted, after some minor modifications, still unresolved were the questions of how, precisely, these concerns about globalization could and should be woven into a theological curriculum, and what standards would be used to grant or deny accreditation of theological educational programs if globalization was not a central priority of an institution.

One of the reasons that such standards may be difficult to construct is that, behind the consensus on these issues and on those of the previous consultations that in part laid the groundwork for this one, lie very difficult foundational issues about which there is very little consensus. They are issues that some of the best minds struggling with these issues have tried to address in systematic ways, as we will see in the next three chapters. Before we turn to them, however, let us briefly summarize some of the remaining perplexities:

1. What is the proper relationship of Christianity to other religions? Here the discussions at ANTS and in Chicago revealed a rather indecent mixture of complexity and confusion. Larry Greenfield of Colgate Rochester stated it most sharply when he pointed out that a good way to induce a heated discussion among large numbers of seminarians and faculty in an ecumenically oriented environment today is to argue that Christians should convert Jews, Muslims, Hindus, and Buddhists because Christian truth in fact grasps the human condition, the nature of God, and the character of history more accurately than any other religion or worldview. It soon becomes clear that most of the students and no small number of the faculty (a) are ignorant of other traditions, (b) doubt that Christianity is any more true than any other religion, (c) do not have a very clear idea of what they would convert anyone to, and (d) suspect that missions and evangelism are mostly a matter of cultural imperialism.

Everyone seems to agree that a dialogical relationship with other religions is a good thing, but there is as yet little clarity about the reason for or basis of the dialogue. Is the purpose of dialogue to clarify divergent stances, to prepare for conversion, to seek a common truth and justice beyond the variety of particular religions, or something else? Further, each call for dialogue, whatever the motivation, presupposes that a common basis for dialogue is present, or, at least, that we can understand what different partners in the dialogue are talking about; but such presuppositions assume a universalistic metaphysical, moral, or epistemological foundation that is reliable and in terms of which dialogue can make sense. What might that foundation be?

2. A second issue about which there is considerable disagreement is the relationship between the individual and the collective in theological formation. In part, this is a question of whether we are engaged in the formation of individuals or the building of community. In our discussions at ANTS, Jane Cary Peck pointed out that posing the question in this "either/or" way, as many do today, is more a reflection of the Enlightenment division of *psyche* from *polis* than the biblical view of person in community. In fact, we are engaged in both, but how one sees the relationship of person and community turns out to be quite decisive for what we do in theological education. When we take up these questions in the midst of reflection on globalization, we are forced to ask what must be involved in the formation of cosmopolitan persons and person-supporting international institutions that can knowledgeably address and find concrete means to express care for those whom we do not know and might not like very much if we did. Further, by what standards can we presume to convert persons or alter societies not interested in becoming a part of global processes? It turns out that the various ecclesiologies worked out over the course of Christian history are decisive models for how this can and ought to be done. The overcoming of factionalism in church and society, for example, demands wide agreement on a theory of how God wants human individuals to live, work, and pray together in community, and a clear view of how authority ought to be structured to sustain such an environment and to form the character of persons who will be interested in taking responsibility for the common life. Clarity and consensus are not widespread on this matter.

3. Still another question that remains quite unsettled is the question of "inclusivity" or "distinctiveness," as Barbara Wheeler has called it.[19] At stake here is not only the question of how open seminaries will be to dissenting groups on matters that others take to be central to questions of faith and morals, but the degree to which pluralism is prized on one side and, on the other, regarded as a threat to distinctive religious identities and senses of mission.

---

19. Wheeler et al., "Mind-Reading: Notes on the Basic Issues Program," *Theological Education* 20 (Spring 1984).

Wheeler's categories also apply to the question of whether particular traditions should be preserved, or whether attempts should be made to broaden the frame of reference to include the wider range of ecumenical perspectives. Even more, in view of the accents just reviewed, we are confronted with the question of whether our sense of religious inclusion ought to embrace social movements and religions that are not a part of any explicit Christian confession or communion but that seem to be manifesting quite concretely the incarnation of hope, purpose, and principle in human communities.

Such questions reflect a growing awareness, over the course of these several consultations, that much of what has passed for first principles and basic criteria may be a reflection of a specific time and place. Thus, what is sought is a way to bring ecclesial, ethical, and intellectual integrity to an enormous diversity of perspectives, but what counts as "integrity" has changed. The debates have moved away from a view that theology is fundamentally about that which transcends the various contexts of the world and must be brought to them, made indigenous to them, and made a living, historical reality in them. This view presupposes that the universal truth of the gospel is knowable and unified even if the ways of the world are broken. The constant task of the church, and thus of theological education, in this view is the "incarnation" of that which is "known" to be metaphysically, morally, and epistemologically valid for the salvation of a broken world.

But now the accent has fallen on a contrary view — that the truth of the gospel is an ever-changing dynamic that is presumptively present, although not always recognized, in the social-historical contexts in which we live. In this view, engagement in and study of particular contexts will themselves reveal the multifaceted character of a dynamic ultimate reality, even if they do not render a clear, universal perspective. The message of the gospel is not something that we bring *to* contexts but something that we derive *from* contexts. And it is variable according to the context. Thus, as we saw also in Chapter 3, contextualism, rather than contextualization, is the tendency. We need but to discern the multiple manifestations of the Incarnation, each one of which will be unique, specific, and immediate; and the greater variety and diversity we can sample, the better. Here again, the fundamental questions of the "realist-nominalist" debate lie just beneath the surface.

4. A related debate has to do with the role that we understand religion to play in civilization. All the voices we have heard hold that religion is — or should be — the moral heart of social history. It provides the inner logic by which the most important as-

pects of civilization operate, with theology as the science proper to its understanding. When religion is transformed, the society changes; when religion falls apart or dries up, not only do people suffer meaninglessness but the civilization crumbles. And theology, in this view, is the mode of reliable knowledge by which religion can be evaluated according to its truth and justice. But also present in this view is the secondary assumption that religion often is — and theology (whether biblical or historical, ethical or practical) may become — little more than reflection on the dynamics of history that do not require the use of categories from religion or theology to interpret them correctly. And since historical life in community is the vital center of all that we humans think, feel, and think we feel, religion is of worth and meaning only when it expresses the vitalities of historical change. In this view, theology is more an art than a science. It is what can give aesthetic form to religious expression.

Under the surface of these consultations is the suspicion that the skeptics of the eighteenth and nineteenth centuries might be at least partially correct: that "educated people" do not really believe that religion is a decisive and indispensable element for personal, communal, and civilizational viability, do not consider theology to be a science in any current meaning of the term, and do not think that there is anything "out there" other than the models we construct out of our partial experiences of the dynamics of historical life. Instead, "progress" (in recent centuries) and "history" (in the current one) are the locus and judge of all that is holy, true, and just.[20] In this view, when society changes, religion must be reconstructed, and the problem is finding the criteria by which to undertake this task. The inner life of historical action is the clue to the meaning of faith; religion is less a cause in civilization than an effect; theology is less a "science" than a particular expression of a historically conditioned moment — and that is as it should be.

5. The question of criteria remains decisive in all these areas of dispute. How would we know what we think we do know? And what should guide our judgments? These consultations reflect a growing doubt about the utility, validity, and reliability of theology as an intellectual activity in itself. Several voices at the ATS convocation in 1984 were quite clear about the fact that theology, if it is to find a new ground, must turn to modes of discourse extrinsic

---

20. See Nicola Chiaromonte, *The Paradox of History: Stendhal, Tolstoy, Pasternak, and Others*, rev. ed. (Pittsburgh: University of Pennsylvania Press, 1985). See also G. G. Iggers, *The German Conception of History: The National Tradition of of Historical Thought from Herder to the Present* (Middletown, Conn.: Wesleyan University Press, 1968).

to itself — to social theory, to hermeneutics, to phenomenology. This idea that theology is not an independent science is of course not entirely new. For centuries it has been the case that some have believed that theology is not and cannot be a universalistic mode of discourse able to cut across cultural, social, or historical divisions. That, in the past, was held to be the case because theology is based on revelation, which, as a privileged mode of knowledge available only to those who are members of a faith community, is simply not available to any to whom the revelation does not come as self-authenticating truth.

Historically, in the West, it has been widely held that, therefore, it is to "nature" that we must turn if we are to find out what was in fact universal. Of course, the ancients turned to the philosophical-speculative study of nature, and the moderns turned to the scientific-empirical study of nature, and these differences are of enormous practical importance. Philosophers want humanity to obey nature; scientists want us to master it. But both believe that only the study of nature, and not the study of anything that smacks of the super- or supra-natural, could provide reliable, general guidance to human understanding and action.

Among the most powerful modern currents of thought lurking in the wings of all the dialogues and consultations are echoes of these views that suggest a nagging question. Is it so that theology has to depend on something other than itself, and thus undercut its own claims to be foundational? At the same time, none of the views we have thus far examined have turned to "nature" as the point of appeal. They seem to presume that our views of nature are no less conditioned by our social situation, by the hermeneutical models available to us, and by the phenomenological dynamics of our interactions with others than are our views of religion. Thus, it becomes necessary for philosophy, science, and theology jointly to inquire again into the basic modes of knowing anything with reasonable certainty. And, as we can see in the several consultations, we are left with the rather painful awareness that we must undertake theological education with an eye to the engagement with civilizations around the world in ways that are ethically compelling; but we are unsure as to whether what we do is valid, whether it is based on what is true, and how we might argue for it if we think it is.

These unresolved issues have been the subject of several outstanding, if finally not fully satisfying, studies in the last few years. These studies became the topics for discussion and debate within the ATS research team and within the faculty. To their strengths and weaknesses we now turn.

CHAPTER 6

Praxis *and Solidarity**

Many of the participants in the dialogues and consultations discussed herein have pressed theological education toward "action" or "social engagement" models of learning and teaching, an accent that has prompted many to explore the term *praxis* in new ways. Indeed, many are so entranced by the "new" emphasis on *praxis* that they forget how old the term is. We should perhaps not be surprised to find a Greek philosophical term at the center of some branches of current theological discussion. Christian theology in the postbiblical periods has always involved a synthesis of biblically derived symbols and philosophical modes of understanding. Indeed, one of the most decisive questions for theology over the centuries has been the question of which modes of understanding are most appropriate to a true and just faith and thus most proper to theological education. All serious theological education is, in some sense, rooted in a philosophical theology even when its governing motifs are taken from Scripture, tradition, or religious experience. Today, many are proposing that *praxis* provides the truest, most faithful, and most ethically responsible way of understanding what Christian theology is all about. It should become the core of both the life of the church and theological education.

In classical philosophy, *praxis* was understood to be one of the three basic ways of knowing, living, and being in the world. It stands distinct from, but in a complementary relationship to, both

---

*This chapter is based in part on research for the ATS team by Lee Harding.

poesis and *theoria*. *Poesis* involves imaginative creation or representation of evocative images. It includes the kind of awareness and orientation to life that can be discovered by aesthetic and kinesthetic experience. *Theoria* involves observation, reporting, interpretation, and critical evaluation. It thus includes all that can be known by analysis, systematic study, reflection, and contemplation. The central issues of *theoria* are less aesthetic or kinesthetic than ontological, metaphysical, and epistemic. In contrast to these, *praxis* involves intentional, practical engagement whereby people seek to do something for the common good. However, the kind of life and world orientation that derives from *praxis* is not unrelated to *poesis* or *theoria*. Social conduct for the common good has moments within it that may demand aesthetic celebration or theoretic reflection on the presumptions and consequences of what is being done. These moments, it is held, can be creatively instrumental to the formation of community. They can clarify, enhance, and give motivation to action. Indeed, the worth of these poetic or theoretic moments is assessed according to their relative capacity to inspire the will to active engagement. *Praxis*, in short, has become the technical term for the "action/reflection" mode of teaching and learning, one that does not focus primarily on either speculative theory or aesthetic expression, but accepts these as possible resources for action. These are sublated into a new synthesis, one that is held to be intimately tied to a particular sense of the mission of faith and of the church, and hence of theological education.

THE ADVOCATES OF *PRAXIS*

Contemporary advocates of *praxis* frequently hold that Western thought has taken some wrong turns, specifically when, in the history of piety, it elevated *poesis* over *praxis*, and when, in the history of theology, it elevated *theoria* over *praxis*. The one becomes preoccupied with religion in its cultic, mythic, and liturgical dimensions; the other with reason in its speculative, abstract senses. Both truncate action. But we shall see that not all major contemporary perspectives are in agreement on this point. Without always using these same classical terms for how humans teach, learn, and act in accord with the matters most important for theological education, some are today advocating a recovery of semiotic *poesis*, which they feel can reintegrate *theoria* and *praxis* in new, creative ways (Chapter 7); others argue that only a new phenomenological *theoria* can include *poesis* and *praxis* (Chapter 8). It is in any case ironically convenient that these three Greek terms represent a typology of current attempts to repudiate the connection between theology and classical philosophy.

One distinctive feature of the new *praxis*-oriented proposals is that those who call for them are deeply concerned about the community background and interests, the "social location," of those who assume particular religious or theoretical positions. In accord with that concern, we should be clear that those who advocate the modern recovery and recasting of *praxis* appear today in a number of groups.

For example, the idea is widely advocated among the staff leadership of "liberal" Protestant and ecumenical churches and seminaries. This occurs at a time when, after centuries during which the Protestant church was a part of the establishment, Protestant church membership, relative to the general population, is declining (as the membership of Roman Catholic and evangelical churches increases), and at a time when alienation between the mainline denominations and the political, economic, and cultural values of the United States is intensifying. This can be seen either as the prophetic disengagement of Protestantism from "Constantinian Christianity," or as the sectarianization of the mainline churches in the face of their loss of influence.

Ironically, a second group advocating a recovery of *praxis* consists primarily of conservative political philosophers who believe that the post-Enlightenment religious, intellectual, and political life is so entranced with the abstract theories of modern science that it loses contact with those basic "natural" structures of human virtues so necessary for any *polis*. These "classicists" often engage in a sharp critique of modernity and call for a return to the "deeper" worldviews of the ancient Greek political theorists and to the days when philosopher-kings defined the virtues of *praxis* in terms of a particular philosophy of prudence and wisdom. While the proposals for return to the worlds of Plato and Aristotle by these most serious of all "neo-conservatives" are seldom accepted by modern theology (of which they are quite contemptuous), their critique of modernity often is echoed by religious leaders who feel that technology, science, secularism, historicism, and socialism and/or capitalism are destroying all human meaning and distorting both *praxis* and *theoria*.[1]

---

1. We have in mind the disciples of Eric Voegelin, Leo Strauss, and Alasdair MacIntyre. The most recent and pompous representative, as far as education is concerned, is Allan Bloom, *The Closing of the American Mind* (New York: Simon & Schuster, 1987).

A third group consists of the "new philosophers of deconstruction," a still rather inchoate group of intellectuals who hold that theology, metaphysics, ontologically based ethics, and classical political philosophy are basically dead topics, as Nietzsche has declared. Radicalizing the "hermeneutics of suspicion," they argue that talk about the true, the good, and the beautiful is basically an echo of faded dreams that were never valid in the first place. These contemporary heirs of nihilism in politics, sadism in sexuality, Dadaism in art, and the Heideggerian protest against the "Western Project" in philosophy claim that humans today are liberated by knowing that *theoria* has no foundations beyond the poetic fantasies of those who play with them, and that *poesis* is basically the *praxis* of the strong, devoid of any pretense that it is rooted in any "objective" vision of the good, the true, or the beautiful.[2]

A fourth group advocating the recovery of *praxis* — and the one that will primarily concern us here — has been and is being indirectly influenced by all the groups just mentioned. But, more directly, it consists primarily of "radical" Christians who share with the other groups a series of presumptions about intellectual and social history. They are seldom concerned about what liberal church leadership says, however, and they doubt that there is much to be learned from the Greeks. Many are quite convinced that religious *poesis* and intellectual *theoria* must be subjected to a radical hermeneutics of suspicion, although few know about or care about the practical implications of modern deconstructionism.[3] Yet these advocates of *praxis* are, like the others, dissatisfied with both abstract theology and modern life. They see the one doomed to failure and the other so laden by commercial interest, media hype, patriarchy, and vacuous pieties that it can do little more than exploit or betray all that makes human life human. At the same time, they find new possibilities among the peoples of the world who are emerging from slavery, feudalism, tribalism, patriarchal domination, cultural imperialism, and colonialism. Among these peoples they find a spir-

---

2. At this point we have in mind Michel Foucault, Jacques Derrida, and Richard Rorty. Rorty is especially interesting because of the ways he links the ideas of these French thinkers to John Dewey's pragmatism and thereby to much of American educational philosophy. The results are artfully stated in Nathan A. Scott, "The House of Intellect in an Age of Carnival," in the *Journal of the American Academy of Religion* 55 (Spring 1987): 3-19.

3. The most important single work representing this view is *The Pedagogy of the Oppressed* by Paulo Freire, trans. Myra Ramos (London: Herder & Herder, 1971); but also significant are the works of Gustavo Gutiérrez, James Cone, Richard Shaull, and Robert MacAfee Brown.

ited assertion of new ways of living in new social solidarities. There, new patterns of action and reflection challenge Western theology and civilization, ancient or modern.

THE ROOTS OF *PRAXIS*

These new possibilities — now found among women, people of color, the poor, the oppressed, and the outcasts of the "Two-Thirds World" — are simultaneously current, concrete expressions of communal solidarity actualized in political movements and kinds of transformed consciousness derived from "seeing things from below" which, these groups hold, engendered the biblical witness in the first place. Solidarity with those suffering the pains of racism, classism, sexism, imperialism, and colonialism, all caused or legitimated by *theoria* or *poesis* from the top down, and solidarity with those new possibilities now emerging from the bloody underside of history is the proper locus of redemptive *praxis*. This is the source of the kind of living and being proper to theological education; this is liberating. This turns the "Western Project" on its head.

The Greeks, and subsequently Enlightenment minds, valued the life of *theoria* above *praxis* and *poesis* as that form of knowing that was most like the life of God. *Praxis* and *poesis* helped make the contemplative life possible, but *theoria* was *the* end in itself. Although Plato and Aristotle attempted to hold together the three ways of living and of knowing, it is widely held that their preference for *theoria* induced a disjunction between the three. This disjunction was taken over into theology when faith adopted Greek patterns of philosophy as its partner in thought. The social and political dimensions of *praxis* became de-emphasized, and *poesis* was made subservient to cultus. Speculative metaphysics became the primary way of viewing the cosmos and social life, all was hierarchically arranged, and other ways of living or thinking were given reduced importance. Indeed, the people who lived by *praxis* or *poesis* were also reduced in ontological status. To be sure, *praxis* was taken up from time to time by various populist sects, but they were crushed again and again.

Many who view Western intellectual and social history in this way hold that a new chapter on how people teach, learn, know, and act was written in the Enlightenment. *Theoria,* in a philosophical mold, was further abstracted from *poesis* and *praxis,* and became so removed from reality that its epistemology had no ontological or metaphysical or material foundation.

In the recent recovery of *praxis,* great emphasis is placed on the ways in which Hegel, and subsequently Marx, reacted against the formalistic and epistemologically centered speculations of the Enlightenment, took up the neglected elements of human knowing and doing in terms of *Aufhebung,* and re-engaged the study of historical reality. The German *Aufhebung* was often intended as a reclamation and recasting of the Greek *praxis* and is related to the formation of political solidarities. According to Hegel, the decisive *praxis* is that of *Geist* as it actualizes itself and comes to consciousness in time, especially in the practical actions of civil society and the nation-state. *Theoria* is thus redefined, and its place in thought relocated. It becomes, in its purest forms, the human attempt to offer an articulation of the patterned dialectic of *praxis* and *poesis.* In this understanding, *theoria* does not guide action but attempts to identify and comprehend the inner spirit of the dialectical logic of action, which is both poetic and practical.[4]

We might note, at this point, that a modified version of this Hegelian view became highly influential in the United States, where it entered into an alliance with utilitarian thought to form American pragmatism. At the hands of William James it was individualistically applied and deeply shaped the definitions of religious experience used in practical theology. At the hands of John Dewey it was applied to democratic theories of education and the formation of the professions, especially teaching. In both forms, pragmatism, as the North American form of *praxis,* presumes that a creative spirit is at work in human progress, and that the purpose of theological, ethical, metaphysical, or moral theory is the exploration of existing conditions to identify possibilities that can be actualized to create values, enhance satisfactions, supply solutions to problems, and lend integration to conflicts. Theories are (as Dewey says) "inference policies" — kinds of poetic expression that are neither true nor false but capable of being assessed according to their pragmatic ability to bring about desired consequences.

It is these motifs that increasingly became adopted in religious circles to form the "liberalism" so influential in many ecumenical churches and in the shaping of the main contours of practical theology in the seminaries — whether these groups are conscious of their own intellectual backgrounds or not. Theology and piety are

---

4. Richard Bernstein, *The Restructuring of Social and Political Theory* (New York: Harcourt Brace Jovanovich, 1976). What Bernstein traces analytically appears as gospel most artfully in Gustavo Gutiérrez, *A Theology of Liberation,* trans. Inda Caridad, Sr., and John Eagleson (Maryknoll, N.Y.: Orbis Books, 1973). Note their similar bibliographies.

understood to be the personal or interpersonal "inference policies" developed out of life experience and immediate practical relationships. Their validity is judged according to whether they help people in personal growth, community relations, and professional success. Therapeutic and managerial criteria define meaning and guide *praxis*.[5]

Marx distrusted the utilitarian claims of American thought and saw them as a mask for capitalist interests. Even more, he resisted Hegel's assumption of a superordinate *Geist*. He replaced it with a specific understanding of humanity's material and social existence, so that human interests might be both stripped of illusion and aided in rational action. He believed that the purpose of philosophy is not to understand reality but to change it. *Theoria* thus becomes a primary way of enabling *praxis*. Humanity, especially those members of it who are the "doers" of the world, the "workers" in solidarity, become the self-initiating agents who constitute history through their activity against those who try to control *praxis* by false *theoria* (and its alliance with illusory *poesis*, especially religion). The *praxis* of human agency in pursuit of material interests becomes the centerpoint of all human meaning and activity. Humans in solidarity are liberated to be truly human. All social realities, artistic achievements, and theories are seen as human artifacts that must construct ideologies to clarify the *praxis*. In this view, those who accent the priority of *theoria* (or, for that matter, of *poesis*) are understood to have some material interest in mind that really determines their claims about what is true (or beautiful), and to use the priority they affirm to dominate, manipulate, and frustrate genuine human self-actualization in *praxis*.

In more recent intellectual developments, these motifs have been modified by a group of remarkable scholars of the Frankfurt School of Social Research in Germany. The driving force of this effort was to combine the *praxis* concerns of Marx (and Freud) with a reconstituted rational theory in the tradition of the Enlight-

---

5. See Philip Rieff, *The Triumph of the Therapeutic: Uses of Faith after Freud* (New York: Harper & Row, 1966); and Robert Bellah et al., *Habits of the Heart: Individualism and Commitment in American Life* (Berkeley and Los Angeles: University of California Press, 1985). Also see Roger Lundin, "Deconstructive Therapy," *The Reformed Journal*, Jan. 1986, pp. 15-20, for a superb essay on how these accents are related to the work of those deconstructionists mentioned in footnote 2. And see Janice G. Raymond, *A Passion for Friends: Toward a Philosophy of Female Affection* (Boston: Beacon Press, 1986), pp. 43ff., for a critique of "deconstruction" from a feminist standpoint. Raymond is alert to at least some of the "whos" who get deconstructed if the theory of *praxis* is accepted.

enment. Most particularly this demanded a new attentiveness to *poesis* in terms of what is necessary for communication. The result is a new "critical theory" intended to reconstitute political *praxis*.[6] Paralleling these philosophical developments, a number of new "political theologies" have also begun to develop — drawing concerns of the liberation theologies of the Third World into the mix.

PRAXIS BAPTIZED

Whether the emphasis on *praxis* is philosophical, liberal, conservative, deconstructionist, idealistic, psychological, pedagogical, or critical (in the "critical theory" sense), it is possible to see the potential for confusion. *Praxis* can mean a way of being in the world that unifies reflection and action; it can mean knowing that derives from engaged living; it can mean a self-actualization that deconstructs all limits; it can mean a pragmatic adjustment of and to life; or it can mean the quest for a new humanistic basis for sociohistorical existence that overcomes the pathologies of modernity. In all cases, these modern uses of the term are shaped by a reaction against what is regarded as a disastrous predominance of theory in a theory/practice dichotomy, and as a neglect of the real human meanings on the part of most of theology, which focuses on theory. What is required, it is widely held, is a new theory and a new practice of religion based on *praxis*.

Matthew Lamb is perhaps the best of several contemporary scholars who have attempted to sort out the possible confusions and to identify the implications of *praxis* for religious studies and theological education.[7] As a scholar deeply influenced by the *praxis*-oriented theory of contemporary liberation theology as well as by the "critical theory" and "political theology" movements, Lamb believes that what the Greeks and, even more, Enlightenment minds generated as theory has in modernity developed into a rationale for imperialistic domination. The fact that much of theology and theological education have become wedded to *theoria* has brought theory to the brink of nihilism.

In his view, there are three basic options for theology, two of which are irrelevant to the recovery of *praxis* that is needed.

---

6. Here we have in mind Adorno, Marcuse, Harkeimer, and especially Habermas, perhaps the most significant "product" of this school. See Habermas, *The Theory of Communicative Action,* vol. 1: *Reason and the Rationalization of Society,* trans. Thomas McCarthy (Boston: Beacon Press, 1984).

7. Lamb, *Solidarity with Victims: Toward a Theology of Social Transformation* (New York: Crossroad, 1982).

The first option could be called "idealist" in modern terminology or "realist" in older vocabularies. This option gives priority to theory grounded in the apprehension of those normative principles of thought and patterns of being that are "absolute" or "necessary" for human thinking and acting in general. Thus, it attempts to understand, interpret, evaluate, and guide practical experience in terms of these principles and patterns. An example of this can be found in pre–Vatican II Catholic theology. This form of theology attempts to specify by deduction what is normative, eternal, and necessary for life and faith. It understands theoretical assent as the highest form of Christian wisdom. *Praxis* is not accorded the capacity to change the principles or patterns of being or knowing that are thought to be grasped by right theory. The role of theology, and hence of theological education, is to proclaim, expound, and develop by logical application the universal truth known by rightly reasoned faith.

A second, empirical or inductive possibility locates the principles and patterns within material reality, which is publicly observable and capable of verification or falsification. This is the direction taken by modern science, which is on the whole suspicious of classically derived principles and patterns, and of normative thinking in general. This way of thinking is often called "liberal," although it can also be found in radical views that accept "historicism"—for example, the "existential" thought of the previous generation.

As Lamb sees it, this view has its roots in Luther's "nominalist" repudiation of speculative theology, in the accent of pietist movements on subjective religious feelings, in Baconian science, and in the Enlightenment's turn away from metaphysics. Theology is understood to have no knowable objective referent, although it may be an expression of the emotive-intuitive, internal noncognitive experiences or the needs of believers. Lamb quotes Avery Dulles's characterization of this position to the effect that religious truth "consists not in correspondence with an outside reality, but in enabling one to participate more fully in the ongoing processive reality with which man is continuous. Creeds and dogmas, therefore, are not to be assessed in terms of the knowledge about God they are thought to convey, but in terms of their ability to help man move beyond the relatively inadequate situation in which he finds himself and to expand his life within the human community."[8] Several of the "secular theologians" of the 1960s and 1970s are cited as exemplars of this direction as it bears on theology and theological

---

8. Dulles, *Revelation Theology* (New York: Herder & Herder, 1972), p. 169.

education. In some ways, it is the most characteristic form of "liberal Protestantism," American pragmatism, and much "practical theology" as currently taught.

The third approach, neither simply deductive nor inductive, neither "realist" nor "nominalist," relates all normative principles and patterns to the structural dynamics of human performance in *praxis*. The decisive debates within this approach are about how, precisely, *praxis* is to be understood in relation to *theoria*, and which dynamics of human practical experience are to be taken as foundational and normative in society.

According to Lamb, each of these three possibilities implies a distinctive interpretation of religion, and hence of theology. The first tends to stress focus on a universalistic sacral realm. The second tends in the long run to deny the existence of a reliable, knowable sacred order altogether. It leads inevitably to secularism and the sovereignty of the human will. But the third attempts to overcome the artificial split between the two, and to provide an alternative to either sacralism or secularism, idealism or experientialism. But Lamb recognizes that relating the sacred and the secular also means knowing that each is not totally the other. And that both the relationship of these realms and the distinction between them demands some theoretical awareness. Thus, intrinsic to any *praxis* theory is a covert theoretical component — one which is not, as Hegel and Marx held, something that emerges as the *logos* ingredient of *praxis* in interaction with *poesis*, but one which is prior to the *praxis* and *poesis* itself. Lamb's work is important in part because he recognizes that theory is not a "moment" of reflection between actions but a component of them. But what that component is and should be is still unclear.

Lamb offers a typology of the most compelling forms of viable theories of *praxis:*

1. Lamb cites early Karl Barth or Hans Urs von Balthasar as modern theologians who attempt to cut through the usual distinctions between theory and practice by pointing to the *praxis* of God. Thus a "revelation model" is rendered. "The reality of God overpowers the shadows of this world, with all its efforts at theory or praxis." Similar emphases can be found in "the pentecostalist experience of the Spirit or the mystic's dark night, or unconditional obedience to the Word — these are the touchstones of truth and life."[9] (We have encountered views close to this one in Chapter 3.)

2. Lamb cites the Niebuhrs, Paul Tillich, Emil Brunner, Karl Rahner, and David Tracy as modern theologians who hold to one

---

9. Lamb, *Solidarity with Victims*, pp. 74-75.

or another form of a "correlation model." In these theologies, the concern is to offer a mediational perspective, one that attempts "to envisage the union-in-difference between theory and *praxis* . . . as primarily established through the elaboration of an ontology which would do justice to both immanence and transcendence, to both the socio-historical and existential demands of Christian faith and practice."[10] These figures are inclined to settle the question of normativity of principle and pattern by a mutual interaction of faith and reason, and provide essentially theoretic unities that point only in an anticipatory fashion to practical unities. Thus, the correlations are primarily metaphysical in character, but with an openness to the empirical sciences, to critical historical disciplines, and to practical engagement in the struggles of finding personal and social identity in a broken world.

3. Lamb's own position is one that he calls "critical praxis correlation." It may well be that it is this view that is predominant in the best liberation theologies today, and is closely related to some interpretations of "contextualism" that we have already encountered. This view has certain affinities with what "correlationists" hold, but it places the emphasis not on identifying theoretic unities or ontology but on compassionate, active *praxis*. The traditional tests of theory that influence the correlationists of an ontological bent — coherence, adequacy, and consistency — remain important, but in this view they must above all be tested by their correlation to, capacity to induce collaboration with, and engagement on behalf of the oppressed and suffering victims of history. The reason for this test is the fundamental conviction that "*vox victimarum vox Dei* — the cries of the victims are the voice of God."[11] This, according to Lamb, is the historical, the *actual* meaning of the gospel. The crucifix is the center of all theology; it is the call to "costly discipleship" that demands a new *orthopraxis*, for in suffering with victims we have immediate, practical, personal, and intimate knowledge of the sacred in the secular.

The experience of suffering with, for, and among the least and the lost is thus taken as the benchmark of all theoretical and practical knowledge. And *praxis* with its implicit theory is to serve the victims in concrete ways that transform and liberate experience. Theologians such as Bernard Lonergan and Johannes B. Metz, from whom Lamb draws many resources, "seek to contribute to the liberation of noetic *praxis* from the oppressive academic, ecclesial and

---

10. Lamb, *Solidarity with Victims*, p. 76.
11. Lamb, *Solidarity with Victims*, p. 23.

social structures which both condition and are conditioned by those [other] theories."[12] They do not invite or drive believers into critical analysis and transformative action for the oppressed. They do not demand that we see the struggles of the many victims of the world to be disclosive of the deepest powers of life, and to be the locus for the ongoing actualization of religion and reason in life. Thus it is not all *praxis* that is the source of, norm for, and test for theory; it is that kind of *praxis* which liberates suffering humans from heteronomous dominations — conceptual, ecclesiastical, economic, or political — and produces genuine communal autonomy, the ability of those humans whose lives are controlled by others or by traditions that have been imposed upon them to define themselves and the structures of their own lives in their own ways. Now we can see the reason for Lamb's title, *Solidarity with Victims*.

Lamb has presented us with a powerful vision. It makes the core of theology available to any who can empathize with those who suffer. All the complexities of theology are reduced to a potent simplicity. It is quite possible that the new proposals for *praxis*-based theological education can give direction to some things that must be done in theological education and in the formation of living witnesses to the gospel in our age. These proposals may also suggest new possibilities for those who, in dialogues and in ecumenical consultations, have pressed us in such directions but left us with a number of unanswered questions. Few would deny that compassionate engagement with and for the oppressed and a demand to transform oppressive structures are integral to the biblical heritage.

DOES *PRAXIS* MEAN *ORTHOPRAXIS*?

And yet, we are obliged to raise questions about whether the new multifaceted advocacy of an *orthopraxis* can serve as a sufficient basis for creative reform of contemporary theological education, particularly if it hopes to take globalization, contextualization, and mission seriously. What if, for example, those who are manifestly suffering have an understanding of the causes of their distress, specifically as it relates to the social, intellectual, and historical conditions that produced their troubles, that is demonstrably in error? Or what if the advocates of the new orthopraxy depend upon a wedding of biblical symbols to a specific political interpretation of society that is likely to produce more suffering? Or what if this

---

12. Lamb, *Solidarity with Victims*, p. 22.

view ties the gospel to forms of reaction against modernity that prevent liberating *praxis* in the long run and inhibit engagement with those "modern forces" that are likely to shape the future? Does compassion require solidarity with bad sociology, poor politics, debatable historical analysis, and ideological exegesis?

What is most clear from the attempt to heed the appeal to *praxis* in one of its most careful forms is that, in fact, *praxis* (and especially an *orthopraxis*) is deeply dependent on a quite specific, highly schematized and synthetic, social and historical dogma. Or, to put it another way, the action of *praxis* and the capacity to learn from it, or to teach it, or to know anything reliable about it demand a previous, and a rather elaborate, *theoria* about what is true and just.

It is, of course, very bad form in many centers of theological education today to raise any questions about the priority of *praxis* or the current forms of intellectual characterization, sociohistorical analysis, and liberation theology that turn it into *orthopraxis*. To let it be known that one might have some reservations about any of these is frequently taken as a failure to discern the movement of the Holy Spirit *(Geist?)* among oppressed peoples of the world, or as a moral blindness to the practical demands of life in favor of the "idealist" ideology of white, male, bourgeois, and Western cultural imperialism. And there is little doubt that some critiques of liberating *praxis* participate in, contribute to, or are driven by these spiritual pathologies. And yet, it may be the best service to genuinely liberating *praxis* and the most creative, engaged form of listening to inquire whether the predominant theory of *praxis* rests on secure foundations. Is it true? Does it lead to justice?

The question of truth may arise at two levels. One has to do with intellectual history and the relationship of certain ideas to social history. At points, very large claims are made about how certain ideas have shaped oppressive structures of civilization. But is it really the case, for example, that the terrors of racism, classism, imperialism, sexism, and colonialism have been essentially engendered by classical and Enlightenment theories, especially as these have been taken up by theology? Have the grand theories of the Greeks and Enlightenment minds not had less influence outside the universities where they have been discussed than have pagan, communitarian patterns of thought and belief in the societies where these terrors exist? It could be that anti-philosophical, anti-theological, contextual religious influences have been much more decisive in the formation of the societies where these pathologies are most rampant than have these philosophies or theologies.

Indeed, it would be easier to make the case that wherever Christianity has taken up selected aspects of these intellectual traditions and utilized them in the formation of a philosophical theology emphasizing the public character of all claims about truth and all definitions of justice, there oppression, violence, exploitation, and discrimination have been reduced. It would also appear that the greatest pathologies of the twentieth century — those leading to colonialism, imperialism, and systematic genocide — have derived from nationalistic and populist idolatries, what Carl Schorske has called "politics in a new key," which protest classical, Enlightenment, systematic, theological, and universalistic thought of all kinds.[13] If so, what the advocates of liberating *praxis* are citing as the causes of evil may be among the best remedies for it. To pose such questions, of course, invites comparative and cross-cultural analysis of how ideas influence social behavior in general and how these ideas have influenced oppressive behaviors in particular. There is no evidence that the new advocates of *praxis* have undertaken such studies or could do so in convincing ways, given their operating presuppositions.

If we do begin to look at the evidence, it may turn out to be the case that in precisely those areas where there are the most victims and where liberation movements are currently the strongest and most needed — areas such as Latin America, Korea, the Mideast, Indochina, and South Africa — civilizational patterns were formed by philosophical and religious traditions that were among the least affected by Greek, Enlightenment, or any other "universalistic" influences. Indeed, they were most affected by anti-philosophical and anti-theological folk traditions, by highly communitarian religions, by ethnic-centered economic and political traditions that constitutionally resisted all "universalistic" claims. In those locations of the greatest systematic victimization of people, dominant groups have been most resistant to these patterns of thought. They have often forced poets, intellectuals, and scientists to sacrifice either their faith or their intellectual and moral integrity by demanding both a solidarity with a communally defined group

---

13. It is highly instructive, in this regard, to read Paul Tillich's newly translated and published open letter of 1934 to Emanuel Hirsch, perhaps the most brilliant German theologian of the 1930s and one who supplied the most powerful theological foundations for the National Socialist movement. It is painful to note that many of the terms used in the analysis of modern society and history celebrated by *praxis*-based liberation thought today were present in Hirsch's work. See *The Thought of Paul Tillich*, ed. J. L. Adams, W. Pauch, and R. L. Shinn (San Francisco: Harper & Row, 1985), pp. 353-88. Note especially pp. 370-74.

and an *orthopraxis* based on national, sexual, ethnic, religious communitarian, political, or economic interests.

If we look elsewhere in world history to contexts where peoples have founded civilizations on the basis of human *praxis* without regulative guides from an "abstract" normative *theoria* that attempts to be universalistic in its view of truth and justice, we find patterns of racism, classism, sexism, imperialism, cruelty, and exploitation produced by Machiavellian manipulations of power that are at least as oppressive as those presumed to have been shaped by too much abstract and universalistic theory. Nor can it be argued that racism, classism, sexism, imperialism, cruelty, and exploitation are absent where the legacies of religions *not* influenced by the biblical traditions are most profound. In such locations, victims may be more numerous and the regular patterns of life producing them more frequent. This is not the place to engage in a systematic survey of the world's civilizations and a comparative analysis of the degree to which reliance on "abstract" theological and ethical *theoria* correlates with suffering. But it is pertinent to observe that the contemporary advocates of *praxis* have presumed a series of cause-effect relationships as a matter of empirical fact that may not be true.

There is also a logical problem at this point. Attributing social pathology to the influence of certain philosophical and theological developments attributes a power of causation to ideas that sounds distinctly "idealistic," something the advocates of *praxis* describe as a false analysis of social history. And yet, it seems that every intentional *praxis* is in the employ of *some* governing theory, and the question is less one of the tension between idealistic *theoria* and *praxis* than it is one of which *theoria* is sufficiently true and just that *praxis* ought to be carried out in its service.

IS *ORTHOPRAXIS* TRUE AND JUST?

It turns out, as we have seen, that what finally controls Lamb's understanding of *praxis* is, in fact, a theological idea of the life, death, and resurrection of Christ. But it is not an idea he states theoretically; he states it metaphorically, symbolically, and evocatively. His basis for an *orthopraxy* is a specific bit of *poesis*. He offers the crucifix as the warrant for his appeal for solidarity with victims. Lamb is quite probably correct that one critical dimension of the meaning of the cross does demand that empathetic response, responsiveness, and responsibility, but nowhere does he make the case for taking Christ seriously as the guide to social and historical analysis in the first place, or for taking this symbol as the core of what the Christian faith is all about, or for interpreting this symbol in this way. The empty cross, for instance, is not something he mentions. Nor does he anywhere point out that the symbol of Christ on the cross used in *this* way has already introduced a highly synthetic theory of suffering into the symbol, one that allies the medieval, mystical meditations on Christ's suffering with the pleasure-pain calculus of the utilitarian moralists as a test of all meaning — a calculus more associated with modernist political economies than with the classical piety that generated this symbol.

The implications are rather far-reaching: why should anyone who is not already a Christian, and not already committed to this understanding of the gospel, accept this view as normative? The only possible answers would seem to be those of the "revelationist" sort offered by Barth and Von Balthasar, or those of a "correlationist" sort offered by the Niebuhrs, Tillich, Rahner, and Tracy, or perhaps some view that would offer a compelling case for the fact that Christ on the cross unveils the deepest truth and widest justice humans can know. Otherwise, we are trapped in an unwarranted fideism, or tempted to utilitarian interpretations of religious *poesis*.

At another level, both Lamb and the liberation theologians from whom he draws much are alert to the fact that what is taking place among the peoples of the Third World is a profound religious awakening, one that all believers can and should celebrate. But there appears to be considerable ambiguity at this point, for *praxis* as a basic way of living and being in the world is an idea obviously derived from the Greeks, who did not show particular compassion for the oppressed, while the vision of "liberation" to which it is most frequently attached is an idea that obviously derives from the Enlightenment drive toward emancipatory autonomy. These philosophical movements most emphatically repudiate the possibility of an appeal to religious *poesis* as a basis for political solidarity. Yet these are the connections Lamb and several liberationists want to make.

A basic presupposition of the Greek understanding of *praxis* is that the *nous*, human intelligence, learns from *praxis*, *poesis*, and *theoria*, and that it is to be the sufficient guide to human meaning and action — without recourse to religion or revelation, which the Greeks suspected of being entirely beyond reliable warrant. And the basic idea of the Enlightenment — whether idealistic, as in Kant, or materialistic, as in Marx — is to overthrow all dependence on any standard deriving from any heteronomous source. Reliant only on unaided human subjectivity — individual and "rational" or collective and "scientific" — humanity is to seize its own destiny and define, construct, and control its own future according to the practical requirements of social living — again *without* recourse to any religious, traditional, metaphysical, or moral standards that are beyond human self-actualization in history. Do these not presume an autonomy for human capacities that makes any appeal to the redemptive significance of the cross (as crucifix or empty) awkward, to say the least?

It is, however, not only reservations with regard to truth that trouble us about the perspectives of those who argue for *praxis;* other reservations have to do with justice. The "solidarity" that is called for presumes a definition of community governed by a "political theory of social life." That is a pronounced accent in the Frankfurt School and among the political theologians from whom Lamb and many liberationists draw. That is a motif that the "radicals" and many liberal Protestants also share with the Greeks and Enlightenment minds. That is, they all believe that the political order refers to the most comprehensive community of all human associations and is subordinate to no other, and that "solidarity" eventually must involve political sovereignty and the political integration of society.

It may well be that, in those countries where liberation movements are most vibrant, political movements will be required to transform or overthrow oppressive regimes that cause so much suffering. What is less certain, however, is whether the most enduring movements of liberation in social history — those that have established pluralistic societies of relative freedom, equity, and peace — have taken place under the influence of philosophies that reconstitute the regime on the basis of a political theory of society. In fact, it can easily be argued that an alternative view of society has more frequently developed the kind of freedom, equity, and peace that justice demands. This is a "social theory of political life." That is to say that politics is viewed as but one indispensable dimension of human existence, but that it neither can nor should comprehend or determine every other institution of society. Indeed, politics is to be the servant, not the master, of society. And society — including at least areas of life such as education, the arts, family life, health care, law, science, technology, the professions, work, commerce, and especially religion — ought *not* to be politicized at every point or controlled by political authority. There is little doubt that responsible participation in societal life includes political responsibility, but some areas of living ought to be exempt from political interest or manipulation, especially since all serious politics finally involve command over, the use of, or the threat of the use of coercive force.[14]

This focus on politics by *praxis*-oriented liberation theology could easily make theology (and religion) into an instrument of power only. There is little doubt that one aspect of theology is always intertwined with power, and that any theology that presumes to guide social and civilizational behavior will have to give criteria for the legitimate use of power. But to give such guidance and to correct the power biases that frequently enter into theological formulations, it is surely necessary to believe that theology is neither determined by power nor centrally developed for purposes of political *praxis*.

In short, there are substantial reasons why many who try to heed the call to liberating *praxis* and solidarity as set forth by Lamb and others do not immediately respond to the call for an *orthopraxis* and gradually grow suspicious of the call itself after the early excitement of being radical and relevant is over: the account that its advocates give of the nature and character of theory and of its relationship to social experience and history seems doubtful and confused. The kind of solidarity that it demands requires action on the basis of a political theory of society that many doubt would bring just liberation, and it may even undercut the institutional pluralism necessary for a just society. However much we could agree that the Greeks and Enlightenment minds distorted some things, however much we believe that identification with the cause of the oppressed is a mandate of Christian faith, however much we recognize the liberation movements as among the most creative and dynamic social forces in the modern church manifesting a profound spiritual as well as social awakening, however much we agree that *praxis* has been too much neglected by many theological theories — regardless, a number of theological educators simply do not believe that such accounts as these tell us why things are the way they are, or that the prescriptions based on them are likely to render the most just, enduring relief. The predominant theories of *praxis* seem to be too much overburdened by the legacy of a synthetic and

---

14. One extremely suggestive theological statement of this "social theory of politics" can be found in Abraham Kuyper's *Christianity and the Class Struggle*, trans. Dirk Jellema (Grand Rapids: Piet Hein, 1950). See also Michael Walzer, *Spheres of Justice: A Defense of Pluralism and Equality* (Princeton: Princeton University Press, 1983); J. F. A. Taylor, *The Masks of Society: An Inquiry into the Covenants of Civilization* (New York: Appleton-Century-Crofts, 1966); and Max L. Stackhouse, *Creeds, Society, and Human Rights: A Study in Three Cultures* (Grand Rapids: Eerdmans, 1984).

questionable European, social hermeneutic that is used to interpret some dreadful experiences in specific ways, while pretending to be drawn directly from the experience of oppressed peoples outside Europe.[15] The interpretive theory, however, appears to be highly questionable in its understanding of history, philosophy, religion, theology, ethical judgment, human motivation, and the nature of intellectual cause and social effect, or how politics works in human societies. To take *this* theory of *orthopraxis* as a new center of theological education could be to commit it to such a mixture of valid concern and dubious analysis that truth, justice, and compassionate engagement would be as much discredited as actualized.

Of course, it has been and can be argued that the reason why North American, white, male theologians (among others) raise these reservations is that we are so caught up in the biases of our social location, so deluded by empty searches for "objective" quests for truth, and so wrapped up in abstract theories of justice that we cannot possibly grasp the existential realities of life as experienced by those on the underside of history. Few doubt that this characterization accurately applies to some parts of theological education at one point or another. But the reservations expressed here are shared at least by members of the ATS research team who do not fit this description.

Besides, if this charge were valid, so that anything "non-victims" think and teach in theological education is irremediably tainted or suspect unless they totally adopt this *orthopraxis*, it would be useless for *anyone* to try to persuade anyone else of the urgency of the situation by talking of these matters. For such a response to these reservations presumes that all intellectual arguments are little more than representations of actual social interests and historical settings. No common standards beyond race, class, sex, culture, position, or material interest could be available so that peoples divided by these forces could come to common judgments about truth and justice. If this were so, theological discourse, dialogue,

---

15. The claim that the various liberation theologies are derived directly from experience has further complications for two reasons. First, no data of experience interprets itself. To be pertinent to *praxis*, it must be ordered by some framework of meaning to guide intentional behavior. Second, were it true that experience could engender a required framework of meaning, the diverse experiences of women, blacks, Latins, and others would likely render sufficiently diverse frameworks of meaning that no common cause could be developed. Solidarity would be impossible, and the attempt to form a common political or social order would be inevitably frustrated by sectarian perspectives incapable of mutual communication. This peril has been the motivating concern of Habermas (see note 6).

consultation, study, listening, questioning, and education would be entirely useless unless they fed the direct participatory experience of sacred, suffering love, linked to the political definition of society to alter that society toward solidaristic community. That, in fact, is what many who undertake liberation *praxis* in theological education often teach and demand of all. Those with other orientations are unofficially excommunicated (by being told that their views represent the consciousness of oppressive classes). Thus, the appeal to *orthopraxis* engenders a new sect of fideist politics for which theology is an instrumental ideology. Some people simply don't believe it, and don't think others should.

PRAXIS REQUIRES *THEORIA*

The final reservation we shall note at this point has already been implied. It is a double-sided point. One side of this point is that *praxis* is itself based on *theoria,* and that the former is only as good as the latter on which it is based. That is a point which the neo-conservative advocates of *praxis* also stress, as we noted previously. And it is against the ways in which the classical (especially Greek) philosophical tradition has influenced Catholic social and political life that the more radical Catholic voices are speaking. Indeed, the most creative understanding of *praxis* seems to be an ethical demand for socially transformative engagement with, among, and on behalf of those who need liberation from oppression so that they can be free from subsistence and terror and enter into the wider and deeper possibilities of human life and meaning that God intends. We are all indebted to such scholars as Lamb and the myriad of contemporary liberationists for demanding attention to this engagement in the face of the frequent neglect of the plight of these people and in the face of theology's complicity in allowing institutions from which it benefits to contribute to that plight. But we have seen that such engagement demands not only compassionate involvement, activism, and commitment, but also normative theological guidance from a *theoria* able to comprehend more than a poetic basis, a hermeneutics of suspicion, an analysis of social location, a political ideology, and power calculations.

The second side of this reservation is also already implied. Philosophy and social theory, with their demands for precision and clarity, may well be indispensable to an adequate theory of *praxis*. But philosophy works primarily with concepts, and works most precisely when each word means one and only one thing, and social theory must comprehend an enormous complex of historical and institutional variables. Theology works primarily with symbols, and symbols are multileveled. They are not — and surely cannot be reduced to — either *theoria* or *orthopraxis*, although they may have enormous significance for both. We rarely understand the full range of the multiple meanings of symbols until they are theoretically sorted and practically applied to a wide range of social interaction. In short, a decent theory of *praxis* will require a deep appreciation of *poesis* for more than utilitarian purposes.

It is one of the weaknesses of many of those who are today governed by a profound spiritual and ethical commitment to the poor and oppressed — just as it is a weakness of those most insistently committed to academic excellence in the classical or Enlightenment traditions — that the rich resources of symbol, the richest of which are inevitably religious, are too often neglected. Symbols not only touch the mind and its conceptions, and evoke action with a purpose, but compel the heart. Perhaps the neglect of symbol is what makes so much of academic ethics and social action so boring. We whittle fine points down to nothing; we recite ponderous bodies of data, citing all the statistics and instances of terror and want among the people; we quote all those scholars who have conceptually worked out this or that scheme of possible interpretations of texts, historical movements, the human psyche, and social fabric — and these are properly recorded and reported back by students in examinations. But rarely are the foundational and motivational warrants for such activities gathered into those symbolic forms that synthesize and evoke the integration of mind and will in individuals or among peoples.

Symbolic discourse is a very peculiar kind of human communication. It is not only cognitive; it is also evocative and relational. That is, it knits diversity and conflict into community and calls to mission. It is at once centripetal and centrifugal. It gathers and it sends. It allows and limits meaning. It cannot be easily manipulated. Symbols seem to be more discovered than invented. Those who try to make symbols come to mean what they want the symbols to mean, as do philosophers who define concepts or activists who define agendas, find themselves captured by more than they can handle.

The importance of these observations at this point is that it turns out that praxis-oriented theories and programs can be shown to be more dependent on symbols than they often pretend to be, as we have seen in the discussion of Lamb. And it is likely that not all symbols are of equal worth, especially if profound symbols are usually religious in nature. If this is the case, a critical question becomes this: Which symbols, which *poesis,* most reveal the fundamental, the true character of reality, and lead to justice? And that question, in turn, leads us once more to the question of criteria. How would we know? Here, again, *theoria* is required. *Praxis* alone, or *praxis* wedded to *poesis* alone, will not suffice.

Such questions will lead us, eventually, to a recognition that an *apologia* for a preferred symbolic framework must, sooner or later, be made; and it will force us to consider whether or not an "orthodox" understanding of a normative symbolic framework is necessary and possible. This, however, we must explore in later chapters. For now, let us examine some major modern perspectives that focus primarily on *poesis.*

CHAPTER 7

Poesis *and* Contextuality

Besides the emphasis on globalization by those in contemporary ecumenical circles, and the focus on a new *orthopraxis* by those committed to political theology and liberation, another major perspective on the issues pertinent to this study deserves direct attention. This is a perspective that focuses on the encounter of Christian theology with multiple cultural contexts, especially in Christian missionary experience. There we find some of the most critical issues of theology as it confronts particular contexts all over the globe. We have been able to find no finer example of this approach than Robert Schreiter's *Constructing Local Theologies*.[1]

Schreiter's concern centers on how we can engage in making sense of the Christian message in local circumstances. He recognizes, in concert with a large body of research in the world religions, that there is a frequent discrepancy between "the great tradition" and "the little traditions." The former frequently centers on perennial or "catholic" theological motifs, but people live their lives in terms of the more temporally immediate, "local" religious accents. Christian doctrines may be thought to be cosmopolitan and eternal, but Christians believe in things local and immediate. Tension is always present between the two. From a theological point of view, a necessary concern is making the perennial and universalistic gospel dynamically present in local frames of meaning; Schreiter is

---

1. Schreiter, *Constructing Local Theologies* (Maryknoll, N.Y.: Orbis Books, 1985). The evaluation of this work was greatly aided by the comments of Lamin Sanneh, J. G. F. Collison, and Gabriel Fackre.

also concerned to preserve and appreciate local religious sensibilities that render succor and hope to people of faith.

To this end, he reviews, with rich cross-cultural references, the various attempts that have been undertaken, or that are presently underway, to make the Christian faith more fully contextualized and less abstract. He traces the development of efforts at "indigenization," "ethno-theology," "inculturation," and "liberation," and he assesses the various strengths and weaknesses that each has thus far revealed. All of them, he argues, involve an effort to make the faith a living, vibrant possibility in the midst of people in their own contexts without entirely alienating them from dimensions of their primary culture that are not incompatible with the gospel.

MODELS OF CONTEXTUALIZATION

Further, Schreiter points out the various models with which missionary movements and pastors have worked in recent years. Most tend to focus on one of two "adaptation" models. The first of these focuses on some key insights or doctrines of the faith that are identified as the "kernel," in contrast to the "husk" of cultural and historical accretion. While the kernel remains, and must remain, constant and pure, the husk of the missionary culture can be stripped away and replaced by the husk of the missionized culture. This kernel serves, then, as the core of the new husk and is also potentially protected by it, so long as we are clear about what is kernel and what is husk. This view presumes that Christianity has a clear and distinct "essence" that can be rather clearly discerned and differentiated from that which is "accidental" to social, cultural, and historical conditions.

The second model focuses on the more dynamic concept of "flowering." In this view, the boundary between kernel and husk is less precise, and the emphasis is on the growth of new possibilities once the seed of the gospel is planted in a new location, inevitably in its old husk. But, once the seed is planted, it will interact with the soil into which it has been planted, and new forms of faith will spring into being. These new forms of faith enrich the whole range of Christian possibilities. (We have already encountered views close to this one in Chapter 4.)

In contextualizing the gospel, Schreiter points out, it quickly becomes clear that particular contexts will be dominated by one of two needs, and these two needs provide us with the key models that should now supplant the "adaptation models." In some places, the problem is the collapse of identity in the face of threats of chaos or change. In such situations, people will need a sense of continuity, of stability, of solidity. In other places, the problem is one of constrictive order, of confining or oppressive control. In these situations, people will need a sense of hope for social change and dynamic discontinuity. It is, Schreiter suggests, the poets who can often articulate that which expresses or reconstructs identity, and the prophets who lead in a recovery of the liberating faith, one that can serve as a fulcrum for structural change when identity has become stereotyped and oppressive. The decisive model for today is the "poet/prophet" model.

Schreiter sees a distinctive role also for the theologian, as the chief custodian of those aspects of the gospel that are of longer duration and wider scope than any local community can fully embody. However, the theologian ought not to dominate the local scene, for such dominance could become simply a new ideational hegemony. The primary agent in the formation of every local theology will be the local community of faith itself. Yet the theologian is an indispensable resource. He or she must live in intimate contact with the community, must know the local dynamics of meaning and patterns of life, and must be in constant interaction with both the poet, who can capture and arrange "those symbols and metaphors which best give expression to the experience of the community," and the prophet, who judges the social environment and the false pieties of the people, including the idolatrous and immoral theologies accepted by communities of faith when they ignore context-transcending standards of truth and justice.[2]

Yet the theologian is always, in one sense, an outsider. The theologian is always an evaluator of as well as a listener to the dynamics of the local situation. Local communities of faith can easily become self-centered, dominated by concerns of tribe, class, life-style, power, sex, or race. Thus the theologian must not only identify with the poet or the prophet. "Poetic insight has to be tested on more than aesthetic criteria or resonance with a community's experience," Schreiter says. And the call of the prophet "must be tested on the touchstone of other churches' experience" in other times and places.[3] In other words, the theologian must have a command of *theoria,* and specifically the more universal dogmas that have been taught over long periods of time by the wider church. These dogmas in some ways transcend every partic-

---

2. Schreiter, *Constructing Local Theologies,* p. 18.
3. Schreiter, *Constructing Local Theologies,* p. 19.

ular *poesis* and *praxis,* although, Schreiter holds, they are themselves constructed, metaphorical generalities derived from the accumulation of a great number of practical particularities. The theologian must be equipped to bring the deeper and broader generalities as one critical resource to each local theology. "To ignore the resources of the professional theologian," says Schreiter, "is to prefer ignorance over knowledge,"[4] but the more important task is learning how to read the context and speak to it concretely in terms of its own needs. That is the task of the "practical theologians," which is to say the actual leaders in every community.

ON READING CONTEXTS

Schreiter's perspective is perhaps more alert than any view we have thus far examined to the variety of methods by which the poet, the prophet, and the theologian can discerningly grasp the structures and dynamics of particular contexts and interpret the faith in a way pertinent to the formation of a local theology. These methods, Schreiter suggests, are in accord with the gospel, with the insights and witness of the wider church, and with the particular needs of the culture in which the theologian works. These methods are rooted in a presumption that the truth of the gospel manifests itself through the power of the Spirit — although often in distorted or fragmentary ways — in both the church tradition and the cultures wherein the church finds itself. Indeed, Schreiter argues, the church tradition is itself a series of local theologies held together by the (often hidden) power of the Word of God and by nurture through the Eucharist. The great dogmas of the faith, at their best, point to these powers.

Every cultural context, Schreiter holds, has its roots in some belief system or worldview, itself produced by a series of spiritual movements over time. Thus, we are constantly confronted by parallel structures of meaning. These reflect distinct spiritualities, with constant confluence, interaction, and mutual correction giving rise to the dynamic formation of new spiritualities. The problem is how the *practical* theologian — as part member of a community and part outsider, as part poet and part prophet — is to understand, evaluate, and guide these spiritualities.

The first task is listening. Every theologian needs to heed the church tradition and the local spirituality. But how are we to listen?

---

4. Schreiter, *Constructing Local Theologies,* p. 18.

Without attuning our ears, we simply pick up noise or that which we are already disposed to hear. Or we might become entranced with a tradition or a culture, become so engrossed with its nuances and rich complexity that we fall prey to total and uncritical acceptance of it, as have many romantic folklorists. What is necessary is analytical listening. At one level, what we listen for analytically are the overtones of the gospel and of the Holy Spirit. These are often present but obscured by many other factors or veiled by language or by patterns of mind and expectation that are so removed in form from the "classic" formulations of the faith that they cannot easily be recognized. If, however, these overtones can be identified, emphasized, and celebrated in terms intrinsic to the culture, they can both reveal new possibilities for extending the church tradition and induce change in a tradition or a context. When what was once present but obscure becomes manifest and clear, change in both the church tradition and the cultural context can be expected. As Schreiter points out, "The Christian message, after all, is about change: repentance, salvation, and an eschatological reality to be realized."[5]

However, it is another level of discussion that makes *Constructing Local Theologies* so important to our topics, for Schreiter presents a fertile and helpful overview of the analytical tools that have been developed since the nineteenth century in the social and anthropological sciences for the interpretation of traditions and cultures. Whereas the theologian once turned to the classical philosophers to understand human nature, the social contexts of life, and intellectual rigor, it is to the best social theorists that the theologian must turn today. Classical philosophy turned out to know less about humanity, nature, and wisdom than it claimed, and contemporary philosophy has lost interest in even these questions. Thus, social theory poses the most important anthropological, sociohistorical, and intellectual issues. Schreiter is well aware that many who are engaged in contextual theological development at present are indebted to the work of Marx and his successors, who have produced what Schreiter calls a "materialist" analysis. And Schreiter knows that in some situations where political-economic issues are of paramount local import, this approach may be useful on certain questions. But he is also aware (as fewer contemporary theologians are who have only recently discovered the importance of social theory) that the work of Marx has been surpassed in many

---

5. Schreiter, *Constructing Local Theologies*, p. 29.

respects, even in regard to material analysis, and that its constitutional preference for conflict-centered orientations makes it seriously problematic when dealing with the deeper spiritual foundations of life and community. Schreiter holds that other major tools of social and cultural analysis are more directly pertinent to practical theology in local situations and must at least supplement these concerns if an adequate grasp of the existential conditions in particular locales is to be had.

Schreiter identifies the "functionalist" school of thought as a major potential resource. This tradition includes — as he charts the intellectual landscape — Max Weber, Emile Durkheim, and Talcott Parsons. The chief concern of functionalist approaches is to understand how the various aspects of society are constituted and interrelated to form cultural wholes. Functionalism is, most often, highly empirical and strongly comparative. It presumes that the chief problem of human existence is the threat of chaos, in part because it works on the basis of a methodological doubt about whether there is any clear metaphysical foundation, provable by scientific methods, which provides coherence and continuity in the face of the enormous variety and constant change of existence. On the basis of empirical research, however, functionalists have shown that beliefs about metaphysical and moral forces play an enormously important role in the formation of communities.

Functionalism (and an influential modification of it, structural functionalism) frequently focuses on how civilizational, cultural, and religious systems, as developed in a society, generate characteristic patterns of personality and interpersonal relations, form a relative stability of structure and meaning, and, if they are successful, provide legitimate ways of adjusting to change that will not bring the threat of chaos. Critics of this school of analysis, noting its focus on relative stability, often accuse functionalism of not being able to deal with or mobilize radical change when relatively stable systems are in place but of apparently fomenting or allowing oppressive or meaningless patterns to continue. Still, as Schreiter points out, functionalists will emphasize holistic concerns, attention to particular and unique features of a system within a larger picture, a concern for empirical detail as it relates to the whole, and the practical import of religious orientation.

Closely related to and sometimes overlapping with functionalism is the second, or "structuralist," mode of analysis. Structuralists tend to focus on the unconscious structures of the mind, often expressed in linguistic, mythic, or ritual forms, which govern the patterns of culture and control their transformations. Claude Lévi-

Strauss and Roman Jakobson are among the widely regarded structuralists, and frequently their work is tied to the work of some psychologists of development, such as Jean Piaget and Carl Jung. In these perspectives, basic structures are seen to be the product of binary oppositions within modes of human thought, conscious or preconscious, which in combination produce particular patterns of personality or culture—male and female, reason and intuition, nature and nurture, cosmos and mythos, and so forth. Less empirical than the functionalists, and more trusting in the possibility that there are universal structures present in and necessary to both the affective and the cognitive dimensions of every human context, the structuralists offer an account of how opposing dimensions of existence relate to one another and, especially, of how they take shape in experience.

THE SCIENCE OF CULTURAL CONTEXTS

Schreiter, however, holds that modern "semiotics" is the best science for contextual analysis, that it is compatible with the best features of the materialist, functionalist, and structuralist approaches, and that it supplies elements necessary for analytical listening to traditions and cultures which other approaches do not adequately provide. Schreiter draws on the work of Clifford Geertz, Mary Douglas, and Victor Turner, who stand partially in the Anglo-American tradition so indebted to Max Weber; on the work of Roland Barthes and Julia Kristeva, who stand primarily in the traditions of French structuralism; and on the work of Jan Mukarovsky, Vladimir Propp, and Viktor Shklovskij, who have attempted to develop new tools of cultural analysis to supplement Marxist analysis in the Soviet Union. In drawing on these materials, Schreiter focuses on the meaning of signs, symbols, metaphors, gestures, and rituals as the basic cultural units for investigation. These are "texts" that appear in oral, behavioral, or narrative forms. They may be written or unwritten (as we have already seen in the work of Carole Fontaine), and they appear in art forms, clothing styles, and cuisine as much as in documents. Nevertheless, these are forms of *poesis* that bear a message. They are encoded in a logic that must be understood if a culture itself is to be understood. Semiotics is the "science of signs" that attempts to understand the meaning of the texts in terms of their encoded logics, their function and structure in the societal context, and their performative power in generating civilizational forms and possibilities.

In such texts, whether literary or popular, whether ritualized or casual, are implicit worldviews — ways of construing reality, making sense out of life, resolving conflict, and evoking novelty. These reveal — perhaps more deeply than any alternative method of analysis, Schreiter suggests — the basic spirituality of a tradition or a culture. These texts shape individuals and define the boundaries of social identity. If these texts are not clearly understood, there is little chance that we will know what kind or quality of spirituality we are dealing with in interpersonal encounter, in crosscultural contact, or in mission or pastoral care.

When a church tradition encounters a particular sociocultural context in mission or ministry, what is at stake is often a semiotic clash between two "texts," each with its own system of signs, symbols, metaphors, and encoded logics. Failure to recognize the complex character of each prevents any serious dialogue. But close attention to the sign system of the respective parties in the encounter allows us to identify possible points of agreement, common frames of reference stated in highly contrasting ways, and points at which genuine tension is unresolved. Even more, it can allow us to recognize that Christianity itself is, in large measure, a semiotic system based on a particular although highly variegated text consisting at least of the Scriptures, the great conciliar and confessional statements, and an authoritative leadership that conducts authoritative rituals. Thus, the theologian is faced with the constant task of reading the signs of the times and places where he or she is present as a practical leader in local situations, *and* faced with the continuing task of attempting to discern, ever more deeply, the "text" of Christianity itself.

We know that Christianity itself has gone through at least two great moments of thematizing the meaning of its own texts: one in which it focused on sapiential knowledge and warranted doctrine as the gospel encountered the Greco-Roman world of thought, and one in which it strove for the sure knowledge of *scientia* developed by the European Scholastics. (We shall encounter these themes more directly in the next chapter.) Further, as we also saw in the previous chapter, the emergence of liberation theologies today suggests a certain dissatisfaction with the notion that previous thematizing is sufficient or exhaustive. For Schreiter, however, liberation thought is less a helpful answer than a sign of a profound question. Or, to put it in terms of his "poet/prophet model," liberation theology may express a need for social change and dynamic discontinuity, but it cannot provide a sense of constructive identity. That will require a new poetic imagination.

What we must now face is the recasting of the gospel in new

thematics — not only in terms of the urgencies of social and political crises, but in terms of the longer, slower process of semiotic sorting of fundamental spiritual meanings. Thus, our task will demand close attention to cultural, linguistic, and ritual texts. We are entering an age of new pluralism in which authoritative thematizing might well be premature. Perhaps we should recognize that people will live in dual systems — between high religion and folk beliefs, between cosmopolitan perspectives and particular loyalties, between centuries-long traditions and immediate religious excitements, between official dogmas and spiritual needs in family, neighborhood, and village — with multiple combinations producing ever and again new syncretisms, new local theologies, and new chapters in the history of faith.

In any case, practical theology is inevitably a local construction, and it is the responsibility of every theologian and every pastor, priest, minister, teacher, and lay leader at the local level to be equipped to listen, analytically, to the spiritualities at hand, to bring as a resource to the local community the broader and deeper perspectives of the tradition in all its amplitude, and to assist the faith community to construct its own cultural-linguistic system of belief and action.

Schreiter's perspective seems to be among the most compelling of the voices we have thus far discussed. It allows — even demands — closer attention to religious sentiments, religious texts, and the inherent content of religious meanings as deposited in religious messages and practices than do several other perspectives we have studied. This view recognizes, as some do not, that these things are of first-order importance. At the same time, the demand for sensitive listening to the messages of the context, coupled with a broad awareness of the analytical tools that are pertinent to discerning spirituality in a given ethos, would seem to prevent any imperialist tendency from attending the effort to contextualize the gospel. The discerning and selective use of materialist, functionalist, and structuralist analysis integrated by cultural semiotics surely provides a less ideological set of resources for intercultural encounter and for a nuanced interpretation of multiple human contexts than is widely in use among theologians. Nevertheless, this view does present some problems that require comment.

CATHOLICITY FORSAKEN?

Most immediately, we note that Schreiter's use of the resources of cultural semiotics is less connected to the selective use of those modes of analysis that accent social and institutional forms than he perhaps intends. If one uses the analytical tools Schreiter proposes, one has no sense that there are normative patterns to guide family, political, or economic life. Schreiter seems to presume that if the inner content of a culture's signs is rightly understood, the structural patterns of life will take care of themselves. Yet many of the most acute pastoral and sociocultural issues are often posed by conflicts, ambiguities, injustice, and oppression precisely in these areas. And it is in these patterns of life that various spiritualities become embodied and reveal their practical meanings.

We should note, in this connection, that Schreiter is writing from within a Roman Catholic framework, and he may be presuming that normative teaching on these questions is more settled than it is in the wider church and world. This whole effort presumes that the chief problem of the faith as it attempts to contextualize and globalize the gospel is that it is too top-heavy in official dogma. That to which the core dogmas point is not overtly and directly challenged; nevertheless, Schreiter believes that "the faith" seldom does or can take account of the dynamics and structures of meaning that are dominant at the local level in highly diverse settings. Seldom, indeed, does the faith open its ears to the immediate felt needs and sustaining spiritualities among the people at a specific time and place. Thus, Schreiter is covertly and indirectly challenging the teaching authority of the magisterium by identifying a problem that is quite pronounced and widespread among many of the great historic communions of faith, and (for quite different reasons) among some evangelical theorists of mission who use many of these same tools of analysis, but who also presume that in Scripture (rather than in magisterial teaching) one can find core doctrines as invariable as those of the dogmas of church traditions.

This is not, however, the special problem that many ecumenically open Protestant seminaries and churches face. For many pastors, denominations, and seminaries, the problem is just the opposite, in part because these modes of analysis have been pursued with great vigor for more than a century, and in part because our "free-church" ecclesiologies have celebrated pluralistic local theologies to the extent that we are unsure whether anything transcends the immediate contexts of ministry. The "liberal," ecumenical-Protestant sense of the larger church tradition and its dogma is often weak or undeveloped. While seminarians must study the history of the larger church, pastors are often unsure how that relates to practical ministry in any context, and neither theologians nor church members are held accountable in any way to what the tradition has held. The sense of doctrine is often attenuated to the point that each pastor or theologian or believer can and does develop his or her own theology which may or may not conflict with the ecumenical and historic teachings of the faith. And what is preached or taught is often accepted in local congregations so long as it does not violate the indigenous sensibilities and cultural styles of the congregation.

In other words, the plea for awareness of local theologies and the contribution they can make is not new to many, and may simply reinforce the subcultural stereotypes about theology that already are widely institutionalized. And, while some might rejoice at this "protestantization" of Catholicism to the point of the sovereignty of the local congregation, Protestants have found that this tendency can also become lopsided in another direction. Local — even individualistic — theologies appear in abundance. In not a few "congregational" and "independent" churches, the construction of local theologies becomes mere provincialism where it does not become local snobbery. It is among the tasks of the theologian to deprovincialize our churches and communities, our poetry, our prophecy, and our practice, as Schreiter knows; but the chief problem is how we might find the grounds to do that. This problem looks different when it is approached from the side of traditions which claim a universality that has seldom been sensitive to local contexts than it does when approached from the side of traditions which are so contextual that any claim of universality seems highly remote as a possibility or even as a legitimate quest.

Closely related is the way in which the tools of analysis proposed by Schreiter — most especially semiotics, but also some aspects of materialist, structuralist, and functionalist methods — are likely to be used if they are adopted. It is also possible that he has not fully recognized how the very tools of analysis he uses so creatively can present problems of a rather severe kind to theology when they are consistently applied. Schreiter uses these tools to relativize false and pretentious attempts to impose the symbolic, cultural, and social systems of one environment on another, for these can show how much of any missionizing tradition is a product of a highly particular series of semiotic and sociocultural systems. This use is the most pervasive one in many contexts today, and the one that Schreiter is concerned to point out. In fact, many of these tools of analysis have been developed precisely for such use.

It is also possible, however, that other aspects of materialist, functionalist, structuralist, and cultural semiotic analysis can bring us to an awareness of the common structures, dynamics, and pro cesses that underlie every human context and every pattern of meaning. That would be a contribution which would be of considerable import among those who are doubtful that there are patterns of cross-cultural and cross-historical meaning. If these common structures, dynamics, and processes can be identified, and if they include religious matters, a basis for direct conversation between the secular sciences and theology proper and among the religions would be at hand.

It is surely something of an irony that tools of analysis developed by modern social and cultural theory to show the relativity of civilizational, societal, cultural, religious, and spiritual formation themselves demand (or rest on) categories of thought that bridge the particular formations they are designed to investigate and celebrate. Protest against the hegemony of Greco-Roman theories of "natural law" and against the universalistic concerns of the Scholastics ended up relying on new understandings of universal "epistemic principles" as grasped by materialist, structuralist, functionalist, and semiotic analysis. In order to use these tools, one would have to believe that there is a *logos* in the world that is more than a series of idiosyncratic particulars in specific times, places, and sociocultural contexts. The very effort to interpret the variety by developing a science to do so implies that there is also a universal logic, potentially present in our various particularities, even if our little logics, our scientific rationalities, and our psychological or sociological rationalizations do not adequately comprehend or reflect it. In short, a certain abstraction is necessary to wrestle with the concrete; a certain realism is necessary to every nominalism; a systematic approach is necessary to every attempt to identify the dynamics of the uniquely local; a trans-contextual logic is necessary to grasp contextual realities. Our abstractions, realisms, systems, and logics may be too narrow, but they will be corrected only by the development of deeper and broader ones, not by renunciation of them. To put the matter another way, the tools of analysis used here to challenge pretentious universalisms end up requiring a kind of epistemological catholicity at another level, one for which few arguments are given.

It is important to stress this point in our reflections on theological education because, as we will see in Part III of this study, it is a critical question whether any attempt to deal with particular spiritualities, with "texts," with religion, with God, and with education about these matters can be treated with intellectual integrity in cross-cultural and cross-historical ways.

This leads us, however, to the final point about Schreiter's study. Schreiter simply presumes, as do many theological educators, that the gospel is true, that it is, for the most part, rightly presented in the Bible and in the authoritative dogmas of the faith, as mediated by the sacraments and by the teaching magisterium of the church. Further, he is convinced that, if rightly understood through the use of cultural semiotics, the gospel will lead the human community to justice. But these perceptions of truth and justice are widely disputed today, precisely by those who have made the most extensive contributions to the methods Schreiter commends, by post-Enlightenment scholarship in the West, and by other religions around the world. That is a troubling fact. At several points, Schreiter comments that what these modes of analysis have rendered cries out for theological treatment, but he does not offer that treatment in any complete way. Like most of the works we have surveyed, and perhaps like most of what goes on today in theological education, Schreiter's work focuses on descriptive analysis and much less on normative analysis, but the decisive issues always turn out to be normative.

The richness of this proposal, one widely held by many theologians and pastors in less systematic and carefully documented terms, can surely inform our contemporary understandings of contextualization, globalization, and mission in theological education. It carries out, in more ordered terms, the implications of understanding the faith in terms of *poesis* in a way not unlike the one Charles Kraft proposed nearly a decade ago in more evangelical terms. In his masterful study, *Christianity in Culture: A Study in Dynamic Biblical Theologizing in Cross-Cultural Perspective,* he too calls for using the many new resources from the social and cultural sciences in thinking about the tasks of mission. Both of these fine studies, however, are governed by a set of presuppositions at one level that might be questioned. That is, they both presume that there is a "Christian message" which is, in some sense, universally valid and which is not *poesis* alone. Schreiter treats this in terms of the power of the gospel and the Holy Spirit as these have been identified by Catholic dogmas and sacramental practice, which have been constructed out of a long tradition of reflection on a series of "local theologies." Kraft speaks of "the Biblical message" in a similar way, as a normative view having an internal meaning that is, by its very nature, universal in import — if it is stripped of the accoutrements of localism that the Western traditions have imposed on it and misidentified with it. Both men are alert to the difficulty of defining exactly what they are pointing to, and are more concerned to prevent the contemporary church from extending too far the scope of what is certain and universal. Still, in one or another sense, each leaves a range of Christian doctrine untouched by the critical analysis he uses. It is only slightly too strong to say that one, finally, reserves a privileged place for a certain *sola dogmata,* and that the other, in the end, does much the same for *sola scriptura.*

Neither of these studies, however, is very clear about what the content and form of that universal or catholic message might be. Nor are they clear about why that message should be exempt from examination with the tools of analysis they bring to every other aspect of theology, religion, and culture. And this is a matter of some importance.

What if, as is not infrequent today, the very tools of analysis employed by these fine studies are turned to the content of the "gospel" directly? Is not the notion of "the gospel" itself a doctrine subject to all the modes of analysis these scholars bring to everything else cultural, linguistic, historical, and social? Is it not the case that all of what believers want to contextualize, globalize, and carry into the byways of life by mission in the name of the gospel would itself have to be seen as but one *poesis* — if a rather large and capacious one — created out of a local and parochial history? And would all efforts to speak of this in the many contexts of the world be but an enormous exercise in cultural imperialism?

DOCTRINE AS A CULTURAL-LINGUISTIC SYSTEM

Fortunately, we do not need to imaginatively construct, on the spot, what such an approach might mean. This approach is worked out with considerable subtlety in George Lindbeck's widely celebrated new work, *The Nature of Doctrine.*[6] His purpose, of course, is not to address our problems directly. He is much more concerned with how it is possible for Christian traditions to engage in ecumenical dialogue when each seems to be fixated on its own particular construal of the Christian message. But, to solve that problem, he attempts to probe deeper into the nature of religious doctrine itself. In the process he shows how we are likely to come to think about "the gospel" if we follow the methods adopted by Schreiter to their logical conclusion.

Lindbeck sets forth a view that he claims is "post-liberal" and

---

6. Lindbeck, *The Nature of Doctrine: Religion and Theology in a Post-liberal Age* (Philadelphia: Westminster Press, 1984).

"post-classical," a view that he indicates has become more and more influential in America (at least) since the work of H. Richard Niebuhr. He argues that modern scholarship has demonstrated that Christian doctrine, like that of every other religion, is a cultural-linguistic system of biblical rootage that may have a certain internal coherence but is ultimately confessional in character. That is, we hold to the system because it is ours, and its terms make sense only when we are socialized into it.

Lindbeck contrasts this view with two alternative approaches to religious matters, both inadequate in his view. One is the "experiential-expressive" or liberal approach to religious matters. It presumes that behind all religions is a common religious experience that involves "getting in touch with" one's deepest feelings to find the common roots of all religions, although each religion will involve different forms of expressing that experience due to various cultural and historical variations. The other is the "preliberal" or "classical" approach. It emphasizes the "cognitive-propositional" elements of religious understanding. This classical approach focuses on questions of truth or falsity, and hence is unable, Lindbeck says, to reconcile differences when basic disagreements occur. Although he shows some appreciation for contemporary and ecumenically influential Catholic scholars such as Bernard Lonergan and Karl Rahner, whom he portrays as attempting to combine the "experiential-expressive" and "cognitive-propositional" approaches, he finally rejects their views also. He believes that we must turn to a "confessional" approach, one warranted by modern cultural-linguistic (or semiotic) research.

A cultural-linguistic understanding of religious — and thus also of Christian — doctrine demands an acknowledgment that, finally, no extrinsic warrants can be given for holding any particular doctrine, dogma, or view of the gospel. It is true, of course, that every person and every community needs a core meaning system to survive, and that some meaning systems have a greater capacity to supply core meanings to more people in more circumstances than do others, primarily because they contain a grammar of meaning of greater amplitude than do some alternatives. But it is not possible to confirm the truth or justice of doctrines by appeal to the deepest emotive levels, or to derive propositions from the textual or communal symbol systems that *we hold as true for us,* or to show that they are verifiable in any sense outside the system as we hold it. Here, neither *sola dogmata* nor *sola scriptura* is taken as the point of reference. Neither the magisterial authority of those who govern the teaching office of the church nor the rationalized use of any "depositum" in authoritative texts defines the core or meaning of religious doctrine. *Sola fide* is the only decisive point of reference. And that can be "scientifically" discerned only by the cultural-linguistic scholar, reflecting on a particular community of religious discourse in its sociohistorical context. He or she can describe how the parts fit together in a poetic whole, how they have developed, and how more integrative ways of seeing things might allow for greater internal cohesion.

But such scholars, the doctrines under examination, and the contexts in which they occur or are examined are able to "affirm nothing about the extra-linguistic and extra-human reality" to which they are presumed to refer.[7] The warrants for doctrines taught are entirely internal to what is believed in the first place, and to the authorities that are taken as valid by the doctrines and the believer of them. "Orthodoxy" is what particular communities decide it is, and "orthopraxis" is what a particular community requires people to do if they are to participate actively in that community's identity. Both would be malleable as any community expands, constricts, or revises its doctrines according to its local needs — even should its "locale" be modern civilization and modernizing cultures.

This, of course, leaves us in some doubt about the nature and character of "theology." Lindbeck makes a distinction between "theology" and "doctrine" — the latter being the topic of his research, of ecumenical dialogue, and of contemporary education. Theology and doctrine may be correlated, but they need not be. The one has to do either with the "explanation, communication and defense of the faith" by means of apologetics (or fundamental theology), or with the application of faith to personal and social behavior (practical theology). The other has to do with the "cultural and linguistic processes and dynamics of communal . . . agreement."[8] Lindbeck is primarily concerned with the latter, and he is restrained, even dubious, about any attempt to engage in apologetics or the attempt to "show" that doctrine may be true or just on practical grounds. He wants to be — and he wants the churches and the seminaries to be — faithful to what is already believed, adjusting it, as appropriate, to new encounters that the historical process brings to us, and utilizing it to absorb the new worlds that Christians encounter. Theological education and mission activity in any context around the globe would involve, essentially, nurture into a given community's ever-evolving set of symbols, and the poetic absorption of

---

7. Lindbeck, *The Nature of Doctrine,* p. 69.
8. Lindbeck, *The Nature of Doctrine,* p. 76.

competing and contradictory symbol sets within it.

Lindbeck is surely correct in arguing that doctrines are set forth in highly symbolic language and that symbolic language not only presents a cultural-linguistic perspective but also evokes, provokes, or enhances characteristic experiences. Indeed, Lindbeck believes that there are ideas we cannot imagine and experiences we cannot have unless the cultural-linguistic system proper to these ideas or experiences is already in place. But why one would want to imagine Christian ideas or evoke Christian experiences remains an unanswered question. "Because it is ours" may well be a temptation to idolatry or imperialism that the cultural-linguistic system of Christianity explicitly resists. The only other possible reason — if apologetic and practical theology are of doubtful worth, of dubious faithfulness, and probably impossible — would be aesthetic. That is, the only reason for being a Christian or studying doctrine would be to enhance experiences or incite ideas that are, in themselves, aesthetically in harmony with the cultural-linguistic system that is confessed. In this view, *theoria* and *praxis* become instruments of *poesis*. The possibility of theology, as a science, a knowledge about divine things, is doubted, and religious education becomes socialization into a preferred confession, as a matter of the poetic definition of personal and corporate identity while "scholarship" becomes a no-nonsense empiricism. Reality is what we (our traditions) decide in dialogue to name it. Nominalism becomes epistemologically sovereign.

It may be no better solution to collapse *theoria* and *praxis* into *poesis* than it is to collapse *theoria* and *poesis* into *praxis*, as we saw in the previous chapter. But we note that the radical emphases on *praxis* and *poesis* both depend upon a distinctive *theoria*. We shall not be able to avoid it much longer. Indeed, in the next chapter we shall turn to one of the most sustained and critical examinations of *theoria* under discussion today.

CHAPTER 8

Theoria *and* Phenomenology

Perhaps no contemporary discussion of theological education has been more widely debated than Edward Farley's *Theologia: The Fragmentation and Unity of Theological Education.*[1] More than any other work we have surveyed thus far, it focuses on the necessity of a certain priority for theoretical issues. Further, it draws on one of the most influential forms of contemporary philosophical thought to call for a substantial reform of theological education, a reform that the author believes would include, and give coherent form to, current concerns about globalization and contemporary accents on *praxis* and *poesis*. Indeed, although Farley's work was written before most of the specific writings so far discussed in this volume appeared, he does treat many of the basic orientations present in them and views them as suggestive, if finally unsatisfactory, attempts to overcome the present malaise of theological education.

THE LOSS OF INTEGRITY

Farley argues that *theologia* has all but disappeared as the unity, subject matter, and end of theological education. This is so primarily because of changes in the "theological encyclopedia," that is, the basic *theoria* of the theological disciplines and their relationship both to the core subject matter of theological education and to each other. This has been brought about by the shift to a

---

1. Farley, *Theologia* (Philadelphia: Fortress Press, 1983).

123

"post-enlightenment, European type of faculty as a group of specialists . . . [and] a dispersion of *theologia* into independent sciences." Farley understands *theologia* in its primal sense to be "sapiential and personal knowledge of divine self-disclosure . . . [which renders a] wisdom or discerning judgment indispensable for human living."[2] It is this particular form of "wisdom" that has been lost. When it is present and vital, it evokes a linkage between commitment and intellect, and an ecclesial involvement of mutuality, participation, and ecumenical scope.

The symptoms of this loss are several. The typical seminary "product" is not a theologian in any serious sense. Scholars in theological disciplines work in isolation. Seminary catalogues list a cafeteria-like series of offerings without a hint of a main menu. And seminary education is experienced as an arena in which *praxis* and *poesis*, both widely celebrated, seldom meet in a coherent *theoria*. Many proposals have been made to address the symptoms, Farley says, but few approach the more basic issues. To do so, we must go deeper historically and analytically than many have yet done.

The deep roots of the present disarray in theological education are to be found in the facts that American theological schools adopted models of theological education from the German university system, and that faculties developed primary loyalties to the specialized "guilds" organized around the specific fields in which they work. In addition, there has been a shift to "professionalism" in ministry — a development that makes it of rather marginal value for students to engage deeply in the fields to which they are exposed, so long as they get passing grades in a required number of courses. These developments have shifted the understanding of what counts as decisive knowledge from a "convictional" or "heartfelt knowledge of divine things to scholarly . . . mastery . . . [of discrete bodies of data]," each with its own methods of study and skills.[3] These deeper problems are compounded by the several problems that afflict many, if not most, of the students currently in seminaries: they find that their previous degrees have not prepared them for graduate-level work; they find themselves introduced to quite different directions of thought and method when they take courses in the different fields of study; they experience a discrepancy between what the churches and the seminaries expect them to be and to do;

---

2. Farley, *Theologia*, p. x.
3. Farley, *Theologia*, p. 10.

and they are not always the most talented individuals in the first place.

Farley traces a series of historical developments that he believes have led to the present situation. He notes that, at root, *theologia* has a double-sided character. On the one hand, it is saving knowledge cultivated by the habits of the heart that render a distinctive "orientation of soul." And on the other hand, it entails disciplined reflection, a kind of inquiry into key texts that are understood to be a "depositum" of truth. This, of course, requires clear and precise methods, and presumes that one can render conclusions or "demonstrations." At this level, *theologia* has a clearly cognitive component. Both sapiential understanding and the "critical-historical" analysis of texts entail real knowledge. Indeed, in the great classical periods of orthodoxy, it was presumed that these would and could be held in concert — in the heart as well as the head, each reinforcing the other.

When, under the impact of the Enlightenment, theological education began to focus almost exclusively on the cognitive grasp of purported universal truths, there was also a "romantic" reaction that claimed that these did not and could not be related to experience. At that point, a major split occurred in the fundamental content of theological education. Thereafter, a major effort was made to reclaim the "practical" side of things. But, in the post-Enlightenment world, this effort produced the modern forms of "practical theology" that are, at base, mostly technique — a kind of technological study of the means to get certain tasks done. For this, neither the wisdom of faith nor the wisdom derived from textual studies is necessary.

These developments can be traced through study of the changing "encyclopedia" by which theological education understood itself. As Farley recounts this material, three developments emerge as most significant.

In the period immediately following the Reformation, the various branches of the newly divided church found it necessary to establish their own legitimacy. Thus, the main reason for reading patristics, church history, and the various Scholastics had to do with efforts to refute the "pagans and heretics," and to show the truth of one particular Christian confession in the face of others. This program dominated theological education at least until the Enlightenment. During the Enlightenment, attempts were made to overcome divisions by establishing abstract, formal principles by which all religious phenomena could be evaluated.

Post-Enlightenment Protestantism tended to see various religions and confessions as historical, correlative to variations in culture and context. Theology came to be understood as one of several potentially "useful" conceptualities by which people expressed their convictions and by which this or that religious community came to consciousness as a sociocultural movement. In this period, says Farley, it was Friedrich Schleiermacher who articulated a new perspective. And it is on Schleiermacher's "encyclopedia" that he concentrates especially. For it is in this period that theological education became "professionalized." That is, what one learns is what is required for certification, for "qualification." Theology is conceived to be something that ministers have to know about, comparable in some ways to what lawyers have to know about the civil code, or what doctors have to know about biochemistry. Theology is "specialized" knowledge, not required among the people for salvation — no more than a knowledge of jurisprudence is required to be law-abiding, or a mastery of physiology is required to be healthy.

In this context, theology becomes redefined away from *theologia,* especially in its existential, sapiential dimension. It becomes the technical, historical, and critical study of a religion's texts, practices, and developments that can be known in a purely cognitive way. Yet, it is presumed — as a continuing legacy of one version of both earlier interchurch polemics and Enlightenment thought — that one can isolate from this knowledge something like an "essence of Christianity" as it has been expressed confessionally by the church, as it is embodied in church laws or constitutions, and as it has been given ordered articulation by professional scholars who direct their sciences to some specific part of the historical whole. Those insights and principles that come from the specific parts of the whole are themselves to be ordered and integrated by the specialized discipline of philosophical theology and thereby woven into the whole fabric of social and cultural meaning. On this basis, cognitive *theoria* has become the way that specialists order "qualifying knowledge."

Closely parallel to this development was the "clericalization" of practical theology. It was widely held, as we saw in quite different connections in the previous three chapters, that "practical theology" was the "culminating branch of theology." But very soon, Farley says, following the Schleiermachian encyclopedia, practical theology became "a cluster of courses which address minister's obligations in church leadership," and these too were fragmented, with "religious education," "pastoral care," "liturgics," "preaching," and so forth soon taking on their own disciplinary trappings.[4] Each

---

4. Farley, *Theologia,* p. 104.

subfield developed its own guild, methods, doctoral program, journal, and literature, with little reference to the other theoretical or practical disciplines. And this occurred while the so-called "classical" disciplines were becoming more and more refined in terms of the periods, regions, themes, and subspecialties studied by professors and taught to students. Thus, theological education became an aggregate of specialties without *theologia,* without coherence, without focus, without integrating sapiential knowledge. The result is the "fragmentation" that Farley refers to in the title of his book.

Structurally, the Schleiermachian model, as it was modified and adapted, produced what Farley calls "the four-fold pattern." All students are to be exposed to the Bible, history, theology, and "practics." This model presumes that each field will inevitably point to the "essence of Christianity," that each part of the pattern will contribute to the whole, and that the historical-critical study of these will "co-inhere" with faith. In view of the actual developments within all of these four areas, however, little unity results. What integration occurs is accidental. In fact, what pastors actually do becomes quite determined by the accidents of their denominational confessions, by their personal styles, and by the immediate demands of their situations. Theology (and ethics) become dominated by the categorical worlds of current philosophies — today led by historicist or social-scientific ones — or by the "agendas" of a preferred group or cause. And preaching, as it is actually done by people trained in the pattern just described, becomes the application of a selected text to some contemporary spiritual or social issue without theological appraisal, careful exegetical study, or clarity about how the contemporary situation is to be discerned. In short, the result of the loss of *theologia* borders on a rampant voluntarism. So pervasive has this influence been, argues Farley, that the result is no less true of conservatives than of liberals, of Catholics than of Protestants.

TOWARD BELIEF-FULL KNOWLEDGE

The recovery of the sapiential knowledge of *theologia,* with its "belief-full knowing . . . [its] certain insightfulness which characterizes faith itself . . . [and its] pre-reflective" sensitivity, could be accomplished by reintegrating the parts in a kind of education that would make faith conscious and self-conscious through "deliberate processes of reflection and inquiry."[5] Thereby a fresh reappropria-

---

5. Farley, *Theologia,* pp. 157, 158.

tion of *theologia* would be possible. To undertake this, we would have to recognize that all processes of reflection occur in three matrices. The first matrix is the actual situation of the believer, which varies from person to person and from culture to culture. The second matrix is the functional situation in which church leadership dwells — namely, the gathering of the redemptive community by "traditioning" and proclamation. These are both aspects of "ecclesial existence," the topic of two previous works by Farley,[6] and they are similar, in some ways, to what we have here discussed in the previous two chapters. The third matrix is scholarship, characterized essentially by that kind of phenomenology which accents the critical hermeneutics of both the "ethos" of the believer and the "mythos" of the church, and their interaction.

The new *theologia* will not be quite like the old one, which is lost for two major reasons. Originally, it was developed in contexts wherein both piety and the authority of "orthodoxy" could be known by study of an authoritative "depositum" in Scripture or dogmatic confessions. But both of these are lost and cannot be resuscitated in their old forms, although some people are trying to do just that with regard to piety through what Farley calls "a flurry of activity . . . about 'formation' and 'spirituality' . . . [that is] not highly credible." With regard to orthodoxy, the old *theologia* relied on forms of authority that had also better be left behind. Those who refuse to recognize that they are gone will end up with a wooden fundamentalism. Thus, according to Farley, the critical question is "whether *theologia* . . . can have a post-orthodox form" — indeed, whether faith itself can have a post-orthodox form.[7]

Orthodoxy moved from text to context, presuming that the "depositum" could be grasped and then applied. Today's newer models — shared by case-study methods, field-based education, liberation theology, and cultural-linguistic studies — move from situation to reflection and back to situation, presuming that the two levels will integrate simply by sequential encounter. Farley believes that while such methods are in some ways promising, they actually maintain the division between theory and practice, even if they have a place for each. Such methods do not tend to take the foundational unity of *theologia* as such seriously. More adequate would be the interpretive grasp of the *ethos* (the situation of the believer)

---

6. Farley, *Ecclesial Man: A Social Phenomenology of Faith and Reality* (Philadelphia: Fortress Press, 1975); and *Ecclesial Reflection: An Anatomy of Theological Method* (Philadelphia: Fortress Press, 1982).

7. Farley, *Theologia*, pp. 160, 161.

and the *mythos* ("traditioning" and proclamation) by a "life process" that is inevitably hermeneutical in character. Where concern for the situation is primary, we read the situation through the reinterpretation of *mythos* (or, as others might say, through *poesis*); where concern for the *mythos* is primary, we reinterpret the myth in light of the life process lived out in the situation (or, as others might say, through *praxis*). In both phases of the hermeneutic, the sapiential knowledge of prereflective faith serves as the primary point of reference. Such "post-orthodox faithing," understood phenomenologically, refuses all absolutizations; it recognizes that all imagery, symbols, doctrines, and dogmas (which constitute *mythos*) are products of former life processes where *mythos* and situations were reciprocally interpreted in religious practice. Thus, the resources of Scripture and Tradition, of confession and creed, are to be treated with a hermeneutics of suspicion until they prove effective in the life process. All this is possible because it is nothing less than divine reality which "undergirds the human life process, pervades it, and lures it to its best possibilities."[8]

As these themes were discussed in our faculty, it became clear that much of Farley's effort is laden with pertinent observation and insight. Farley is surely correct, as was stated forcefully by professor of evangelism Jerry Handspicker, that we do suffer from fragmentation, and his description of what students and faculties in seminaries experience is remarkably accurate. More important, Farley has recognized that how we conceive of theology *per se* is ultimately determinative for how we work together to form individuals, communities of faith, and the fabric of our "ecclesial" existence in a center of learning. Farley has, more than any other voice, put the discussion of theological education on another, important level. Moreover, what he calls for is a careful theoretical statement of key issues that many who are concerned about contextualization, globalization, and mission in theological education are today trying to formulate. It is well worth our time to wrestle with this material.

DISSATISFACTIONS

As became clear in the discussion of this book by the ANTS faculty, however, many are in fact dissatisfied with the prescription, even if it does reflect much of what is practiced by numerous seminary professors and advocated in a good deal of current scholarship.

---

8. Farley, *Theologia*, p. 54.

This is so because certain key questions appear to have been avoided in both the diagnosis and the prescription. The first question is, as church historian Eleanor McLaughlin posed it, the decisive question of epistemology. How do we know much of anything with security if we take this view of knowledge? Is it not the case that what this method renders is but another "technique" of selectively correlating our widely varying perceptions of our situations with widely divergent readings of the *mythos*? A related question, stated most sharply by systematician Gabriel Fackre, is this: What, specifically, does this view have to do with the great affirmations of historic faith? A general kind of "faithing" may be necessary to every and all kinds of understanding, but many pre-reflective "faiths" have little or nothing to do with the truth claims of Christianity — or of any other great religion. Are these claims to be taken only as potential resources for contemporary "traditioning," useful only if they meet the pragmatic needs of our present "life process"? Still a third question, voiced by professor of preaching Eddie O'Neal, has to do with the relationship between education in this way and "vocation," the calling to be a minister — a calling that has to be discerned by the community of faith and may not coincide with training in the philosophical hermeneutics of situation and the *mythos,* and may call us to judgments against either or both.

In addition, several others, led by Earl Thompson (pp. 17-18 herein), questioned whether Farley had really made his case regarding key historical influences that have shaped contemporary theological education. Is it not true that he ends up with but an alternative rendering of the Schleiermachian proposal, one that has put the dynamics of philosophical phenomenology in the place of nineteenth-century "essentialist" theories of *mythos* and "confessionalist" theories of our ecclesiastical situation, but has changed little else? For one who wants to take the situation seriously, Farley tends to ignore the rather critical difference between the role of *mythos* in a society with an established, territorial church intimately tied to governmental structures of taxation, and the role of *mythos* in a society that is pluralistic, with churches organized as "voluntary associations." In short, for all his concern for analyzing the situation, Farley's understanding of "situation" is abbreviated to the point that it is hard to know what systems of meaning and life process we are dealing with. The point is especially telling if we wish to wrestle with diverse contexts around the globe or have become familiar with the various tools of analysis one may use in attempting to define this, or any, context. And, finally, Orlando Costas (among others) wondered whether this kind of perspective could render any sense of mission, or whether it would not be equally valid for every possible religious point of view.

Behind these questions is the rather acute issue of whether there is anything very distinctive about theological education, phenomenologically understood, in the first place. The hermeneutics of situation and of the governing *mythos* through a phenomenology of "life process" takes place in families, in neighborhoods, in political parties, and in a wide range of academic courses in literature, psychology, and the social sciences, all of which require a connection between "commitment and intellect" and, in Farley's words, a kind of "wisdom or discerning judgment indispensable for human living." Seldom are these seen as intrinsically and necessarily connected with *theos* or *logos*.

And here we face one of the critical issues of our study. If it is in fact true that many areas of life and of academic reflection require this kind of "wisdom" or "discerning judgment," then any sort of phenomenological study in any field of inquiry would suffice. Surely one of the particular responsibilities of theological education, at least as it takes place in seminaries or departments of theology, is to lead people to know something reliable about God. It is less *mythos* in general that concerns theology than those dimensions of "traditioning" and proclamation that can be held to unveil, point toward, or in some measure grasp what is ultimately reliable because it can be reasonably shown to be, or point to, that which is divine, true, and just. Is it not so that *theologia,* if it is to be held with integrity, must provide a basis upon which to stand as we respond to the life process, selectively embracing or resisting dimensions of both the life situation and the governing *mythos?* And is it not true that *theologia* must provide the criteria by which the precognitive faith from which we preach, teach, evangelize, and organize in the life process can be evaluated and condemned or approved as warranted? And is it not the case that *theologia* must function thus in the multiple contexts of a world in which other situations and interpretations of *mythos* provide alternative hermeneutics of and for the life process, and direct the entire matrix of personal, historical, and civilizational existence into conflicting channels?

It is notable that Farley offers no discernible doctrinal content as a core part of his proposal. He speaks of "post-orthodox" *theologia,* and hence there is no discussion of the authority of Scripture, of the propriety of taking the classic creeds (such as the doctrine of the Trinity) seriously in "traditioning" or proclamation. Nor, for that matter, is there any hint of the normative content of conscience or confession or cultus (such as we saw in Schomer and Thomas), or any normative direction for mission or ecclesiology (such as we found in the reports on globalization). Nowhere does Farley speak of the demand for sacrificial love and solidarity in *praxis*, which Lamb called for, and the idea of an *orthopraxis* would be as doubtful to him as the idea of orthodoxy. And Farley does not even offer a focus on a normative confession *pro nobis* in *poesis*, as accented by Schreiter and Lindbeck in distinctive ways, although he is closer to them than to others we have surveyed.

It is true that Farley speaks of "the situation as God undergirds. . . [it], pervades it, and lures it to its best possibilities," as already mentioned. But such a pantheistic, or possibly "panentheistic," metaphysic is not self-evident, and would be subjected to sharp criticism by nearly every voice to which we have thus far attended. It is also true that Farley calls for direct engagement in the human situations of life, as many voices already noted have also done, but Farley gives little sense that we would undertake this task with any profound sense of justice, righteousness, peace, or obedience. It is not that Farley is against these; rather, it is that he seems simply to presume that perfectly adequate, if inevitably only temporary and hypothetical, definitions of these would emerge from a proper phenomenological analysis of ecclesial interactions between *ethos* and *mythos*. But there is little hint of what a normative ecclesiology for ecclesial existence would look like, what terms of analysis might be used in understanding the concrete situations of believers, or what criteria might be employed in guiding "traditioning" and proclamation. Farley seems to have convincingly established the need for a certain priority of *theoria*, but that which he provides seems to be less any specifiable knowledge of or about God than a kind of "awareness" of the sacred in life in general. Nevertheless, in dealing with life in general, Farley shows little focused or articulated concern with global perspectives of the kind that could enhance our hermeneutical understandings, support the primal "sapiential" faithing, or correctly grasp the dynamics and structures of the life process. Yet disputes over these matters are surely decisive for his effort as well as for our own questions.

SCHLEIERMACHER STILL?

Finally, Farley's direction offers only a procedure for, and no sense of the substance of, *theologia*. It is not clear that he has escaped the post-Enlightenment concerns out of which the Schleiermachian "encyclopedia" was born. Phenomenology in this mold may manifest the nominalist, historicist, and romantic tendencies of modern theologizing more than it corrects or stabilizes them by showing the possible validity of sapiential knowledge. In short, the question is whether this "post-orthodox" *theologia* does not leave the door open to every passing heterodoxy, heresy, spirituality, and agenda that Farley too opposes.

In our faculty discussion of this material, a number of participants, each in her or his own way, were more inclined to accept certain key emphases of our international consultants as reported in Chapters 3 and 4. One of the points that Nantawan Boonprasat-Lewis stressed is that contextuality and universality are, most profoundly understood, not poles but mutually interdependent concepts. If seen at their deepest levels, they point to intercontextual communication of the sort that leads ultimately to the question of who God is as the One who gives coherence to all contexts and their relationships. At the core of Frank Collison's paper are three universalistic affirmations which, if assessed to be true, are of global significance: (1) Humanity is alienated from God; (2) All particular ills derive from this alienation; and (3) Christ overcomes this alienation. In his presentation on translation, Lamin Sanneh maintained in a series of arguments both that there is a real, objective content that is translated and translatable, and that, in all languages into which translation contextualizes content, a universalistic potentiality is present that allows indigenous cultural structures to both receive from and contribute to the human comprehension of that which is translated. To return to the theme that George Peck, the president of ANTS, accented in his inaugural address, "transposition" is possible because there is something to be transposed and a coherent framework into which and through which it can be transposed. And it is precisely because of the lack of attention to this, in contemporary phenomenological studies, that theological education experiences the malaise that Farley and this study attempt to address.

In contrast to the notions that theological education should be structured around an *orthopraxis,* or a cultural-linguistic *poesis* grasped by semiotics, or a sapiential wisdom requiring a phenomenological hermeneutic in this mold, it is possible that quite different approaches are today required. It may be that the pervasive nominalism in all of these ideas, plus the contemporary fear of orthodoxy and the current suspicion of any "depositum" or "demonstration" in matters theological, has prevented some of the best minds of our time from wrestling with normative criteriological issues in theological education.

It is not the case that no one is posing these questions. Don Browning's collection of essays on practical theology does just that.[9] So also do the superb new work on Christology by S. Mark Heim,[10] Gabriel Fackre's work on "the Christian story,"[11] Elsie McKee's work on *diakonia* in Calvin,[12] and a number of efforts to articulate a "public theology."[13] In these several ways it is argued that certain key affirmations of the classical evangelical, catholic, reformed, and orthodox traditions of Christianity can be stated in clear form, can be defended in the public and intercultural marketplace of ideas, and ought to be acknowledged by those who do not hold these views at present.

Is it possible that major figures concerned about contextualization, globalization, and mission have — like those concerned with *praxis, poesis,* and *theoria* — broken prematurely with the very notion that Christianity involves anything heretofore thought decisive for Christian *thinking* and *sound* faith? It appears that a full and integrative vision of theological education is today replaced by efforts to theologize that cannot be judged to be right or wrong in their content. Farley in particular shows that this dimension of theological education earlier involved disciplined thought that could render demonstrations and conclusions for the establishment of "right doctrine," and that it involved the grasp of truths beyond those of immediate experience that ought to be related to, be planted in, and give shape to experience. But, Farley argues, this has been lost; it cannot and ought not be reclaimed. In this, he seems to represent a consensus among contemporary ecumenical theologians.

But it is just this consensus that we have had to question in our research team for this study, specifically because we are deeply concerned for theological education in an ecumenically oriented way around the world. Is it not possible that the chief vocation of theological education, today and always, everywhere, is to give an

---

9. *Practical Theology: The Emerging Field in Theology, Church, and World,* ed. Don S. Browning (New York: Harper & Row, 1983).

10. Heim, *Is Christ the Only Way?* (Valley Forge, Pa.: Judson Press, 1985).

11. Fackre, *The Christian Story: A Narrative Interpretation of Basic Christian Doctrine,* rev. ed. (Grand Rapids: Eerdmans, 1984).

12. McKee, *John Calvin on the Diaconate and Liturgical Almsgiving* (Geneva: Librairie Droz S. A., 1984).

13. See David Tracy, *Analogia* (New York: Seabury Press, 1984); James Gustafson, *Ethics from a Theocentric Perspective,* 2 vols. (Chicago: University of Chicago Press, 1981 and 1984); and Max L. Stackhouse, *Public Theology and Political Economy: Christian Stewardship in Modern Society* (Grand Rapids: Eerdmans, 1987).

account of — indeed, an *apologia* for — the faith we have, to "demonstrate" that some of its key claims may be of universal validity, and that, without acknowledgment of these, the various life processes, efforts at hermeneutics, and primal apprehensions of sacredness are doomed to become trendy or fanatical, and possibly idolatrous? And is it not also the vocation of theological education to forthrightly state that, if it cannot offer such an account, it must give up the appearance of being either education or a discipline, and stop pretending that it can be conducted on the basis of ecumenical activism, an *orthopraxis* that is essentially a matter of political solidarity after the model of the Enlightenment and the French Revolution, or a localistic construction of confessional meaning?

Farley has demonstrated that the malaise of contemporary theological education will not be overcome until we come to a viable definition of *theologia*. Further, he knows that, to be viable, the definition must involve ecumenical-ecclesial dimensions (as we also saw, in different terms, in Chapter 5), a demand for engagement in the practical situations of life (as we also saw, in different terms, in Chapter 6), and an appreciation for the cultural-linguistic character of *mythos* (as we also saw, in different terms, in Chapter 7). Moreover, Farley is alert to the fact that *praxis, poesis,* and *theoria* must be related. For all these contributions, we are in his debt. In our judgment, he is unsurpassed as a diagnostician. What remains to be developed is a compelling prescription to cure the disease. In the next section of this work, a series of proposals will be offered to move theological education beyond what we have thus far encountered.

PART III

A Proposal

CHAPTER 9

Apologia

Thus far, we have attempted (in Part I of this study) to recount the main themes and perspectives that surfaced in an episodic dialogue in an ecumenically oriented, and primarily Protestant, faculty of a Christian seminary. The dialogue took place not only among the members of the ANTS faculty, but also with international consultants on the topics of contextualization, globalization, and mission. We found, among other things, that the preferred ways of dealing with matters that we, as individuals, use were not always as widely shared or as free from difficulty as we wished. This was true whether we spoke of text and context, doctrine and practice, realism and nominalism, or theology and the social and historical sciences. We discovered that we did not have a very clear idea of what it is that binds us together as "theologians," or what makes us a part of that peculiar overlap of ecclesia and academia called "theological education."

As we discussed and debated the responsibilities that we have to reach out to the world, to learn from it in new ways, and to offer our resources to it, we realized that we must reach greater clarity on these points than we have heretofore. Thus, we also have attempted (in Part II of this study) to look in some detail at key representative views of theological education that are presently under discussion and that do try to think systematically about the issues relevant to our dialogue. What we have found is that the contemporary ecumenical, liberationist, semiotic, and phenomenological perspectives that are so widely influential today contribute rich resources for contemporary reflection and action. From each of these perspectives and approaches we have gained much. But we have also noted that the views we have encountered do not all agree with one another on how contextuality, globalization, mission, and theological education are to be understood. Further, we have found that each one of these approaches entails ambiguous presumptions, unanswered questions, or unsatisfying implications in at least those respects that we have attempted to specify.

What are we to make of all this? If there is some degree of confusion among us, and we cannot find consistently compelling orientations elsewhere, only a few options are open to us. We can ask what is lacking in these views and see whether it is possible to supply what is missing. We can attempt to plumb deeper than we think we or others have heretofore done and find a well from which we can all drink. We can celebrate diversity and pluralism, cultivate as many views as time, energy, finance, and life allows, and let a thousand flowers bloom. Or we can muddle through with the more or less adequate compromises allowed by faculty interchange, the requirements of the churches and our students, and the fruits of international contact. We can, in other words, seek our future by anticipating a sequence of one relatively workable consensus after another, trusting in the providence of God that we are going somewhere and in something like the right direction.

It is likely that we shall choose the latter option. Most theological faculties do. But it surely would not be without merit to explore the other options in hopes that we might discover clues, principles, or themes that could guide us in our efforts to find a consensus that not only works reasonably well within the limits of time, energy, finance, ability, and personal foibles, but has some discernible foundations and articulable directions. In fact, it may be that something of a consensus already exists, but that by failing to make it explicit, articulate, and central to our teaching and research, we allow an unnecessary confusion to remain. Deep, enduring, and ultimately irremediable "dissensus" is hard to find, even if we believe that the only way to take conversation partners (such as those of Parts I and II) seriously is to point out areas of disagreement. Perhaps by making explicit certain possible core presumptions behind the implicit consensus, and critically examining them to see the degree to which we can make a case for them, we will be able to find those integrative reference points by which to order the multiple insights we have uncovered in our dialogues and in our wider study. Of course, it is also possible that, once we articulate a proposal about core presuppositions, some will decide that they do not really like them — at least in the form that this portion of the study will use to set them forth.

To call for such an identification and critical examination of basic presuppositions is to focus on a distinctly academic and intellectual task. And to include them at this juncture is to suggest that intellectual and academic work is the primary point of departure for theological education. Above all else, that is why faculties are brought together. Whatever bonds of friendship, allegiance to some church or confession, depth of commitment, or "role models" — of race, class, gender, culture, or ideology — individuals may represent, the indispensable reason for forming a faculty is intellectual and academic. Theological faculty members are called to be talkers — academic, intellectual talkers — capable of offering warranted views about what can and cannot be reasonably known about God, humanity, and the world, about faith, eternity, and history, about scriptures, traditions, and practices, about the cure of souls, the clarification of truth in the face of ignorance and distortion, and the overcoming of injustice in civilizations. Whatever else students and the churches may require of a theological faculty (and the list is sometimes long), if it is not a center for the formation of the mind through academic training, it will have failed in its primary task. Faculties, students, administrations, boards of trustees, the churches, and the world — all know that knowledge of the sacred Scriptures and traditions, spiritual maturity, moral character, intensity of faith, sociopolitical commitment, a passion for ministry to neglected or oppressed groups, public speaking abilities, managerial skills, compassionate care for individuals, and therapeutic sensitivity are by no means limited to theological seminaries or theology departments in universities. Indeed, on every faculty thus far assembled, people are appointed who are deficient in one or several of these and still are viewed as qualified to teach because of their intellectual and academic qualifications. The decisive issues of theological education have to be addressed at this level in order to give a firm foundation to the other levels.

WHAT IS MISSING?

Do the views reported in Parts I and II of this study lack anything intellectually and academically that can and should be supplied, and is it possible to make a case for that which is needful? It may be. Most of the views we have examined do not argue overtly that religion makes a fundamental, objective difference in the real world, or that we can reliably know anything about the relative truth and justice of any religious claim. That somewhat flat way of stating several complex matters points to a very common feature of contemporary thought that has in some ways invaded our consciousness and pervades academic literature about religion and theology: Religion is understood to be a derivative or epiphenomenal expression of something else — something more fundamental, more objective — that is thought to make all the difference in the world, and that can be used to assess the relative truth and justice of religion.

That "something else" may be identified with psychodynamic or sociodynamic forces, with interests determined by race, sex, class, culture, or power, with the structural ways the human mind works, or with the functional needs of community survival. It may be stated in terms of the ways religious texts are thought to be generated by sociocultural contexts, the way religious *theoria* is held to be an instrumental phase of social and economic or political *praxis,* the way general beliefs are viewed as the artifacts growing out of a particular *poesis* of experience, or the way theologies are treated as the linguistic or confessional residues of one or another expression of group identity or institutional need as these emerge developmentally in history. Such views run counter to what has been assumed in most cultures in most of world history, and among the major anthropological, sociological, and comparative-religions studies of civilization. All of these presume that religion itself is an "independent" and not only a "dependent" variable in social, cultural, and intellectual life.

Not all of the views we have surveyed fit such characterizations in all respects. And not all disciplines in theological education are as prone to these interpretations of religion as others. Perhaps the reaction against the superordinate revelationism of neo-orthodoxy has driven theologians of our day to re-emphasize the conditioned character of all religions, including Christianity. Or perhaps the fact that most of contemporary academic life in the West is conducted on the grounds of Enlightenment presuppositions, which relegate religion to a matter of the second order, has prompted those who hope to be scholars and religious to treat their own religious convictions on two distinct and seldom related levels: within a framework of personal or communal confessionalism in their private lives, and within the conventional frameworks of modern academia in scholarly teaching and research. These individuals thus subordinate their deepest convictions to other considerations in what they pass on to the next generation, as if their convictions are not or could not be defended intellectually. Or it may be that in theological circles Romanticism has entirely carried the day. In the Romantic movement, religion was thought to be the expression of the soul's hidden rhythms—always intensely personal and entirely beyond the grasp of cold reason or stifling institutions. Whatever the reasons, a sometimes hidden and often overt presupposition of many who work in theological education is that, under critical examination, religion as an intellectual or social reality turns out to be a second-order, derivative, and epiphenomenal matter in human life, although the teachers of religion hold religious matters to be phenomenal in their own lives.

To be sure, a number of scholars on our faculty whose ideas we have studied recognize that, once a religion is established in a human psyche, in a society, or in a civilization, it becomes itself a motivational or cultural force in life, and may enter into a dialectical process of interaction with those "original," primary forces that gave it birth, influencing them as it is influenced by them. Others seem to hold that religion is important and interesting because its symbols, codes, and organizations can be "unpacked" to get at the "truly" significant or "more" interesting factors that they express, or because its coalesced symbols, codes, and organizational resources can be mobilized to help accomplish some "real" purpose in life—therapeutic wholeness, social integration, cultural cohesion, or a political-economic program. In any case, these understandings reinforce the view that the content and truth claims of a religion are not, in themselves, matters of the first order.

The problem can be stated this way: Religion is based on a fundamental presupposition that there is a metaphysical-moral realm that is real, transcendent to the empirical world, and simultaneously sufficiently present to human reflection and experience that it can be taken as the decisive point of reference for the understanding and guidance of empirical life and historical existence. Further, religion (all religions) presuppose that this metaphysical-moral reality has been sufficiently unveiled (that is, either revealed or discovered) so that humans can know something about it with enough clarity and security to take it as the foundation for belief and action without intellectual fraud or ethical duplicity. Thus, religion presumes a first-order reality of a metaphysical-moral sort, epistemologically accessible, that can be used to interpret and guide all second-order matters—such as therapeutic wholeness, social integration, cultural cohesion, and political-economic programs.

Many of those who work on questions of theological education today either invert the ascendancy of first-order and second-order matters, or quietly proceed as if it were perfectly clear to all that religion is a first-order matter, and that all we need to do is spell out its implications. That has been the dogmatic approach of every age and nearly every religion. Today, however, there are pervasive doubts that religion is of first-order import, or that, if it is, we could know how to make the case for its import in view of the great variety of religions that we can find in the world. These doubts create a suspicion about the sufficiency of this approach, one that raises questions about the character of any teaching or learning that deals with religion.

Views suspicious of first-order claims are not, of course, brand new. One can find them in philosophies of religion at least since Feuerbach, in theories of history at least since Marx, in epistemology at least since Hume, in aesthetics at least since Nietzsche, in the natural sciences at least since Darwin, and in the human sciences at least since Freud.[1] In all cases the doubt about religion involves a two-pronged argument: religion presents a false view of reality, and religion distorts morality. To be sure, religion may have some emotive import in that it poetically states the mystery of existence and touches the recesses of the heart, or it may provide the motivating zeal to resist oppression; but the metaphysical and moral claims are basically the residue of inadequate efforts of the past to cope with matters now best understood on other grounds. The sooner we can overcome religion's intellectual errors and its moral terrors, the better.

Such views are present not only among learned scholars who are the cultured despisers of religion. They are present in the churches, in the methods of seminary education, and among the students from all those cultures deeply influenced by European and American intellectual and social history. Even more, such views are officially established in the so-called Second World, and are being increasingly exported to the Third World (in somewhat different forms) at the hands of both the First and the Second Worlds, as well as by the adoption of these presuppositions on the part of Third World scholars, managers, political leaders, and revolutionaries. In many contexts, these views are used to explain or interpret the pervasive character of non-Christian religions. Theological educators often draw on these perspectives to expose the preconscious

---

1. This is not the place to enter into a prolonged discussion about the relative merits of Feuerbach, Marx, Hume, Nietzsche, Darwin, and Freud, of their precursors, or of their overt or covert heirs. A good bit of quite compelling literature already exists with regard to the basic argumentation. See, for example, Brian Hebblethwaite, *Christian Ethics in the Modern Age* (Philadelphia: Westminster Press, 1982). His footnote references are as valuable as his arguments.

biases in views held by the students or prevalent in the culture or to "unmask" what is "really going on" in the rise of various sects or cults. Such perspectives are of great help in acquainting people with some of the nonreligious influences and pressures that have shaped and do shape religion. The problem is that it is very difficult to take religious questions with fundamental seriousness if the methods by which the teachers teach and the ways in which students perceive that which is taught convey the notion that the content of religious claims is not of first-order importance on its own terms.

There may be, at present, no way to bypass the power of the Enlightenment and its Romantic aftermath. What may be very helpful here, however, is to suggest that the issues implicit in modern doubts about religion as a first-order matter ought to be made quite central to theological education so that students can understand what they are getting themselves into if they are also systematically exposed to the argumentation that raises questions about the adequacy of these views for understanding religion. Physicists, biologists, psychologists, anthropologists, economists, and political scientists are not reluctant to argue that the matters they investigate are of ultimate and decisive importance to life and well-being. Seldom, however, do seminaries or departments of theology consciously make the case for what they are about in the face of pervasive, critically based suspicion. If theologians are to carry on their tasks with a good conscience, and to nurture the next generation of leadership into matters that are truly and objectively important, then a self-conscious *apologia* will have to be developed.

IS RELIGION REALLY IMPORTANT?

It is possible that three approaches would be fruitful in laying the groundwork for an *apologia*. One would be to adopt the critical methods that have been developed on nonreligious or anti-religious grounds, and to see how far they can go in explaining and interpreting civilizational and cultural history, reported human experiences of transcendental reality or ethical demand, and cosmological perspectives on the meaning of the cosmos. This might properly be the special province of university departments of religion, and be a necessary prerequisite for seminary education. Several accents would be of particular importance: (1) the study of the history of civilizations with particular emphasis on the role that religion has played in shaping those civilizations; (2) the study of religion and the social sciences — that is, the psychodynamics, sociodynamics, and cultural dynamics of religious belief and the role that religion has played in shaping such dynamics; and (3) the study of the philosophy of myth and symbol, particularly as they enhance or inhibit the understanding of the cosmos and the place of humanity in it, and as they shape the way philosophy itself is undertaken. There are two reasons for studying religion through the spectacles of history, the social sciences, and philosophy, with a focus on the reciprocal influence of religion on civilizations, cultural contexts, and systematic thought. The first is that such study introduces religion to modern academic study and provides basic information about religions in relationship to the structures and forces thought to influence them or be influenced by them. The second reason for such study is that it poses the question of whether religion is a first-order matter that cannot be reduced to the study of history, anthropology, or philosophy.

If, in fact, these disciplines can account for religious phenomena rather exhaustively, then those of us who have given our lives to theological commitments, institutions, and scholarship should be quite frank about it and give up what we do. There is no reason to have centers of theological education (except as a kind of training ground for "party hacks" among those who share an unwarranted and indefensible opinion) if modern critical methods have in fact shown the derivative and epiphenomenal character of all that we do, think about, and teach. If, however, these critical methods cannot give an adequate account of such things, if religion is decisive for an understanding of civilizations, anthropology, and the cosmos, then it is incumbent upon us to make the case for what we do by turning the critical methods to their own presuppositions and showing that what they consider to be of first-order import is in fact of second-order import. The second approach, then, would be to show that religion (or some kinds or some aspects of religion) would have to be seen by historians, social scientists, and philosophers as itself of first import, and therefore necessary to every effort to interpret history, human individuals and societies, and philosophies. Given the pervasive suspicion about religion, these grounds would have to be argued not only metaphysically and morally, but in terms of the history of political economy, technology, law, and the arts, in terms of human psychology and community formation, and in terms of what can be philosophically defended.

In short, religion must be shown to be important for these areas of life. If religious leaders are not or cannot be prepared to understand and make these cases in the public domain, religion not only will be but ought to be relegated to secondary import, and what will be contextualized, globalized, and carried around the world with missionary zeal will be ideologies based on nonreligious foundations — ideologies that are sociopolitical, psychiatric, managerial, or technical, or based on race, class, nation, or gender.

Of course, if religion makes no fundamental difference, we should not fret about it; but if it does make a basic difference, then it should be a matter of considerable concern to all education. Further, if religion does make a difference, then theological education would demand a rather dramatic revolution in how we think about what we do — in our seminaries and in the churches and in the universities.

A third approach to religion and religious teaching would surely emerge out of efforts to move in this direction. It would be an approach that would admit candidly that much of what is called religion is indeed an epiphenomenon of other matters, deeply freighted with the projections of psychological, sociological, and anthropological needs or interests onto a cosmic screen, and claiming a metaphysical-moral universal truth and ethical validity that it does not have. But, to keep this approach from leading to the results of the first one, it would have to be claimed that not all religion is of that sort, that some of what we call religion is in fact a manifestation of a metaphysical-moral reality that can be, in some sense, known with relative clarity and security, and shown to be inherently true, at least in principle, and just in its effects when adopted. A critique of what is not valid requires some acquaintance with what is valid. Otherwise, we have only competing opinions, none of which can claim greater validity than any other. Such an approach requires that we ask whether there can be religions or specific religious matters within any particular religion that are more or less true and just as compared with those that are more or less false and wrong, and whether we can know the difference in ways demonstrable in scholarly discourse.

At this point, we need to note that insofar as theological education is genuine *education* in and about religious matters — and not indoctrination into a cult, a leap of blind faith, socialization into a subculture, mobilization for political action, or an exercise in therapy — and insofar as theological education is conducted as a *scholarly* enterprise for which we give academic degrees to certify that some people are prepared to preach and teach these matters in public — and is neither initiation into an arbitrary and idiosyncratic worldview nor a sophistical learning of skills about how to influence people without regard for the validity of what we say and do — theological education must, above all, center its life on the question of what is objectively true and just in religious matters. However widely indoctrination, socialization, political mobilization, therapy, initiation, and the development of skills play a role in learning, they are to be subordinated to, and subjected to evaluation according to, the intrinsic worth of their metaphysical, epistemological, moral, and sociohistorical content, which in the end must stretch beyond any particular malady or interest, local context, or cultural heritage.

Of course it must be acknowledged that — given the frailties of the human mind, the levels of our ignorance, and the constant perils of bias — much of what we identify as true and just is distorted and of less than universal import. And, since religious matters are often coalesced into highly complex symbolic forms with multiple levels of potential meaning, the difficulties of avoiding distortion are immense. In this whole area, we know that often the best we can do is to achieve some relative approximation of what is true and just, or, at the very least, to identify that which is least false and wrong. Nevertheless, it is of decisive importance whether we think what we are about is simply articulation of our own or our own group's condition-determined opinion, or whether we think that warrants can be given for that which we hold to be true and just, warrants that allow us to disqualify other opinions.

Decisive at this juncture is the question of what the criteria might be to discern the difference between that which is religiously true and just and that which is religiously false and wrong. The question is decisive because if it is not possible to know anything about the criteria with any degree of certainty, we are each trapped in our own religiously solipsistic world, and the critical assessment of religious matters in education is a fraud.

CAN THEOLOGY JUDGE RELIGIONS?

Simultaneously, insofar as theological education is *theological* education, it must surely take *theos* as its essential subject matter. This has a number of implications. For one, theological education must presume that what is true and just in religion is to be judged on the basis of whether or not the criteria are of God and capable of being "logically" discussed. Any theological education that does not take God and the *logos* of God as the central referents of all that it does is properly suspect as theological education. This, in turn, demands a second presumption: that some reality properly called *theos* exists and can be known in sufficient measure to be recognized as the central source and norm of what is true and just.

Still further, theologically focused education must presume that what it discusses is not the same as what is discussed on historical, social-scientific, or philosophical grounds, although it may be relevant to these, may learn from these, and may use similar methods in ferreting out decent warrants and criteria for what is true and just. These modes of cognition may, indeed, help establish the validity of claiming that religion is important, but it is doubtful whether they can finally aid in establishing the relative validity of any particular religion. In short, *theos*-centered education also presumes that God is not the same as history, humanity, or society, or our speculations about the cosmos, even if God, or the *logos* of God, is seen to be present in the world and decisive for the critical assessment and knowledge both of religion, as it exists in the world, and of the world itself. Were this not the case, we would not only have nothing to teach or learn in theological education beyond our own opinion, and nothing to call us to mission, nothing to globalize, and nothing to contextualize beyond that which we already are, have, and do. We would be trapped in the closed walls of "this-sidedness," confined to our own contexts, celebrated and codified in "contextualisms."

If it is possible to speak of theological education in these terms, then we may have found the deeper well from which all participants in our dialogues and all those views that we have surveyed can draw, for then we would have a basis for knowing what should be contextualized, globalized, and carried in mission; then we would have a basis for knowing something about spirituality, *praxis*, the construction of local theologies, sapiential knowledge, and the formation of identity in reflective practical ministry. Indeed, we may have found that center of indispensable knowledge that above all else needs to be mediated to every context in mission around the globe. For that would surely be of universal import and universal in character.

If, of course, it is not possible to know, study, teach, or learn anything about God or God's *logos* that can be discussed and taught reasonably, if it is only possible to have contextually conditioned opinions about God that could not, in any sense of the term, be "scientifically" warranted, then we may still wish to confess our faith, engage in our preferred rites of worship, tell other people about our beliefs, share our stories with as many people as will listen, and organize our lives around them. But we should be clear that our focus is on ourselves and on what we hold as opinion or folkway or folklore, just as others may hold atheistic and nonlogical positions with equal degrees of commitment and sincerity, or still others believe in multiple deities and spirits, each with its own stories and ritual obligations. If this is our focus, then our attempts at contextualization, globalization, and mission are surely a rather sophisticated form of religious imperialism.

One of the most subtle yet most significant shifts that has occurred in the last several hundred years of theological education is the shift in the very definition of the word "theology." It once meant the "science of God" but now means "reflection on faith." Whether we attribute this shift to Anselm's "faith seeking understanding," as some do, or to subsequent developments — Descartes' *cogito*, Hume's *dubito*, Pietism's *professio*, or Romanticism's *confessio* (as others have) — it has meant a relocation of our focus of concern. Many of the views that we have encountered in the first two parts of this study have a decided anthropocentric focus of the sort recently challenged by James Gustafson, among others.[2] They all seem to reflect a modern skepticism about theology as a science of God or of divine matters. In one sense, this skepticism today borders on the anti-intellectual protest against treating religious matters as having intellectual and cognitive content of any fateful importance.

It is reasonable to believe that many who are engaged in theological education are in fact convinced that they are involved in genuine education about that which is true and just, and that the decisive core of what they teach and learn is genuinely theological in that it "scientifically" represents what is reasonably to be said about God (and hence about God's "logos" — the "word" of freedom, love, grace, providence, care, law, purpose, self-disclosure, activity in history, etc., as Christians say is best known in Jesus Christ). Many may also hold that theology is the decisive way of assessing religions and the ordinary ways of human life and thought in the world. But it is doubtful whether many theological educators today have self-consciously made the case or even tried to make the case that such terms are proper ones to interpret the world. They may speak in these terms in chapel or at prayer while avoiding them or offering nontheological interpretations of their possible meanings in the classroom. Insofar as nontheological expositions of the meanings of theological terms allow the recognition of the importance of religion and bring normative categories to bear in the analysis, assessment, and ordering of historical, anthropological, and cosmological realities, few objections could be raised. Yet, if theological

---

2. Gustafson, *Ethics from a Theocentric Perspective*, 2 vols. (Chicago: University of Chicago Press, 1982 and 1985).

educators believe that a "science of God" is possible, they are seldom certain about how one would make a case for it, about what their own discipline has to do with it, and about the importance of conveying to theological students the warrants for taking what they teach about such matters with the seriousness that material may well deserve as a part of any such science.

Still, theological educators engage in such regular acts as evaluating papers, sermons, studies of historic figures or movements, and treatments of various religions and ethical arguments, and doing so not as if these were simply variant confessional statements to be assessed on the grounds of their internal coherence, consistency in argument, accuracy in the use of sources, literary excellence and clarity of expression, or their accord with what fits the situation of the author alone. Instead, grading involves assessment according to the relative truth and justice of the stances taken. Coherence, consistency, accuracy, clarity, and pertinence to the actual conditions and loyalties of the author count in any kind of written or oral expression, and incoherence, inconsistency, inaccuracy, lack of clarity, and irrelevance suggest that false, wrong, or bad work has been done. But theological educators also evaluate work done by students and colleagues according to standards that involve assessment of the metaphysical-moral adequacy of the confessional stances taken and of the conditions from which the author speaks. In the processes of assessment, it is presumed that what is produced by the student or scholar or pastor is more or less true or false, more or less right or wrong, and more or less good or evil in its implications; that it can be judged accordingly; that it is not simply a matter of opinion, preference, or background; and that it makes a difference in the church and the world. Indeed, the best theological educators presume that students and colleagues can offer insights or arguments that are not in accord with the ones the educators have taught but that are more true and just than what they previously thought, and consequently the educators must alter their views. What is unclear today is whether there are any warranted foundations for doing what we know we must do when we don't know how we know this or why we must do these things.

It should be candidly admitted that much of what has been said thus far about what would have to be included in a decent *apologia* — with all it involves in terms of responding to the critique of religion since the Enlightenment, the privatization of religion in Romanticism, and the general crisis of whether there are any foundational points of reference in education at all — is rooted in modern Western intellectual history. But the questions are not Western only.

They are simply exacerbated by the experience of peoples around the world who are acquainting themselves with a wider ecumenical community, growing more alert to imperialistic, ethnocentric, and androcentric tendencies in their own pasts, interacting in new ways with the world's religions, and seeking a global vision that must be inclusively sensitive to multiple contexts and yet compelling in regard to truth and justice.

WARRANTED WISDOM

It may be useful to provide a somewhat alternative account of the history of theological education than has thus far been presented, and to ask whether the central dimensions of that larger history have, or should, now come to an end. As most of the voices we have heard have already indicated, how we view the past has rather extensive implications for how we view the present and the future. That will also be the case here as we try to present an interpretation deeper and broader than we have heretofore seen. This interpretation may allow us to see our present situation in a somewhat different light than some of our faculty members, consultants, and theorists have suggested. It will also lead us into our next chapters on the nature and character of "orthodoxy" and "praxiology."

The core thesis of this interpretation is quite simple: in the history of Western Christianity, and hence in the dominant patterns of theological education, there have been two great moments since biblical days, and they are related. Within these great moments, there are a rather large number of smaller changes, some of which have been taken to be of greater import than they are. And the question before us is whether the changes we now face in the new accents on contextualization and globalization ought to be understood as some of the smaller changes, or as a new great moment inviting us to set aside, or to recover and recast, that which the two preceding great moments have rendered.

We have previously referred to the two great moments. The first one is the encounter of the biblical tradition with the Greco-Roman world to form the roots of Christian thought, ethics, and organization, and in some respects the foundations of Western civilization. This "moment" can be characterized as the Mideastern and Mediterranean moment, and dated from the Council of Jerusalem — which approved the encounter of the biblical tradition with non-Christian peoples, philosophies, and practices — to the General Council of 451, after the fall of Rome. It stretches, in other words, from Paul to Augustine. The second moment involves the recovery and basic recasting of that heritage in the transition from the Middle Ages to the dawn of modernity. This "moment" can be dated from the Council of Constance to the founding of the missionary societies in the late eighteenth century. It reaches, in other words, from Wycliffe and Huss to Jonathan Edwards and includes the great reformations of Europe and the Americas. Each of these "moments" is obviously quite elongated, and each has been treated in enormous detail. But for our purposes, certain salient features can be identified.[3]

The first moment was formed by the convergence of several major developments. On the basis of a profound quest for a coherent *theoria* of *praxis* and *poesis,* Greek philosophy developed; on the basis of the urgent need of the Roman Empire to hold its vast territories together, a new cosmopolitan polity developed; and on the basis of a new revelation of God's *logos* in time that both confirmed the Hebraic expectations of redeeming grace in historical experience and made the truth of the God of the Hebrew Scriptures accessible to all the peoples of the world, a new religion arose. Many were caught up in the spirit of this movement. They took its claims to be true and just and therefore necessary for the salvation of humanity from the mere "this-sidedness" of life, from ignorance, sin, and death, and they propagated these claims in missionary activity in a great number of contexts throughout the world then known to them. These believers adopted Greek philosophy and Roman polity to express and give ordered coherence to the core of their religious vision. They also found that the truth and justice now unveiled and grasped by *theoria* could not be organized, expressed, or put into practice without drawing from the resources

---

3. A somewhat parallel account of these two moments is also decisive for liberation theology, as one can see in Gustavo Gutiérrez, *A Theology of Liberation,* trans. Inda Caridad, Sr., and John Eagleson (Maryknoll, N.Y.: Orbis Books, 1973), pp. 4-6. Gutiérrez argues that "theology as wisdom" first developed essentially as "a meditation on the Bible, geared toward spiritual growth . . . [and in] dialogue with . . . Platonic and Neoplatonic categories . . . [wherein] it found a metaphysics which stressed the existence of a higher world." That broke down, he says, when "spirituality" became separated from the theological task. Subsequently, he argues, "theology as rational knowledge" developed as an "intellectual discipline, born of the meeting of faith and reason." That, in turn, broke down when theology became "an ancillary discipline of the magisterium of the Church." In the face of these breakdowns, Gutiérrez calls for theology as "critical reflection on praxis." He then turns to those modes of thought already examined in this volume (especially in Chapter 6) as the core of the present and the future, although the question is whether what he presents is the core of the necessary reconstruction, as he claims, or a continuing manifestation of the breakdown.

of *praxis* and *poesis*. Using the resources of *praxis* and *poesis* to articulate key presuppositions of *theoria* in a way that could be understood outside Hebraic frames of reference, the leaders of the movement refined and critically assessed what was essential and universal and what was accidental and merely contextual in the new religious movement itself, and exposed the false elements of the numerous other religious orientations and movements that were widespread in that ancient context.

This movement produced a book — indeed, a number of books, and included those in a new testament — that, over time, the movement determined to be of definitive importance because it pointed accurately to that which was, in fact, universally true and just. In that book we find direct continuity with the Hebraic traditions from which it drew. Indeed, as the book met challenges, it became increasingly clear that the Hebraic Scriptures were not to be set aside but were to be seen as indispensable to the understanding of what was true and just also. In shaping that understanding, however, the movement did not simply repeat the contents of that book. It thematized the contents in the formation of authoritative teaching by the critical use of *theoria*.

Simultaneously, the movement developed organizational forms that drew from the synagogue structures of those who followed the Hebraic Scriptures, and from the polity and conceptions of ethics and law that governed the Roman Empire, especially under the imprint of the heirs of the Greek philosophers, the Stoics, who held that there was a universal, knowable moral law. The movement found that if aspects of its message could not be stated, defended, and enacted universally in multiple contexts, then they were not essential to the message.

Not all knew the Scriptures, Greek philosophy, or Roman polity. For many, cultic practice was the mark of religion. And in such matters, major decisions had to be made about what forms of ritual best expressed the truth and justice claimed, and what policies should be developed toward local cultic practices.

There were many debates about the proper conjoining of these traditions, and many such debates continue today. Further, we know that many of the efforts were distorted by misogyny, ethnocentrism, economic interest, and temptations to cultural imperialism. Many variations existed, and a great number of them seem to have been accepted as being within tolerable limits, if not taken as normative for all. Nevertheless, there were boundaries, and judgments were made when the variations seemed to be idiosyncratic or when some local belief or practice was projected as absolute.

What is important for our purposes is that all theological education has its roots in precisely this conjunction. Other religions also have teaching and training methods and insightful content developing out of the interaction of several religiocultural traditions. But here was the formation of a body of doctrine, understood as "warranted wisdom," linked with a powerful piety, held to be important for all humanity — including, but not exclusively for, those who were ill-educated, poor, oppressed, weak, female, and outcast — and used as a guide for the definition of normative thought, experience, and *praxis*.

What was taught to and by leaders of the movement in the patristic and apologetic writers and in doctrinal development was an amalgam of the Hebraic *logos* of *theos* as actualized in time and history and articulated in the canon, Greek *theoria,* Roman polity, and elements of cultic practice from the then-known world religions, all of which were selected and assessed according to the best standards of universal significance that could be found. Leaders were systematically exposed to these materials so that they could effectively discern what was true and just about religion and what was not, so that they could contextualize the truth of the movement's message among peoples who were not otherwise a part of it, and so that they could bring the critical tools of assessment to bear on other religions and on the ways in which the Christian message was appropriated and implemented in life. The dominant concern was that understanding, experience, and practices be of catholic significance. Religion on this basis attempted to give inner coherence to one of the most complex, cosmopolitan civilizations the world has known. And it almost succeeded.[4]

Finally, however, this religion was not fully equal to the task. It is quite possible that the *theoria* of the Greeks, the polity and law of the Romans, and the cultic policies of the religions in that environment were less universal than they pretended to be and than the movement thought they were. Insofar as the *logos* of *theos* became subordinated to these, the movement had to oppose as many features of its context as it could support, especially when the elites of that civilization attempted to use that religion as a tool, a cement, to hold together what was grounded on these less-than-universal foundations, and tried to impose it as universal. Here again, as we see in such writings as those of Athanasius, attempts had to be made to discern that which was in accord with universal

---

4. See Max L. Stackhouse, *Ethics and the Urban Ethos* (Boston: Beacon Press, 1973), especially chaps. 5-7.

truth and justice, and could thus be foundational for personal, cultural, and civilizational formation, and that which was not.

Whether or not these believers or others made errors is not at issue at the moment. The point is that a "warranted wisdom" of theology was created, rooted in the church's discernments of certain Scriptures as authentic witnesses to God's *logos* and utilizing in the process the best available theory, polity, and cultic policy these believers could discover. This creation of theology as "warranted wisdom" carried on in an organized community for the sake of the whole world represented one of the most important contributions any religion has made to the history of civilizations. All branches of Christian theological education — and, indeed, all forms of religious education that claim to have something to say that is defensible in the public domain and in intercultural terms — draw, through the use of *theoria, praxis,* and *poesis,* from this elongated "moment." Here is the root of *apologia.*

The moment came to something of an end when the Greco-Roman world collapsed under the pressures of civilizational failure. Much of what we now call the West reverted to various local paganisms, but what had been achieved was preserved in missionary efforts and in scholarly monasteries, later to be resurrected in the second great moment.

GROUNDED *SCIENTIA*

In the late Middle Ages, the missionary, monastic, and intellectual centers of Christianity found that the surrounding contexts of life were in such disarray that they were able to begin reasserting that which had lain dormant and protected since the collapse of the Roman Empire. And from those centers emerged the idea of a new, coordinated synthesis of learning which not only could allow the movement's organization — the church — new freedom to follow its own principles, but could begin influencing the exterior patterns of culture and civilization in new ways. This began the reconstruction of intellectual, organizational, and cultic life, the bases for the transformation of family life, of economic institutions, of law and government, of music and medicine. Rooted at first in papal reform, it soon gave rise to new conciliar development.[5]

The first task in carrying out this reconstruction was educa-

---

5. I have tried to point to the universal importance of these developments in my *Creeds, Society, and Human Rights: A Study in Three Cultures* (Grand Rapids: Eerdmans, 1984), especially pp. 40-48.

tion — indeed, theological education. The importance of this development has been noted by historians for centuries, but it has played little part in modern reflections on theological education. But, in some ways, as most recently documented by H. J. Berman, this "revolution in the church" was "closely connected with the revolution in agriculture and commerce [intimately related to what were to become technological and corporate patterns of economic life], the rise of cities and of kingdoms . . . [and therefore eventually of "nations" in the modern sense], the rise of the universities and of scholastic thought, and other major transformations which accompanied the birth of the West . . . during the next eight centuries."[6]

What happened in this process can be accounted for in substantial measure by the rediscoveries, re-examinations, and receptions of the ancient texts in which the deposits of the first great "moment" were to be found. However, the legacies of Israel, Greece, and Rome survived less by the continuity of their direct influence (since they were no longer living, immediately clear options in life) than by the fact that they were adopted and adapted in a critical and selective process, put together in new combinations with each other and with the ideational, cultic, and cultural practices of their new (mostly Continental and to some degree English) environments. Believing that religion is the most significant aspect of life, and holding that knowledge of the *logos* of *theos* is possible (within limits), modern theology was born — the first of the litter, and in some ways the mother of those forms of modern jurisprudence, art, medicine, astronomy, physics, and social sciences that are universal in influence. The new combinations were worked out on the basis of theologically grounded *scientia,* the systematic study of a body of learning undertaken to gain reliable knowledge by bringing specific information under general laws and discovering new truth by trustworthy methods. On this basis was founded a new kind of *apologia* for the basic beliefs and normative practices by which life was to be governed — a "critical *apologia,*" one usually in continuity with the warranted doctrines of the earlier moment but sometimes in sharp tension with them.

The story is much too complicated to tell in this study. What

---

6. Berman, *Law and Revolution: The Formation of the Western Legal Tradition* (Cambridge: Harvard University Press, 1984), p. 23 et passim. Berman provides not only a valuable argument but an indispensable bibliography for understanding the importance of this period. Compare especially Max Weber, *Economy and Society: An Outline of Interpretive Sociology,* 3 vols., trans. E. Fischoff et al., ed. Guenther Roth and Claus Wittich, 4th ed. (New York: Bedminster Press, 1968), 3: 1212-1367.

can be suggested by this sketch, however, is that theological education was decisive for the history of what we now call "the West," and that it is, indeed, as much the progenitor of the West as any other single influence. This is not to say that it succeeded. In fact, it often failed and failed miserably. At every point along the way, the new combinations of the legacies of Israel, Greece, Rome, and the European peoples were interpreted in the most self-serving ways to make them little more than the ideological mask by which to legitimate the interests of one or another people, class, race, gender, or political group. Some of these combinations ended up being little more than biblicism, echoes of Greek humanism, or new forms of imperialism such as Rome had embodied. Further, it can of course be pointed out that the French Revolution, the Industrial Revolution, and the Communist revolution were also major, and often better-remembered, sources of modernity. But what is notable about all of these is that they based their cases on one or another kind of *scientia* that was founded in this new form of critical *apologia*. That is, what bound all these movements together was the underlying conviction that there was something like a universal truth and justice that could be known in sufficient measure to base normative thought and practice on them, and that anyone who was to be taken seriously had to make the case for her or his view on grounds that could withstand critical scrutiny. But positions taken and actions planned that do meet this test can be — ought to be — contextualized everywhere.

The reputed decline of the influence of religion, and indeed of theology, in the modern world may well be due to the fact that theological education began to think of itself, and to allow the world to think of it, as utterly beyond the range of "warrant" for its "wisdom," and without a "ground" for its *scientia*. It allowed itself, for a time, to become trapped in the protest against all universalistic criteria. The nominal, the immediate, the direct, the subjective, the existential, the historically variant, the pietistic, and the particular became the focus, and we are today reaping the whirlwind in the form of a number of highly sophisticated contextualisms; as the wisdom of the first great moment became temporarily obscured by the resurgence of paganism in the "Dark Ages," the *scientia* of the second moment has been fractured into a thousand fideistic sects, none able to tell us why we should take them seriously. Indeed, some forms of Romanticism have celebrated this situation as the triumph of diversity, pluralism, and "natural" spirituality over all pretentious claims about truth and justice. Nevertheless, it is beginning to dawn on theologians today, as it did on theological faculties of the past centuries, that nearly all if not all the enduring contributions have been made by those who have attempted to instruct the church and the world about what would and could count as warranted wisdom and grounded *scientia*. At their best, these were linked with profound piety, sensitive to contextual realities, and dedicated to a mission of global reach. That has been the real stuff of theology and of education. Lesser views have come and gone with great rapidity, as a great number of the current fads are likely to do.

COSMOPOLITAN APOLOGETICS

If anything like this sketch of the deeper roots of theological education is accurate, it suggests that we may be on the brink of a third great moment. In some tribal areas of the world, to be sure, something like the recapitulation of the early church's experience is taking place as peoples learn how to encounter universalistic philosophies and polities not based on tribal or ethnic identities. Some of these battles are being fought in terms of cultic practices. Can traditional drumming be used in worship? Should weddings be performed on astrologically inauspicious days? On such issues, warranted wisdom is being sought. And, in other areas such as the Iberian peninsula, Latin America, and the Philippines, a belated Reformation of dramatic proportions is taking place as Catholicism emerges from a residual "Dark Ages," this time in alliance with various attempts to link Christianity with new theories of social solidarity and nationalism. Many are seeking a grounded *scientia*, but are likely to find, as have several branches of Protestantism, that science and nationalism joined to one or another form of social orthopraxy or cultural-linguistic poetics will bring little more than fragmentation into competing enclaves of confessionalism. Indeed, the "protestant" character of the transformations now taking place in many regions of the world dominated by magisterial Christianity is what makes these regions presently fascinating to those branches of theology still echoing the sixteenth century, Barth, Bonhoeffer, and Bultmann.

It is possible, however, that the front edge of a new, third moment is at hand also. It may well be that we can date this moment, anticipated by those parts of the missionary movement that resisted imperialism,[7] from the Tambaram Conference of 1938.

---

7. See William R. Hutchison, *Errand to the World: American Protestant Thought and Foreign Missions* (Chicago: University of Chicago, 1987). See also Max L. Stackhouse, "Missions/Missionary Activity," in vol. 9 of the *Encyclopedia of Religion*, ed. Mircea Eliade et al. (New York: Macmillan, 1987), pp. 563-70.

There, near Madras in South India, Christians from those great and complex cultures deeply influenced by Hinduism, Buddhism, and Islam met in a world conference for the first time. They recognized that they would have to wrestle, as most of their Western colleagues had not done, with the meaning of "the Christian message in a non-Christian world,"[8] and with the importance of the church as essential to the message. M. M. Thomas has recently summarized the significance of these developments:

> It was through grappling with . . . [these accents], and going beyond [them] that the churches in Asian-African lands had to develop their own indigenous forms of Christian theology, church life and social and evangelistic mission, in which devotion to ultimate Truth, Jesus Christ, could be kept central and religious values and secular ideological insights from other sources could be reinterpreted and affirmed. Meanwhile, movements of church union . . . [reversing centuries of fragmentation and division] got strengthened . . . ; and the churches launched their own missionary societies. . . . All these could be done . . . because . . . [Christian theology] also kept the vision of the ecumenical character of the church and the universality of the gospel before all the churches.[9]

The point of all this is to suggest that we face a new cosmopolitan age, one significantly different in scope and complexity than Christianity has ever met before, and yet one that has strong similarities to what has gone before. Christianity now faces world religions that are deeper, richer, and broader than any that it has previously encountered (or developed). Further, Christianity now confronts cultures and civilizations which have also developed complex systems of philosophy, law, technology, and science that have been — in shaping people's minds, societies, and natural environments — as powerful and pervasive as any in world history. The question is whether, in such a moment, a cosmopolitan *apologia* is possible. Christianity faces again the old question in the presence of new pluralisms: Why should anyone believe it?

Note that we face the question *again*. That is in fact the question which the two previous great moments of the faith faced. And they answered by making the case as well as it could be made — in the face of all doubts, suspicions, and contrary views — that Christianity is basically true and just. That is, it is internally

---

    8. This phrase is, of course, the title of Heinrich Kraemer's famous lectures delivered at Tambaram and published by Harper & Row (1938).
    9. Thomas, *Recalling Ecumenical Beginnings* (Delhi: I.S.P.C.K., 1987), p. 67.

coherent and consistent, it corresponds to reality, and it is, rightly understood, more compelling to the mind than any other metaphysical-moral claim. Further, it is just. That is, it not only contains the fundamental vision of how life ought to be lived, but it leads those who believe it to seek a righteous, peaceful, and compassionate pattern of life. The first great apologetic effort to struggle with these questions left us with a vision of warranted wisdom, the second with a quest for a grounded *scientia*. On the whole, our forebears took on the questions and thought patterns of their era, and showed that Christianity could more adequately respond to the issues of their ages than could any other way of understanding life. Their answers respond less well to the questions of our era, and that is why we must have a renewed, and genuinely cosmopolitan, apologetics today. But we too shall have to meet the twin tests that every apologetic must face. Does it tell the truth, so far as humans can tell it? And does it lead to justice, so far as humans can live it?

As we shall see, the question of whether we shall be able to develop such an apologetics forces us to ask the question of orthodoxy and the question of praxiology. That is, we shall have to inquire whether we think we can reliably say anything cross-culturally and cross-religiously about what is theologically true. Orthodoxy, taken up as a question, is the issue of whether some views, opinions, claims, and — finally — religions are more true than any others. And we shall have to ask whether it is possible, on Christian grounds, to know what is just, to develop a basic theory that can and should guide human behavior. That is the question of praxiology. We shall take up each question in turn in an attempt to identify what we would have to believe if we held that a Christian orthodoxy and praxiology, and therefore a Christian apologetic, were possible.

CHAPTER 10

Orthodoxy?

In the previous chapter, it was argued that modern thought and education demand an *apologia* for any who take religious matters as normative, for those who believe that religion is an independent variable in the formation of individuals and civilizations, for those who think that theology is the proper science to critically evaluate religions, and for those who recognize that we face a new era of encounter with the world's religions and cultures. Two issues are at stake, as we have seen. First is the issue of whether "ideas," especially those of a "metaphysical-moral" character, are in fact influential forces in the dynamics of life and social history. And second is the fundamental issue as to whether it is possible to develop criteria that are "warranted" or "grounded" or genuinely "cosmopolitan." Such an *apologia* demands encounter with and knowledge of the world's religions and how they influence the life and thought of individuals and of entire civilizations. Further, insofar as these matters are treated in the context of advanced, or professional, education, and not simply as primary nurture, socialization, or acculturation into some specific faith (which also has its place), the metaphysical-moral vision that is the constituting core of every particular religion demands assessment on its merits. That is, it has to be shown that what any particular religious vision points to is either more or less true or false, and that it either enhances or inhibits a just moral life.

It was also argued in the previous chapter that the way in which religion is to be tested in these matters is theological, a term by which we mean the ordered discipline rooted in reliable knowledge of that which is ultimately and universally real (God), although different from both material reality and human invention, and accessible to reasoned discourse *(logos)*. Unless theology in this sense is possible, theological education is impossible and ought to be given up. And, finally, it was suggested that theological education involving "warranted wisdom" and "grounded *scientia*" is the product of the two great historic fusions of biblical, philosophical, sociocultural, and cultic materials which, over long periods of time, deeply influenced the formation of modern, cosmopolitan civilization, although these efforts were partly defeated by fragmentations, distortions, and repudiations of these fusions, and by their frequent premature identification of the truth and justice of God with one or another highly relative aspect of philosophical, social, or cultural life. Finally, it was proposed that a new cosmopolitan apologetics is required to face the challenges of our era, to be faithful to our past, and to secure the foundations for theological education.

WHAT'S AT STAKE?

To put these issues another way, the question is whether theology as the warranted knowledge of God and the *logos,* of what is ultimately and universally metaphysically true and ethically just, is possible. Such a question is fateful for all forms of religious studies and theological education that do not reduce the object of study to something other than itself and do not reduce education to indoctrination into some unwarranted or unjustifiable contextualist perspective.

Let us note, however, that in speaking of the history of theological education, we pointed not to the multifarious forms of religious training that have been developed among the world religions and the many philosophical and sociocultural contexts in which these appear, but to Christian religious history in its philosophical and sociocultural environments. That is because theology as *warranted* wisdom and theology as grounded *scientia* survived, developed, and flourished primarily in the context of this particular religion. To be sure, we should remember that in the medieval period, theology also developed to quite profound, and in some ways unsurpassed, levels in Islam and Judaism. And we should bear in mind that both Hindu and Buddhist philosophers and commentators have, in their own histories, reached intellectual subtleties quite as astounding as those that can be found in anything produced by the West. It simply cannot be said that Maimonides,

Abū 'Alī ibn Sīnā (Avicenna), Nāgārjuna, Shankara, and Rāmānuja are any less profound religiously than, for example, Augustine, Thomas, and Calvin. It is also the case that classical, Renaissance, Enlightenment, and contemporary Marxist philosophers have developed metaphysical-moral visions (or at least epistemological theories implying such visions) that have influenced individuals, civilizations, and education as profoundly as religious teachings have. And it cannot be posited or believed that the piety of Christians is any deeper or wider than that of adherents of any of these other religions, or that Christian holy texts are held in any greater or lesser regard as "unveilings" of ultimate truth and righteousness than the texts to which these religions turn. Nor should it be held that philosophies are less nuanced or more pure in religions other than Christianity, or that human wisdom is less insightful or more free from the taints of interest. This being the case, it will not suffice to engage in an *apologia* for religion or theology in general; we will have to show why, if we call for globalization and contextualization concerns, we should engage in *Christian* theological education. Why not adopt one of these other perspectives, or refuse to engage in mission wherever they are alive and active?

The answer to this question is important, for what is at stake is not only the study of religion and its importance, not only the claim that criteria can be found by which to assess that which is true and just in religion, and not only that these criteria are to be found in the *logos* of *theos,* but specifically whether it makes any difference whether we are Christian. Is it in any fundamental sense important to truth and justice in civilizations that the Christian religion be embraced around the globe and contextualized where it is not already present? The answer is also important for understanding what Christian theological education is about as it purports, at least, to train ministers and missionaries what and how to think, to do, and to be in ways that they can carry Christianity to others. The direction of thought taken in the last chapter and in this one, as prompted by those discussions reported in Parts I and II of this volume, implies that preparation for ministry in mission in a contextually sensitive and globally aware way involves familiarity with those essential matters that are distinctive to Christianity, and the ability to account for their importance in the face of the strongest contrary views.

While many other responsibilities inevitably fall to any institution that undertakes Christian theological education — such as learning how to sort out complex emotional conflicts, preparing people to communicate effectively, and developing skills for the conduct of worship and public prayer and for the management of ecclesiastical institutions — Christian theological education that does not put a high priority on preparation for these wider and deeper encounters in a way that can also be conveyed to simple believers is neither serious nor alert to contemporary life. For people in churches all over the world do and increasingly will encounter these challenges to Christianity through business, legal, medical, scientific, and international labor organizations, and through the much less exalted forms of pop psychology, the mass media, new neighbors of a different faith, and the "new religions" (that is, the "evangelical" forms of Hinduism, Buddhism, and Islam proselytizing around the world, such as Hare Krishna, Transcendental Meditation, Sakka Gakkai, the Black Muslims, etc.). In other words, the chief reason for seminaries to exist is to prepare individuals for adult religious education in a specifically Christian theological mode, to benefit both those who are already members of the Christian churches, and those clerical and lay missionaries who minister to those who are not. And that, above all else, is what ministry must involve if contextualization, globalization, and mission are to be taken as touchstones of our common vocation.

This implies, of course, that ministers are first of all to be theologians and theological ethicists in residence among people of multiple contexts, equipped to preach and teach, organize and persuade, critically evaluate and defend as appropriate, and represent in cultic forms of *poesis* and concrete forms of *praxis* those genuinely cosmopolitan theories of God's truth and justice that can be reliably known and contextualized in every culture, society, and civilization, in the face of alternative religious, philosophical, and social orientations that are less true and less just.

It is obvious that such a focus demands asking whether or not there is some correct understanding of religious truth and some kind of living that involves the right practice of justice. If a center of theological education is a Christian one, the presumption is made that some basic Christian doctrines are universally true and that some basic Christian guidelines for behavior are, on the whole, accurate reflections of how the true God wants us to live rightly. These are held to be so in a way that other religions and metaphysical-moral visions are not, or at least not fully. We call right belief orthodoxy. This is not to say that all that passes as orthodoxy among Christians is in fact true. Indeed, some things that have been said to be orthodoxy are frankly ridiculous, indefensible, and demonstrably not faithful to core affirmations of the faith. Nor is it to say that there is empirical proof that Christians have greater knowledge of the truth simply because they call themselves Christian, or are more intellectually honest and more committed to justice than adherents of other religions. That mildly contrite body of sinners whom we call Christians surely fail to apprehend the deepest truths of their own commitments and betray the principles of their own vision of justice at least as often as do adherents of other religions or the most subtle of philosophers. To make these judgments, of course, one has to have a vivid sense of what is defensible, not ridiculous, faithful, and demonstrable — or, in other words, a sense of what *is* orthodox.

It is possible, in fact, that under modern conditions Christianity is more culpable on these points than are other religions and philosophies, precisely because Christianity — believing that it is the most true and most just of all religions and having shaped a civilization with immense intellectual, technological, economic, and political power — is inclined to use its extraordinary power to demand obedience to its misapprehensions of truth and its betrayals of justice as much as it demands obedience to its genuinely warranted and critically examined doctrines and moral principles. Christians may also celebrate the earlier influences that the faith has had on the foundations of modern life and allow those aspects of modernity that remain pagan or that have escaped any continuing rootage in anything of theological import to be uncritically baptized. The public policies and political rhetoric that emerge from so-called Christian nations and are frequently wrapped in the sanctity of Christian language make this point rather obvious.

Nevertheless, there is little reason to have a theological school that is self-consciously Christian and dedicated to contextualization, globalization, and mission if its wisdom is not genuinely warranted, or if the chief tenets of this religion are not grounded in a *scientia* defensible in public discourse, or if it makes no great deal of difference whether or not one believes its purported truth rightly in disparate times and places. And there is no justification for a theological school to teach leaders of the next generation to engage in witness for justice in the social, political, economic, and technological arenas of life that it finds increasingly all over the world if its ethics are not just, demonstrably important for historical existence, and decisive for ordered, free, compassionate, and responsible living in human communities.

In short, theological education must not only take the importance of religion as a primary topic, and seek the foundational criteria by which the adequacy of particular religions can be assessed in a scholarly way proper to education. It must not only take *logos* and *theos* as points of reference, presuming that something reliable can be known about these in all contexts of the world. Theological education must also claim that the specifically Christian vision of metaphysical-moral reality is normative, can be learned and taught in a disciplined fashion, and is decisive for how other fields of knowledge may be organized, for how every sector of life might best be lived, and for dialogue with the other philosophies and religions of the world.

These are rather large claims. Here they are stated in quite direct terms — terms that many theological educators today shrink from using. We are aware that a pretentiousness can attend the making of such claims, and that vicious intolerance has sometimes been unleashed by some who have made comparable claims. And yet, when these claims are not stated so forcefully, they tend to remain just as operative, only less open to discussion, examination, and assessment. Or, without such clarity, Christian theological education in fact comes to an end, and one or another form of sectarian or confessionalist indoctrination is all that takes place. Today, the latter is the case in numerous instances.

The most visible arena where this is true is in the fundamentalist Bible colleges. There it is not doubted that religion is important, or that metaphysical matters are discussible, or that the foundation for all learning is *theos* and *logos,* or that Christianity contains the final truth. But these schools have not yet passed through the second "moment" of theological education. They develop no *scientia* that is grounded, even if they rely on Scripture and selected bits of "warranted wisdom" and develop elaborate rationalized schemes to explain everything in biblicistic terms. Thus, they provide no basis for new encounter with the world's philosophies and religions; for engagement with modern jurisprudence, science, music, or medicine; for evaluation of the Enlightenment or the new secular religions, including Marxism; or even for grasping the meanings of the Reformation — from which they draw only the principle of *sola scriptura,* but do so in a way that the Reformers would consider heretical. Their primary response is overt repudiation of all other options and covert eisegesis in the practice of this one. Certain contemporary developments in Roman Catholic seminaries which demand that the preparation of priests for ministry be confined to indoctrination into that which the magisterium has promulgated, and that it not be subject to a critical *scientia,* tend in somewhat the same direction, although obviously in different terms. Here, the emphasis (as we saw earlier in Chapters 4 and 7) is not on *sola scriptura* but on *sola dogmata.* Neither will suffice.

More subtle, but just as insidious, is the opposite tendency (as we have seen also in Chapters 7 and 8). This is the widespread tendency to engage in sectarian indoctrination of a quite different sort. Here, neither *sola scriptura* nor *sola dogmata* is taken as the point of reference; *sola fide*, in the form of *poesis*, is. In this view, neither the rationalized use of proof texts nor the magisterial authority of those who govern the church defines the core meanings of doctrine; such definition is done by the cultural-linguistic scholar or the phenomenologist, reflecting on a particular community's religious discourse in its sociohistorical context. But as we saw, and as George Lindbeck notes, doctrine in this view can "affirm nothing about extra-linguistic and extra-human reality."

If either the fundamentalist or the magisterial view or these representations of "post-Liberal" views are the case, theological education is crude or subtle indoctrination, a raw or sophisticated form of catechesis. The warrants for the doctrines taught are entirely internal to what is believed in the first place and to the authorities taken as valid by the doctrines. Orthodoxy is what a particular community or communities decide it means to participate in their identity, and is malleable as any community expands, constricts, or otherwise revises its doctrines.

As such perspectives have been debated and discussed in this seminary over the past few years, grave doubts have been raised about their adequacy. The difficulty is less what they include than what they exclude. No one, I think, is unaffected by one or another of these perspectives. It does seem to be the case that some experiences simply are not accessible unless one has a cultural-linguistic framework in which to experience them. It is also surely true that basic frameworks of meaning modulate over time and in encounter with new peoples, perspectives, and problems. Who can doubt that it is unlikely that one can comprehend the meaning of any doctrine if one does not know its grammar, its intratextual and intracontextual references and relationships? And that there is an inevitable confessional element in all religious belief is beyond dispute.

But questions have been raised about whether this view does not in fact exclude too much. Doctrines are almost always set forth in highly symbolic language, and symbolic language not only is useful in guiding *praxis*, not only presents a cultural-linguistic perspective, or broadens our phenomenological horizons and evokes and provokes profound experiences. It also grasps or points to (as other modes of discourse do not) what is held to be real — ultimately, universally, metaphysically, and morally. And because reality is at stake, symbols and doctrines can surely be tested in substantive measure by their capacity to reveal, evoke, lend coherence to, and evaluate profound experience and the right ordering of thought and intentional action. Only insofar as symbols and doctrines do this are they normative. The symbolic structure, if it is to be judged as valid at all, contains multiple levels of cognitive content that can be sorted and tested, in some measure, by conceptual analysis and propositional formulation.

In relation to the issues central to this study, it has become increasingly clear that most of the perspectives we have examined probably cannot provide a basis for mission — even if they can aid in understanding some dynamics of contextualization and globalization. Instead, another step will have to be taken, which could be called the quest for a post-Liberal orthodoxy. It is an attempt to show that key Christian doctrines are, in fact, true and just and important for all peoples in all conditions. We are aware that a case has to be made that what Christian theological education is about is of sufficient universal significance that we can be relatively certain that we have something worth bringing in mission to various contexts around the globe.

Note that in our stating of this concern, a language shift has taken place. We do not here speak of fundamentalist, evangelical, Roman Catholic, liberal, or conservative perspectives. The adjective is "Christian." The use of this term attempts to point to those doctrines on which theological education hinges: if they are not held to be true, theological education cannot be held to be Christian. In this, we follow the "minimalist" hints suggested to us by Collison in Chapter 4, although we take them in somewhat different directions.

FOUR DOCTRINES

The way that Christians try to articulate truth and to set forth the guidelines for *praxis* is by doctrine.[1] In sacrament, prayer, communion, ministry, and mission, Christians attempt to encounter the truth as a living reality. But when Christians want to write or talk about truth, as we do in all formal educational settings, we turn to doctrine. Doctrine, of course, means teaching, and every act of teaching is the "highlighting" (or "glorifications") of an "opinion," a *doxa*. At its best, not only is teaching faithful to what has been

---

1. See Charles Hefling, Jr., *Why Doctrines?* (Cambridge: Cowley Publications, 1984).

taught, but warrants can be given for it; it can be tested in experience, and it is able to withstand critical examination. When this is the case, it is "straight" — orthodox — teaching.

What passes for orthodoxy is not always so. Various churches and religious writers have set forth, as orthodoxy, doctrines that are parochial, pedantic, far from universal in significance, and sometimes simply tawdry. Furthermore, there has always been a tension between those who see orthodoxy as a total diagram for thought and life, and those who see it as a setting of exterior boundaries within which a wide variety of doctrines and opinions may be set forth. In the latter view, orthodoxy is not a total game plan for thinking and living, but the delimitation of a playing field within which serious and reality-oriented discourse can take place with justifiable confidence. Insofar as the church over the centuries has stimulated or allowed or been forced to allow the formation of orders, denominations, and communions, each formed around one or another particular emphasis in doctrine, and insofar as the church has continued to regard most of these specific formulations as within the limits, the second understanding of what is meant by orthodoxy has prevailed. It is the understanding that shall be used here, and that obtains in all ecumenically open yet clearly Christian centers of theological education.

Strictly speaking, only four doctrines appear to have been accepted by the whole church over its entire history and to provide the boundaries of what it means to be Christian: (1) that humanity is fallen and in need of salvation, (2) that revelation takes place in history in the way that the Bible authoritatively indicates, (3) that the doctrine of the Trinity accurately points to how God can best be understood in non-Hebraic terms and what that means for life in the world, and (4) that Jesus is the Christ — the way, the truth, and the light. Precisely what each of these means has been a matter of considerable dispute, and most of the disputes are not finally settled. Various parts of the community of faith have given these doctrines quite particular meanings, and have wedded their meanings to other doctrines that are not agreed upon or to subdoctrines or to particular inferences of one of these that are interpreted quite differently by other parts of the church. Debates over these lesser points have often led to hostile splits in the community of faith. Yet, again and again, many of those who cast others out, or who have been cast out, have been gradually reincorporated into the whole. Subsequently, their witness has been assessed as a testimony to some part of the whole portrait of what is indeed orthodox that was in danger of being neglected, or as some testing of the boundaries and ground rules that brought clarity and humility to the whole. The representation of some part of the whole as the whole has been the bane of Christian history, and is a still-unfinished story. Nevertheless, it is difficult to understand as Christian any position that does not accept the reality of sin and the necessity of salvation, the Bible, the Trinity, and Jesus Christ.[2]

That a community of faith — even a very broad and ecumenically open one — develops doctrines, and identifies some of them as orthodox and pertinent to all humanity, and then attempts to structure and test all thought and life on the basis of what it has developed — all this is very complex. To many, it simply proves the circularity of any argument for orthodoxy. Does it not mean that some things are true because the church says they are? Or does it mean that some things that are true can be seen only by those who already believe them, and thus are privileged knowledge? Or is it possible that out of certain quite specific circumstances, in a long and rather complicated historical process that is not yet fully understood, a particular and special unveiling of truth and justice has in fact taken place, one of such universal significance that it demands wrestling ever anew with a transformed view of religion, of every metaphysical-moral vision in every context of the globe, and one that is nevertheless in principle accessible to those who do not share the context, the history, the religion, or the philosophical orientations that were present in the process that gave it birth? When they are most consistent with their own presuppositions, Christians tend to hold to the latter view, and it is surely important for theological education that this view be theologically examined with all the rigor that can be mustered. Where the view can be shown to be valid, it must be defended and propagated.

1. Sin and Salvation

In some ways, the first of these orthodox Christian doctrines — that sin characterizes human existence, and that we need relief from it — is the least distinctive to Christianity, and the simplest doctrine

---

2. It may seem curious to some that I have elsewhere argued for "ten basic principles" on the basis of "four touchstones of authority" instead of this particular set of doctrines. (See *Public Theology and Political Economy: Christian Stewardship in Modern Society* [Grand Rapids: Eerdmans, 1987], chaps. 1 and 2.) The difference has to do both with a specification of those matters more pertinent to modern political economies as compared with those most central to the foundations of theological education, and with a sense of what central doctrines kept coming to the surface in our ATS team and our ANTS faculty discussions.

to prove by appeal to theory or experience. Everyone knows that ignorance, death, pride, oppression, alienation, and evil abound in life and thought, and that it is utterly naive to hold otherwise. Nevertheless, as Reinhold Niebuhr has shown in what is surely one of the most important studies written in the mode of *apologia* in the twentieth century, the "easy conscience" of modern humanity, when understood in Enlightenment and post-Enlightenment terms, finds this a most difficult doctrine to accept.[3] But Niebuhr convincingly demonstrates by appeal to basic human experience and to the fundamental theories of both rationalist and Romantic modern thinking that the denial of this doctrine leads to more theoretical and practical problems than does its acceptance. Niebuhr does not extensively discuss the conceptions of sin in the world's religions, nor does he accent heavily the understandings of humanity that could be drawn from sustained reflection on the experience of suppressed peoples of the world (including women, as a number of contemporary feminist theologians have made clear), but what he argues for in terms of Christian orthodoxy could easily be extended in these directions. It is, in substantial measure, in accord with what can be found in all those religions that see a need for salvation, redemption, or transformation of the "natural" way in which things are in the world.

The claim that sin and salvation are central has been challenged throughout Christian history, from outside and from inside. This double suspicion of the claim appears among the opponents of the tradition stretching from Paul to Augustine in the early church, among the opponents of the reformers from Luther to Edwards during the second great moment of Christian thought, and again among opponents of apologetics, orthodoxy, and normative religious ethics today.

The first of the two sides can be found among those who agree that Christianity demands belief in the reality of sin and the need for salvation, but who do not believe that this reflects the basic human condition. The problem, they say, is not sin but ignorance. To blame some impersonal force, like "sin," for the faults of the world and to expect some superpersonal force, like God, to remedy those faults is to remain passive or even resistant to what we can learn from philosophy and science to overcome ignorance. Thus, Christianity (or any other purported "salvation religion"),

---

3. Niebuhr, *The Nature and Destiny of Man*, 2 vols. (New York: Scribner's, 1941, 1943).

with all those doctrines of sin and salvation, is the core of the problem.[4]

Within the community of those claiming to be Christians we also find those who deny that sin and salvation are chief characteristics of Christianity. In this view, it is precisely the attempt to interpret the faith in this way that has prevented recognition of the goodness of creation, and inhibited or repressed those creative potentialities inherently present in human existence that can be cultivated into a consciousness of completed and fulfilled spirituality.[5]

Today, not only will we have to continue to wrestle with these challenges, as they come from very influential streams of philosophy and religiosity in the West, but we will have to recognize that major schools of Hindu philosophy and spirituality, as well as much of Confucian philosophy and Islamic mysticism, have worked out these perspectives more consistently, institutionalized them more extensively, and built more extensive civilizational and cultural patterns on these foundations than any other belief system in the past. The classic struggles with what the early tradition called "Pelagianism" and "Gnosticism" and the age of reform called "Humanism" and "Spiritualism" are but anticipations of the debates to come on this issue. And, of course, it should be clear to all that if the "orthodox" Christian view (that sin is real and salvation is necessary) is false, theology can and should be supplanted by philosophy or spirituality, and there is no reason for theological education.

To believe that sin is real and that salvation is necessary does not, however, deny the importance of philosophy or spirituality. It does suggest that both can and should be guided by the reliable knowledge of supra-natural reality, and that both become misguided when they are not. Moreover, theology, as the science of this supra-natural reality, gives a more adequate account of why ignorance and false spirituality (or the denial of potential goodness) have come into existence than do philosophy and spirituality. Thus, in the final analysis, speaking of sin and salvation implies the fundamental necessity of having a "supra-natural" perspective on reality, a view that is indispensable to theology.

The greatest of the world religions may differ with Christian-

---

4. The most important modern representative of this position is Leo Strauss, father of the most profound forms of neo-conservative thinking in America. See his *Natural Right and History* (Chicago: University of Chicago, 1953).

5. Perhaps the best summary of this point of view as it currently influences Christian thought is Matthew Fox, *Original Blessing: A Primer in Creation Spirituality* (Sante Fe, N.M.: Bear & Co., 1983).

ity on what the precise character of sin is, and what it is precisely that brings salvation, or what could serve as a mark of salvific experience, just as social activists in a particular context or a philosopher who feels compelled to write and publish might identify some fundamental fault afoot in the world that needs desperately to be overcome. Further, these understandings might even converge with Christian understandings to broaden and deepen both. But none deny the necessary, primal recognition of the fact of sin and the need for salvation. The question is what criteria ought to be used in discerning the fundamental character of sin and salvation. And, at this point, Christians have a hard time denying that the three remaining doctrines — Scripture, Trinity, and Christology — are orthodox.

2. Biblical Revelation

The doctrine of revelation, specifically with reference to the Bible, is more difficult. It is well known that the Bible is the church's book; the church developed it, canonized it, and included some materials from the early movements of Judaism, from the ancient mystery cults and philosophies of the day, and from a number of early Christian social contexts. In the decision to include some materials, others were excluded. In this regard the Bible is not unlike the sacred texts of any other community of faith. Further, different groups within the whole community of Christians assess the authority of the Bible in quite different ways, in part depending on which view of revelation they hold. Some subordinate Scripture to doctrines developed in the postbiblical traditions, such as the Trinity, Christology, or ecclesiology, while others accept these doctrines because they seem to have some warrant in Scripture. Further, some have viewed the Bible's meanings more typologically, some allegorically, some spiritually or therapeutically. Some have perceived the Bible as a charter for social prophecy, others as the normative source of law and polity, and still others believe that it can best, if not only, be understood through the eyes of modern critical scholarship, laden as it often is with post-Enlightenment, Romantic, or existentialist understandings of life, history, and meaning. These differences, although worthy of considerable debate, are nevertheless intermural disputes from the perspective of the primary questions: Has there been revelation of the fundamental character of sin and the real foundations for salvation, and can it be found by referring to the Bible?

Whoever takes the Bible as authoritative has already made at least three very substantial judgments. First, this stance implies that those who formed the canon — who wrote it, edited it, translated it from (at least) one form of Hebrew to another or from Aramaic to Greek, or drew up lists that meant that some possible texts were included and others excluded — made essentially correct decisions. Indeed, given what everyone knows about human sin and ignorance, the only way to account for the massive range of correct decisions that must have gone into the whole process is to speak of revelation or inspiration. Any view of these texts which holds that they are of such universal importance for all contexts as a source and norm of truth that we attempt to translate these texts into all the languages of all the peoples of the world and for every period of history implies also a view about inspiration. It implies that the early authors, redactors, and so forth did accurately discern something that was of the *logos* of *theos,* and did so, intentionally or not, under the influence of a reality much greater than the human creativity that attends the composition of most writings that have been produced over the course of human history. Therefore, we should agree with their discernment.

Second, taking the Bible as authoritative means that what the biblical compositors selected in substance contains a history — one full of myth, law, prophecy, wisdom, narrative, proclamation, poetry, social comment, folkways, interpretation, and argument — that in a basic way accurately portrays the fact that a transcendent reality, God, created the world and everything in it, granted dignity and freedom to humankind, has been present in the midst of the struggles of human life, and has shown what is required for knowing truth and doing justice. Among other things, this means that any and every Christian orthodoxy must be informed both by decisive and constant themes in all human existence — for example, creation, the Fall, liberation, covenant, vocation, and redemption — and by a sense of story, a story that recounts how people who willfully distort their own character, the structures of the world around them, and the very image of the One who called them into existence are also called out of subservience to sin into communities of fidelity and hope in accord with the will and the providential care of that God. These people — and by implication, all people — fall away from truth offered to them, relying on pretentious trivia, and are nevertheless undeservingly and repeatedly offered a new chance to grasp what is true.

Third, when anyone takes the Bible as authoritative, this belief further implies that that individual, or the community and tradition of which he or she is a part, is sufficiently inspired by the spirit of truth, or has a capacity to discern validity when it is at hand, and is so driven by a concern for ultimate things that he or she can recognize that the truth is in these texts in a way that does not obtain in other texts or simply from the contexts of life.

A Christian orthodoxy may have within it a high regard for the scriptures of other traditions. The Vedas or the Gita of the Hindus, the Pali Canon of the Theravada Buddhists, or the Koran of the Muslims, for example, may be studied and compared with the Bible, and honored for their wisdom. Similarly, Plato, Aristotle, Kant, Hegel, Confucius, Mencius, and a host of other philosophers can be deeply appreciated. Nor is it necessary to turn only to such high and literary sources: the insights of the neglected, oppressed, unlettered, and bypassed peoples of the earth undoubtedly contain sensitivities and perspectives that anyone interested in universal truth would be foolish to neglect. Indeed, modern biblical critics claim that materials included in the Bible may well have come from just such sources as these.

But, finally, Christian orthodoxy requires some acknowledgment that what is contained in the themes and histories of the Bible is somehow more valid than any of these other sources, and that these lack something when they are without the biblical framework. It could at least be argued that the ways in which biblical authors drew on, recast, and transformed material that derived from Egyptian, Babylonian, Greek, and other sources provide the normative model of how authentic interaction takes place between truly inspired religious traditions rooted in the knowledge of the true God and the significant wisdoms of the world. When some nonbiblical perspective comes together with the history and themes from the Bible, mutual reinterpretation may well take place. But what does, can, *and ought* to happen, for the sake of truth, is that the Bible ought to be recognized as providing the governing history and thematic framework whereby the other perspectives are put in a new framework of meaning and on a new foundation that is — in fact, in principle, and in terms of its metaphysical-moral accuracy and epistemological adequacy — more able to unveil the whole of truth than is that which is encountered.

It may be readily granted, as has been the case in most of Christian history, that the way in which the Bible expresses one or another point or tells some part of the story may be incomprehensible to some particular people, to some time or location in history, or to some religious and philosophical points of view, given the prevailing patterns of understanding that are present. It may also be acknowledged that the ways in which Christians have understood one or another part of the Bible have often turned out to be entirely without warrants. And that to insist on one specific interpretation of the story or one of its themes in the face of such credulity may lead to a dogmatism of falsehood more dangerous than the non-Christian or nonbiblical perspective Christianity is disputing. In such cases, patient dialogue and clarification of presuppositions as well as restraint and modesty about what can be known with precision and certainty must surely dominate all discussion, teaching, and preaching. Even more, the use of coercive methods to enforce one or another version of what is orthodox is surely unwarranted in religious matters at this level.

Nevertheless, the dominant reason that the Bible is, and can be, a point of appeal in theological education (in systematics, ethics, pastoral care, and the like); the governing reason for wanting to contextualize, translate, and introduce the study of the Bible among the peoples of the earth; and the sovereign reason for bringing it to the whole globe in mission — these are all rooted in the conviction that confidence in the Bible's contents is justifiable. Just so, the reason for patient dialogue and the eschewing of coercive means to make the Bible's contents enforced articles of faith is the conviction that, in the long run, people will see that the Bible is true, that it contains an indispensable source and norm of right teaching, valid understanding, and honest reflection that accords with the widest experience and deepest reason that humans can know. If this is not the case, theological education has no reason to conduct biblical studies as if they were objectively important to the true understanding of life, and could just as well turn to the study of any of the great texts for their greatness of human insight and poetic eloquence. And there would be no reason to appeal to biblical sources as we engage in mission.

3. The Trinity

The third unavoidable doctrine is that of the Trinity. This doctrine, when it is taken as orthodox, indicates that the foundation of all reality and truth is ultimately unified and transcendent, but can nevertheless be known in some measure and is best understood as differentiated unity. The ground of holistic intellectual and spiritual life, both personally and socially, is to be essentially discerned as a community of individuals inseparably bound together in an ordered pluralism that refuses to fall into monolithic arrogance, dualistic divisions, unlimited pluralism, or chaotic relativism. The symbolic complexity of this doctrine has meant that it can be applied and understood in a wide variety of ways without violation of its essential meaning.[6]

Further, this doctrine is particularly important because it is clearly a "postbiblical" doctrine. To be sure, there are hints and glimmers of the doctrine of the Trinity in some biblical formulations, but it was in the postbiblical periods of Christian cultic development, liturgical formulation, and debates about "warranted wisdom" that this doctrine was more fully articulated. Thus, to accept the Trinity means to acknowledge that the Christian tradition, concerned of course with the question of sin and salvation and informed by the Bible, was able to articulate in brief and highly symbolic form something fundamentally true about the inner structure of God's reality, and about the ways in which God relates to the world, well *after* the Scriptures were written and using concepts *not* intrinsic to the Bible. When, in other words, a biblically informed movement encounters formal philosophies and cultures beyond its own boundaries, and when it is challenged to thematize its contents in a form that allows it to state its core metaphysical-moral vision in propositional-symbolic form which it can then use to interpret its own story and themes and those of others it encounters, it can do so. Also implied is the denial of the view that it is only in and from the biblical revelation that truth can be grasped. Anyone who accepts the doctrine of the Trinity has already acknowledged that something outside of and beyond the Bible can be true in a fundamental way — a truth equal to, or nearly equal to, the truth found in, through, and by encounter with the Bible. Indeed, the doctrine of the Trinity shows that ultimately reliable truth about God and God's relationship to the world can be, and has been, discerned and stated in nonbiblical ways.

This is not to say that all aspects of the doctrine of the Trinity are settled once and for all. A number of major attempts have been made to articulate the basic meanings of the Trinity — especially as can be seen in the classical creeds of the churches — and many possible implications and nuances of the doctrine are under dispute. A series of distinctive models of what the doctrine might mean have been offered. In our own context, for example, Gabriel Fackre has catalogued the main alternatives (psychological analogy and social analogy as they relate to "immanent" and "economic" views of the Trinity) and correlated these with characteristic sym-

---

6. See my *Ethics and the Urban Ethos: An Essay in Social Theory and Theological Construction* (Boston: Beacon Press, 1972). See also Jürgen Moltmann, *The Trinity and the Kingdom* (New York: Harper & Row, 1981).

bols that are frequently used to portray its meanings — triangle, trefoil, triquerta, and so forth.[7] This is not the place to rehearse all of his arguments, but it can be said that many have found them to be a compelling statement of the Christian claim that the concept of Trinity is, finally, one of the essential, indispensable, and correct ways to portray the basic character of the one true God and the way God perennially relates to the world. Whatever other portrayals of the Divine may be utilized and deemed appropriate in particular times and contexts (God as the Rock of Ages, as Love, Lord, Father, Mother, Being, Becoming, Law Giver, etc.), this one is held to be of universal import. Indeed, this portrayal orders and lends coherence and corrective balance to all the others.

The doctrine of the Trinity allies Christianity with many other religions. The first person of the Trinity, as it is usually spelled out, has to do with both the creative or generative dimension of God, and the provision by the Creator of an ordered law in both creation and morality. All religions that view empirical reality as having been created by a moral Creator are allies of Christianity on this point. The second person of the Trinity points to the compassionate and sacrificial love which is the *logos* of God, and which is present to humanity as a personal savior. All compassionate messianic expectations in history are, in principle, potentially related to this dimension of the Trinity. And the third person of the Trinity implies a Spirit of God that moves among the peoples of the world, comforting, sustaining, inspiring new possibilities for sainthood and community, and opening new vistas of freedom, peace, righteousness, and recreative novelty. Insofar as the religions and philosophies of the world hold that something like these realities are part of the ultimate character of the universe, they are allies, not enemies, of Christianity in this regard.

But Christians hold that these three "persons" — "motifs," "substances," "dynamics," "realities," "powers" — are distinguished from one another, are related internally to one another, are ultimately unified in the Godhead, are distinct in the way they indicate God's relationships to the world, and must be understood as being simultaneously unitary and plural. Even more, Christianity presumes that the Trinity is both a mystery and a sufficiently reasonable concept that it can be articulated, argued for, and shown to be at least as coherent as any other fundamental view of God or the ultimate character of the universe. These aspects of the doctrine

---

7. Fackre, *The Christian Story: A Narrative Interpretation of Basic Christian Doctrine*, rev. ed. (Grand Rapids: Eerdmans, 1984).

set Christianity apart from various modern forms of deism, pantheism, and panentheism, and from all nontheistic religious traditions such as Buddhism and Marxism (which can be understood as "secular" religions). This doctrine even sets Christianity apart from its closest religious relatives, Judaism and Islam, which share some of the same Scriptures and a monotheistic view of God. The doctrine of the Trinity also makes Christianity somewhat closer to selected aspects of Hinduism, as Raimundo Panikkar has shown,[8] and to selected aspects of Hegelian philosophy, as George Rupp and Joseph Prabhu have demonstrated.[9] Both of these metaphysical-moral interpretations of reality recognize that the world and its meanings are constituted by a unity that is pluralistically ordered; the former does so metaphysically, the latter in terms of a logic of history. Christianity finally is distinct from these, however, insofar as the former tends toward tri-theism and insofar as the latter swallows constancy into a prematurely schematized logic of change.

Christian understandings of God may be enriched by these or other modes of religious and philosophical reflection, and Christianity may even have parts of its various confessions corrected by them, both in language and in substance. Yet, however these comparisons and contrasts are adjudicated by philosophical and cross-cultural religious studies in the long run, Christianity would surely have to claim that the true, living God has to be understood in a Trinitarian fashion or something fundamental is missing. A center of theological education that does not take the Trinity as a basic point of departure has difficulty claiming that it is Christian, as does any missionary effort, analysis of the human context, or global perspective that is not so based.

4. Christology

The fourth distinctive and indispensable doctrine that Christians claim to be orthodox has to do with Christology. It is, for many, the most difficult doctrine to grasp, although its main contours are already implied in what has thus far been identified as orthodoxy. In Jesus Christ we understand the fundamental meanings of sin and salvation; in Jesus Christ the central meaning of the Bible is to be found; and in Jesus Christ the second person of the Trinity

---

8. Panikkar, *The Trinity and the Religious Experience of Man* (Madras: C.L.S., 1970).

9. Rupp, *Christologies and Cultures: Toward a Typology of Religious Worldviews* (Mouton: The Hague, 1974); and Prabhu, "Hegel's Philosophy of Christianity," Ph.D. diss., Department of Philosophy, Boston University, 1981.

makes personally real the decisive character of sacrificial compassion and the decisive fulfillment of messianic expectation in paradigmatic human experience. Further, according to Christianity, it is only when this second person of the Trinity is clearly understood that the fuller meanings of the first and third persons of the Trinity — indeed, the very character of the Godhead itself — can become most clear. And finally, in this regard, it is a dimension of the Christian understanding of Jesus Christ that he can be known in and through a personal relationship, one that accords with the most profound understanding of sin and salvation possible, with the main point of the themes and story of the Bible, and with the propositional-symbolic meanings of the Trinity. Thus, a cognitively laden apprehension of the compassionate truth of God's *logos* is accessible to all persons in principle. At the same time, it can be pointed out that if someone says that he or she knows Jesus Christ in a personal way but does not grasp the reality of sin and salvation, or the meaning of scriptural themes or story, and does not believe in the Trinity, it can be seriously doubted whether or not that person actually knows Jesus Christ at all.

In his recent book, *Is Christ the Only Way?* S. Mark Heim has posed the issues of the meanings of Christology in a pluralistic world in a particularly compelling way. He is concerned, above all, with "whether it is objectively *true* that Jesus Christ is the way, the truth, and the life. It is not just a matter of whether we [Christians] ought to preach Christ, but of whether people ought to believe us. Is Christ the only way, the definitive truth, the abundant life?"[10] He acknowledges that this way of approaching matters is rare and suspect both in the contemporary environment of philosophical skepticism about the universality of particular religious claims, and in a world where multiple religions seem to demand that kind of tolerance in which speaking of the relative truth or falsity of one religious stance vis-à-vis any other is considered bad manners at best and imperialism at worst. Heim is fully aware that the notion of truth is decidedly out of favor in modernity, especially in regard to any area which deals with ultimate beliefs, and he realizes that Christians must bear a tremendous burden of guilt for what they have at times done in the world in the name of Christ.

Nevertheless, Heim patiently and carefully takes up the multiple charges and suspicions leveled against Christianity in regard

---

10. Heim, *Is Christ the Only Way?* (Valley Forge, Penn.: Judson Press, 1985), p. 8. See also his "Thinking about Theocentric Christology," his forthcoming critique of Paul F. Knitter's *No Other Name? A Critical Survey of Christian Attitudes Toward the World Religions* (Maryknoll, N.Y.: Orbis Books, 1985).

to its understanding of Jesus Christ by culture, philosophy, other religions, and the victims of Christian injustice, and attempts to show that none of these finally can provide grounds for dismissing the claim that Jesus Christ is the way, the truth, and the life. Indeed, in the course of his critical analysis of the presuppositions of those who oppose Christian orthodoxy on this point, Heim raises numerous questions about whether those presuppositions can themselves meet the tests of metaphysical, moral, and epistemological — let alone biblical and doctrinal — adequacy. He does not claim infallibility for either his own or the tradition's formulations of Christology, and he is quite open to dialogue with those whose allegiance is focused on the Buddha, on Krishna, on the revelation given to Muhammad, on the religio-scientific writings of Marx, or on the newer insights of various liberation theologies and spiritualities. Nevertheless, Heim shows what may well be required if modern theology is to make the argument that it is reasonable for Christians to go unto all peoples in all contexts of the world with the message that Christ is the only way.

A REVIEW

This chapter is not the place either to recapitulate or to enter fully into the discussion of what arguments, in detail, might be made to give warrant to Christian understandings of sin and salvation, revelation as portrayed in the Bible, the doctrine of the Trinity, and Christology. The point here is not to attempt all the work of Christian theological education but simply to identify what needs to be taken into account if theological education is to prepare people to teach, preach, and engage in mission in particular contexts all over the globe. It is to suggest that, on at least four matters, Christian theological education requires a wrestling with the problem of orthodoxy in ways that point to something true not only for those who already believe it, and not only for those formed in a particular socio-cultural-historical-linguistic system, but for everyone, everywhere. And it is to suggest that focused discussion and critical evaluation of at least these matters of Christian orthodoxy are surely necessary for any profound religious education, for all serious theology, and certainly for Christian theological education. Whatever else theological education may well entail, if it does not take such matters as these as core concerns and as an organizing center, it is of dubious value as education and as theology, and of dubious value to Christianity, and hence to the world's religions.

In other words, there is no possibility, so far as we have thus far been able to discern, for Christian theological education to proceed without (a) accepting at least a modified realist view of the nature of truth, (b) accepting the responsibility of attempting to make a realist case for the core claims of Christianity in the face of philosophical doubt, resurgent spiritualism, religious pluralism, and cultural suspicion, and (c) showing that the attempts to contextualize and globalize these concerns in mission are intellectually, theoretically, metaphysically, and epistemologically viable. All this implies that theological education must not only confess its warranted wisdom, as did the first "moment" of its development by the early church, and engage in a critical *scientia*, as theology attempted in its second "moment" of "classical" reformulation. Theological education must also show in a widened, more pluralistic, and more doubtful world than has ever existed before that truth makes a difference and that the core truth claims about which it speaks are ones in which it is possible to have justifiable confidence.

Of course, seminaries and departments of theology may have other tasks as well. Personal nurture, development of skills, formation of character and community, and worship are all important. That is assumed in all that has been said. And it may be that evangelical, conservative, liberal, ecumenical, liberationist, Catholic, Protestant, Methodist, Baptist, Presbyterian, and other seminaries may want to show that their particular understandings of sin and salvation, the Bible, the Trinity, and Christology are the ones most compelling in terms of the warranted wisdom and grounded *scientia* of old, and in terms of the new dialogical engagements of our expanded conversations today. But if the case cannot be made that these orthodox points of reference are true in some basic sense in the first place, it is doubtful that Christian theological education is taking place.

Again, if we cannot defend these points of reference, we should either fundamentally alter what we are doing and the directions in which we are moving, or cease calling ourselves Christian centers of theological education, or both. But if we do the latter, we would implicitly accept the view that we are simply preparing to impose our idiosyncratic and accidental views on others in a world where no reason can be given for the views we hold except that we hold them and find them meaningful for us. That could drive us to organized forms of testimonial gatherings, but such could hardly be viewed as either theological or educational in any basic senses.

Of course, many argue that the relative validity of any purported framework of meaning, doctrine, truth claim, or orthodoxy cannot be shown in the abstract, but can be known only by the effects it has on individuals and society. That raises again the question of *praxis*, to which we now turn.

CHAPTER 11

Praxiology?

We have already seen (in Chapter 6) that several of the most articulate theories of *praxis* are laden with both practical and theoretical difficulties. One predominant reason for this is that they tend to shift Christianity from a religion of orthodoxy to one of orthopraxy. Yet, while Christianity demands *praxis,* with all that entails in terms of the intimate interaction of theory and practical experience, it cannot easily be said to involve any specific orthopraxy at all. That is to say that there is no prescribed set of actions, cultic or ethical, individual or social, that can bring about the salvation from sin of which Christianity speaks or that can be identified as a clear and certain mark of whether, in the eyes of God, an individual or a congregation or a people is or is not within the community of faith. Christian orthodoxy is in part distinguishable from its closest religious relatives, Judaism and Islam, by its doubt about the spiritual, moral, personal, or societal efficacy of what are pejoratively called "legalistic" prescriptions of behaviors. Nor does it prescribe ritual actions or practices that claim to guarantee psychophysical potency, spiritual consciousness, or harmonious and enduring social existence, practices frequently found in primal religions, Hinduism, Buddhism, and Confucianism.

To be sure, Eastern Orthodoxy and Roman Catholicism in much of their histories and Protestantism in various periods and branches have become both legalistically and ritualistically prescriptive in tedious detail, at least as popularly understood. Certainly there are some specific actions by individuals or groups that clearly have violated or do violate what Christianity stands for.

Deceitfully dealing with church resources in ways that benefit a family and not the community of faith (Ananias and Sapphira), burning incense to Caesar, selling indulgences, slaughtering Jews in the name of Christ, burning witches and engaging in bloody crusades, establishing and defending racial segregation or apartheid on the grounds of a purported Christian theology, relegating women to second-class status — these are some of the more dramatic examples. But it is more than interesting that these are negative examples. It cannot be said that there is one and only one orthopraxy with regard to handling financial matters, giving to Caesar what is properly Caesar's, dealing with forgiveness, or structuring social-political life to include pluralistic groups.

Indeed, it should be admitted that whenever detailed prescriptions have been accented, Christianity has been properly discredited both by its exterior critics and by its own internal orthodox presuppositions. We have in mind here some areas of orthopraxy prescribed for human sexuality, Sabbath-keeping, iconoclasm, and so forth. Certainly, there have been ways of understanding the sacraments that have involved such ritualistic precisionism that they have become almost magical incantations, with the weightier matters of truth and justice neglected. Orthopraxy in this sense has always violated the first principles of Christian truth and justice.

Such emphases have always clashed with the deeper dimensions of Christianity in a way that is less clear in a number of other religions. There are two reasons for this. One is that Christians, if they are at all orthodox, know themselves to be sinners. They may also know themselves to have been forgiven by the triune God through Jesus Christ in accord with the testimony of Scripture, but they are aware that they remain sinners. Accordingly, they know that humans are incapable of achieving salvation or perfection or spiritual power or harmonious and enduringly just societies by their own actions alone. And the second reason is that nothing in Christianity relieves the believer from using conscience and judgment in decisions about what ought to be done in particular circumstances. No doctrinal, ethical, legal, social, or ritual system, no matter how elaborate, can prescribe the precise *praxis* that must be undertaken. Even in complex situations where it is clear what ought *not* be done — such as some of those situations previously listed — it is less clear what *must* be done.

THE FOUNDATIONS OF *PRAXIS*

Thus, there is always a Christian reservation about too much focus on any specific orthopraxy. At the same time, there is a deep recognition that Christian freedom from such legalisms may not mean disengagement from *praxis* or normlessness in it. Christianity offers more a coherent foundation to guide *praxis* than it does a prescribed orthopraxy. Faith, hope, and love, for example, are taken to be formative virtues that incline people to justice, and all social dynamics can be evaluated accordingly as they are faithful to the laws of God, anticipatory of the purposes of God, and compassionately representative of the mercies of God. However, such a way of understanding Christian ethics implies that the debate is always, in some measure, an open one regarding which actions, precisely, are the most complete embodiments of these virtues or principles in any specific context. To judge some one or some group to be beyond the pale of God's justice because they do not immediately endorse a particular orthopraxis is to prematurely preclude the exercise of Christian conscience and open ethical debate about public decisions.

This is not to say that Christianity is not concerned with "right action" that links theory to practical experience. On the one hand, Christians know that words without deeds are empty. Genuinely held orthodoxy demands engagement, living the faith, implementing its truths in life — in personal relationships, social forms, and civilizational histories. The perils of idolatry in orthodoxy have their direct parallels in the perils of hypocrisy in regard to belief without action. On the other hand, action is its own kind of witness to the truth claims of the faith. For example, in missionary situations, it is not always the case that all the matters discussed in the previous two chapters play the primary role in bringing people to Christianity. Sometimes it is the quite practical evidence of concern, compassion, and care that commends faith. Justice may as often be the prelude to orthodoxy as it is its necessary implication.

Even where Christianity is established, just commitments, actions, and engagements are, for many, decisive evidence of the truth or untruth of a position held. Many believers are little concerned with all the nuances of orthodoxy and with what an adequate *apologia* might entail. Many will leave the more subtle questions of truth to theologians and pastors, trusting that these individuals would not lie about such things. They expect that pastors and theologians have thought these matters through, know how to sort valid from invalid claims, and will teach only what can be taken as reliable guides to belief and action. This is not to say that lay people will not judge and evaluate what is taught or preached, or that they automatically trust those holding pastoral or teaching offices. But it is to say that many will trust and accept orthodoxy if and when it makes concrete sense in people's lives, and that they will distrust it when it does not or when it seems to be betrayed by the behavior of the teacher or the pastor or by the unjust consequences of trying to practice what they preach and teach. When and if that which is set forth as orthodoxy allows people to develop character and a sense of dignity and justice with discipline, to find meaning in their family lives, to become responsible participants in economic and political institutions, to have courage in times of crisis, and to discover purpose when sacrifice is demanded, these claims will be accepted. In other words, Christianity demands *praxis* that rightly guides life both because it is implied in orthodoxy itself and because Christianity, like every other religion, must be accepted by the people who will evaluate any and every religious claim according to "practical" criteria as well as by the more theoretical criteria suggested in the previous two chapters.

The implications of this for theological education are, perhaps, already clear. A seminary or a university department of theology is not a church, a political party, a voluntary association for social change, or a judiciary or legislature prescribing "right actions" for the world, although it may be related to all of these. As we shall see, the distinctive function of theological education in this area is one of interpreting, learning, and teaching how theory and practice are related and ought to be related through the clarification of that kind of justice which can, and ought to, guide *praxis*.

Two points leap to the fore at this juncture. One is the fact that Christianity not only claims to reach the mind, the understanding, with its concern for truth; it also claims to reach the will, the heart, which is the mainspring of practical action for justice in the world (as we saw in Chapter 5). This point presumes, of course, that people, alone and in organized groups, have some real freedom. People can make choices; they can, by the exercise of will, direct the actions they undertake in some measure, and thus they can be held accountable before God and other humans for the choices they make. The anthropological assumption behind this view is that people are not fated—by genetics, by social conditioning, by historical circumstance, by the accidents of being in a specific context, by directives from theologians or church leaders, or even by God's ultimate control of the universe—to act in only one predetermined way when action is required. Although many forces do influence the exercise of freedom and limit it, people can choose to act according to belief, and the belief ought to be well founded. A praxiology will offer reasons for choosing to act in some ways rather than others, but will recognize the inevitable freedom of those who act.

This point leads to a second. The action must also prove, in the practical experience of the people, to be socially and ethically valid. If we are able to direct our actions and to evaluate both our own actions and those of others, we must have access to some basic principles of what is right and wrong, good and evil, and fitting and unfitting in the actual conditions in which we find ourselves. In sum, action must render justice as well as protect freedom. It must give practical guidance about how to live justly — not only how to survive, but how to live fairly, peacefully, and compassionately as individuals in an increasingly global society and in the midst of pluralistic communities who must structure the common life so that neither chaos nor tyranny may reign.

Those who do grasp the root meanings of sin and salvation, of the biblical witness, of the Trinity, and of Christ feel themselves called to serve God's righteousness, God's purposes, and God's mercy in the world. That is what it means to be faithful, hopeful, and loving — as is claimed by numerous treatises on the "theological virtues." Heteronomies of all kinds must be overcome, but justice is not fully realized by efforts to gain autonomy. Beyond heteronomy and autonomy stands the possibility of theonomy.[1] And that is the fundamental clue to justice. And, although there are few specific behaviors prescribed, there are broad areas of action that are to be undertaken in ways that must accord with God's justice, but that are simultaneously to be adapted appropriately to the capacities and contexts of believers and churches and peoples everywhere. These broad areas of practical concern can perhaps be summarized by briefly outlining the kinds of practice implied by piety, polity, policy, and program. These are the foundations of a Christian praxiology centered on justice.

1. Piety

Every orthodox religion rests, in its historical manifestations, on the quite personal commitment of its members to its source, truth,

---

1. These terms are drawn from "liberal" Paul Tillich, "evangelical" Helmut Thielicke, and "Catholic" Hans Küng. See *Theonomy and Autonomy: Studies in Paul Tillich's Engagement with Modern Culture,* ed. J. J. Carey (Macon, Ga.: Mercer University Press, 1984); Thielicke, *Theological Ethics,* vol. 1: *Foundations* (Philadelphia: Fortress Press, 1966); and Küng, *On Being a Christian* (New York: Doubleday, 1976).

and righteousness, and on the regularized patterns of action by which individuals, alone or in concert with others, express that commitment. Every profound piety implies that life, as it is lived in the world, is freighted with peril, pain, evil, wrong, and death, and that recourse to a reality beyond history and nature is required for relief from these. Piety implies that the only final remedy for sin is divine salvation. And among the decisive practices that derive from this piety are prayer and worship. It is through the practice of prayer and public worship that the personal spirituality of adherents and the general *ethos* of a culture are often shaped. Thereby the people are empowered to take responsibility for those innumerable pathologies of human existence which, with God's help, not only are remediable within the limits of time and creatureliness, but may well point to ultimate salvation.

In addition to prayer and worship, some religions see mission as a necessary and proper dimension of piety.[2] In this, Christianity is more similar to Buddhism and Islam, the other great missionizing religions of the world, than to Hinduism, Judaism, Confucianism, and the primal religions. All of the great missionizing religions of the world hold to some great "unveiling" of ultimate truth believed to be of universal import. This "unveiling" induces a passion for transcendent justice; it frees adherents from localistic practices, from the absolute claims of contextual loyalties, and from conventional social conditions. It induces a certain "homelessness," a divine alienation — a willingness to adopt practices that are more just than what may be found at home, an eagerness to bring all other individuals into contact with this new truth, a desire to carry the universal message to peoples and nations who do not yet know of it and to transform personal identity and whole societies on the basis of its justice.

While it is difficult to see how anyone or any group that does not engage in prayer and worship can consider themselves to be Christian, there is also little demand that prayer and worship be conducted in any single, prescribed manner. It is true that worship practices are more public, and that there have been major disputes about and varying interpretations of which are the most appropriate and important ways to conduct worship — ranging from an Eastern Orthodox Easter liturgy, to a Roman Catholic mass, to a Protestant preaching service, to a free-church Bible study and tes-

---

2. See Max L. Stackhouse, Erik Zuercher, and Stephen C. Neill, "Missions," in vol. 9 of the *Encyclopedia of Religion,* ed. Mircea Eliade et al. (New York: Macmillan, 1987), pp. 563-79.

timonial. But there has never been a time in Christian history when significant variety was not acknowledged as legitimate, even if limits have been drawn whenever worship practices threatened to deny one or another aspect of orthodoxy or to violate theological virtue or the principles of justice.

The impetus to mission is, for many parts of the church, less pronounced as an integral part of piety. Yet mission, like prayer and worship, is rightly seen as a manifestation of belief in and loyalty to an order of justice that is other than, and not derived from, natural, social, psychological, and historical contexts of life. Indeed, mission involves the willingness to change the contexts of life — even the prevailing patterns of prayer and worship — for the sake of that other order of truth and justice. And, even in the least missionizing parts of the church, evangelism and proselytism have been regularly practiced. What is involved in this process is not simply maturation through the "natural" stages of physical, intellectual, psychic, social, moral, and spiritual development, but the attempt to bring individuals and groups into an awareness of a spiritual and moral reality that does not derive only from that which is already within us.

Further, in every age and setting of Christian history, wherever the faith has been alive, specific groups of people supported by the wider church have been sent out in mission to neglected populations or to the farther reaches of the known world, taking with them the orthodoxy that is the basis for practice. But few actions are specified when it comes to how missionary activity is to be done. The range of methods used is enormously variegated, often eventuating in rather dramatic innovations in patterns of prayer and worship according to the ways in which these are contextualized in the various places where the missionary activity occurs.

In other words, Christianity sees piety as a basis of *praxis,* one that includes at least prayer, worship, and mission. These, however, are to be understood in a rather permissive way, so long as they are governed by and point to orthodoxy and do not lead to injustice.

2. Polity

Piety cannot survive in an organizational vacuum. Each religion must form an authoritative office, community, or company of religious leadership that is given responsibility for clarifying and articulating orthodoxy, for cultivating piety through prayer and worship, and for undertaking missionary activity. Christianity deals with the question of polity in terms of ecclesiology. One foundation for *praxis* demands intentional community organization and the recognition that the most important communities of life are not identical with the "natural" institutions that can be found in every civilization. No society can survive without at least some family structure to deal with sexuality and the nurture of children, some political structure to deal with threats to law and order from within and without, some economic structure whereby the necessities of food, clothing, and shelter are provided, and some means of communication — at least a language, but also including song, poetry, gesture, dance, and the arts. Complex civilizations also have differentiated legal, educational, medical, and technological and business institutions. The fact that Christianity demands an *ecclesia* which is inevitably related to these but which is not the same as any of these and may not be reduced to any of them means that the formation of the church as a place of and for prayer, worship, and mission introduces a particular kind of organizational polity into every civilization informed by it.

This differentiates Christianity in principle from those religions that define their polity primarily in terms of family (clan, caste, tribe, *ethne*), politics (nationalism, territorium, imperium, or "state religion"), class (master or servant, male or female, rulers or ruled, bourgeois or proletariat), or cultural-linguistic grouping. It also differentiates Christianity from those religions and cultures in which religious laws and civil law are indistinguishable (as in much of Islam), in which religious education and secular learning are identical (as in Confucianism), in which religious devotion and medical treatment are inseparable (as in Christian Science or "faith healing"), in which worship and technical achievement are confused (as in Freemasonry, in a formal sense, and in a less formal sense, among technocratic "workaholics"), or in which religion becomes identified with an economic system (as in socialism or capitalism). Some of the greatest difficulties of Christian history have come from episodes in which the differentiation of *ecclesia* from these other areas of institutional life has been obscured.

What is implied here is the notion that humans can, in some measure, know something about how God wants them to live together. Because of sin, and because of some knowledge of God's will through Scripture, through tradition (especially the doctrine of the Trinity), and through Jesus Christ, we know that some possibilities are ruled out. Monolithic absolutism and anomic licentiousness are both wrong. Further, the right order for polity is not and cannot be simply found in the state, the family, a class, or one linguistic-cultural system, although some forms of governance, sexual relationship, class behavior, or cultural expression may be less troublesome than others. Nor may Christian polity be reduced to or fully identified with the laws of any judiciary, the wisdom of any philosophy or social science, the therapy of any health-care profession, or the methods and structures of any technological or economic system. However useful these may be in describing one or another dimension of human activity, from a Christian perspective they can never be taken as the basic guides to action. The decisive clue to the meaning of social history and the most important guidelines for a just polity are to be found in ecclesiology. This is the normative model and interpretive pattern by which the other arenas of human organization are to be assessed.

In Christian ecclesiology, at least three practices are seen to be normative: baptism, celebration of the Eucharist, and ministry.[3] To be sure, many debates remain about these, but they are widely acknowledged as critical to Christian practice. This is not the place to enter into a full theological or historical treatment of the meanings, implications, and significance of these three practices, or to show how some traditions would augment the list with other sacramental practices that they hold to be decisive. But before we look at these practices briefly, we can note that whatever list of sacraments or rites are taken as normative within one or another branch of the Christian church, there is formal or informal recognition that certain moments in the life cycle require ritual and symbolic religious attention. These are usually treated as critical matters of "practical theology."

Certain moments of life—birth, the transition to adulthood, marriage, the experience of guilt, shame, anguish, or suffering, and especially death—require sensitive, loving response from the religious community and religious leadership whether or not there are full-fledged sacramental theories to govern these moments. Not only is it necessary to have the meaning of these events interpreted in terms of the governing orthodoxy, but the quite practical expression of concern through prayer, worship, and compassionate empathy in joy or sorrow demands that someone, on behalf of the mission of the church, offer the ritualized words that place these events in the largest theological framework. Where this does not occur, people dream up interpretations of the significance of these

---

3. See *Baptism, Eucharist, and Ministry,* Faith and Order Paper no. 11 (Geneva: World Council of Churches, 1982).

events without reference to any transcendentally based understanding of truth and justice, sometimes with false and drastically unjust results. In this connection, it is more than fascinating to note that where modern Protestant traditions have not developed extensive understandings of sacrament to guide these moments, modern forms of "practical theology," often dominated by modern psychiatric assumptions about human nature and development, have supplied them. In many instances, these psychological or psychiatric practices have, along with their anthropological presuppositions, become the centerpoint of ministerial practice. Some forms of these practices are intimately related to a clear, theologically based orthodoxy, but others are more governed by contextually derived theories which are then used to interpret all theology and ethics.

Baptism, in its several ritualized forms, involves a highly symbolic practice that is laden with orthodox themes of sin and salvation, the authority of Scripture, the doctrine of the Trinity, and the decisive importance of Jesus Christ. In baptism is implied not only membership in that company who have taken the truth and justice of God as the governing principles of life, but the notion that God's justice requires the equal status of all who come to live under God's truth, whether strong or weak, wise or foolish, male or female, rich or poor. It also identifies a membership, one set aside from the natural contexts and cultural conventions of life, that is dedicated to prayer, worship, and mission for the sake of the truth and justice of God.

Communion implies the notion that humans must live in community sustained by the shared fruits of the earth as shaped by human hands, and transformed in substance or significance by the meaning and presence of Christ in human life in anticipation of a fully transformed reality yet to come. The Eucharist implies sharing in and being empowered by material stuff understood through the central themes of salvation history in a way that points toward the final consummation of the truth and justice of God beyond our present prospects.

Ministry implies the necessity of a clear polity with structures of accountability ordered according to a just structure of authority. No one doubts the necessity of some kind of organized and authorized leadership, but the precise character of it — who is admitted to it, the degree of authority given to it, and how the ministry of those given responsibility for overseeing it relates to the ministry of all those who are baptized — is a matter of continuing discussion. Here the dispute is of long standing. It can be found in the Bible as a tension between those who advocated a more charismatic leadership arising amidst the people, an idea dating from the days of the ancient judges of Israel, and those who advocated a more monarchic leadership from the days of Saul, David, and Solomon. It can be found in the early Christian Scriptures, where diaconic leadership in local congregations was in some tension with the more centralized authority of bishops. And it can be found in medieval debates about the relative authority of councils and popes. The modern parallels to these disputes remain between the democratic polities of the "free-church" traditions and the newer "Christian base communities" on the one hand, and on the other, the more hierarchical and patriarchal structures of those polities that find their shape in feudal patterns. In short, it must be said that here again a certain pluralism is allowed, although disputes are likely to continue into the centuries ahead.

Yet it can be argued that polity is one of the decisive foundations for *praxis,* one seldom accorded the attention it deserves for societal questions of justice. We know, from the study of comparative religious history, that the structures of polity that come to dominate a region where a specific religious piety is accepted by the people make an enormous difference in the ways in which justice, human rights, and legitimate power are structured in the host civilization.[4] And we also know that recent, official Roman Catholic critiques of liberation theology have ecclesiological matters of polity as at least part of their concern.[5] In both cases, we can recognize that when a religious polity is seen as the way God wants people to live their lives together, other institutional patterns of life are inevitably affected, and their legitimacy is either reinforced or undercut. At the very least, family life, political institutions, economic patterns, and cultural life are deeply affected. Religion, both as piety and as polity, often provides legitimizing guidance to the fabric of civilization, and if it is structured in ways that are contrary to the most cosmopolitan senses of the truth and justice of God, the entire civilization will be seen as false and oppressive, and religious forces will marshal their powers to overthrow it.

At Andover Newton, some basic decisions have already been reached on questions of polity. Indeed, they are so deeply rooted in the presuppositions of the institution that they are seldom exam-

---

4. See Frederick G. Lawrence, "Political Theology," in vol. 11 of the *Encyclopedia of Religion,* pp. 404-8; and Max L. Stackhouse, "Politics and Religion," in vol. 11 of the *Encyclopedia of Religion,* pp. 408-23.

5. See Joseph Cardinal Ratzinger, "Instruction on Certain Aspects of the 'Theology of Liberation,' " Origins, 13 Sept. 1984.

ined critically or recognized as a major issue for *praxis*. As a seminary formed by the Congregationalist and Baptist traditions, and now deeply involved in ecumenical and conciliar relationships, we have chosen to accent the judges' tradition rather than the monarchic one, the diaconal tradition instead of the episcopal one, the free-church tradition in contrast to a more patriarchal one. We are heirs of those who, in biblical times and again in the "free churches" from the Middle Ages to the present, have held that polity is a decisive issue at the very center of faithful *praxis*, and that the true, most just polity will be one that disperses authority and opens up full possibilities of participation in authoritative judgment. We recognize that there will appear to be perils of anarchy in this choice, but we have a greater confidence in the people to recognize and respond to the truth and justice of God than those who demand control at every point. Further, we are convinced that these accents in polity are to be not only enacted in the church but also carried out in all the various social institutions of civilizational life.

However, we have not denied the fact that those who have chosen differently may be orthodox Christians. They are in our student body, on our faculty, and in conciliar bodies that we support. Nevertheless, we tend to believe that Christian praxiology implies a more democratic polity than has often been the case in Christian history, and that this demands the democratization not only of ecclesiological structures but of political, economic, familial, and cultural patterns as well. And we take it as a point of mission to our ecumenical colleagues in the faith as well as to the multiple contexts throughout the globe that may or may not be Christian to develop, wherever possible, those forms of prayer and worship and those patterns of baptism, the Eucharist, and ministry that evoke and provoke the contextualization of inclusive, participatory, and diffused structures of authority. Further, we tend to work with those para-ecclesial and social movements around the world that promote democratic and participatory structures in civilization and to oppose those authoritative structures of the right or left because we believe that a democratic polity is the most likely structural manifestation of God's justice, whether or not those who struggle for it fully embody the patterns of prayer and worship that piety requires.

We must admit, however, that we seldom pause to make the case for this polity or to show its warrants and justifications in terms of the basic reference points of Christian orthodoxy or its significance for justice in social and cultural affairs. Insofar as we nurture, cultivate, and develop this foundation for *praxis* without careful and constant attention to the questions of whether it is true and just and whether or not it has direct implications for truth and justice, we allow our students to erect some temporarily valid practice into an orthopraxy disengaged from both ultimate and long-term questions. The students are inclined to become functionaries of various contextual practices that they are not equipped to assess, defend, judge, or transform. Their *praxis* becomes subject to cultural drift, without direction or intensity. Piety and organizational habits are maintained, but without principle or purpose. Thus, when basic questions of polity appear, especially as they demand attention to issues of justice, the students, the churches, the laity in the communities of faith, and the wider world become convinced that Christians have nothing pertinent to say. All too often that is a reliable judgment.

3. Policy

Every religion interacts with social and cultural patterns in its immediate context to mediate its view of what is orthodox and to carry out the *logos* of practice in *praxis*. And here, every religion is confronted with critical decisions. Will that community of faith resist the social and cultural patterns of its civilizational environment, and try to isolate itself from social and cultural influences by intensifying its focus on piety and internal polity? Or will that community recognize structures in the social and cultural environment with which it can work and by which it will attempt to mediate its distinctive piety and polity to the world?

This is the question posed, in one way, by the tradition of monasticism, which often saw the possibilities of a true piety and polity as viable only in terms of a policy of withdrawal from the world — a policy that has had its counterparts in particular Protestant groups such as the Shakers, who practiced celibacy, the Quakers, who have refused to use the coercive violence always present in political life, and the Mennonites, who have resisted using modern technology in their economic life. Today, many who are not heirs of these traditions nevertheless accept their negative sensitivities. Many oppose the established structures of family life, the use of force in political questions, dominant structures of economic life, the values represented in the mass media, and so on.

The question of resisting or embracing the structures and dynamics of civilizational life was also posed for modern scholarship in more sociohistorical and analytical terms by Ernst Troeltsch and Max Weber early in this century. They pointed out the perennial tensions between religious critiques of "the world" and churchly "compromise" with it — between, in other words, the prophet and the priest.[6] The same question was posed in another typological form a generation later by H. Richard Niebuhr in his analysis of the major possible relationships of "Christ and culture."[7] And, most recently, a series of Third World theologians have expressed a similar question in terms of the relative degree to which God's truth and justice may be found in radical movements for social change.[8]

The decisive theological-ethical issue behind these questions is whether God's justice is present in the world outside the piety and polity of Christianity — and if so, where. Or, to put it another way, where in the world can we discern the *praxis* of God so that it becomes decisive for humans to endorse it, participate in it, celebrate it in prayer and worship, and adopt its dynamics as a part of our policy in order to live in accord with God's justice?

Even the most monastic, "sectarian," "Christ against culture," or "prophetic" approaches will find that some aspects of culture (such as language and music) and some aspects of society (such as roads and police protection) are required to maintain piety and polity. Thus, total isolation for the sake of "purity" is seldom possible. Christian orthodoxy knows that every social and cultural pattern is laden with sin, and in need of salvation. Yet the assumption that God's justice can be found only in those forms of piety and polity that totally oppose social and cultural life has been seen as a denial of the universal sovereignty of God. If God's justice is in the world, but not everywhere in it to the same degree, and if human sin is in the world, but not everywhere without also the promise of salvation, and if the distinction between the two is decisive for what we do, we had better be clear about what we endorse and what we resist.

We know that when Christian missions in the past have converted people and planted churches on the basis of a piety and a polity that have entirely segregated the new community from the questions posed by the surrounding culture, orthodoxy has not been contextualized. Very quickly decisive questions of policy have sur-

---

6. See Troeltsch, *The Social Teaching of the Christian Churches,* 2 vols. (London: George Allen & Unwin, 1931); and Weber, *Economy and Society: An Outline of Interpretive Sociology,* 3 vols., trans. E. Fischoff et al., ed. Guenther Roth and Claus Wittich, 4th ed. (New York: Bedminster Press, 1968).
7. Niebuhr, *Christ and Culture* (New York: Harper & Row-Torchbooks, 1951).
8. See, for example, *Theology in the Americas,* ed. Sergio Torres and John Eagleson (Maryknoll, N.Y.: Orbis Books, 1971).

faced. Most often they have shown up first in areas of pastoral care. How are ministers to deal with the cultural phenomena they confront — marriage practices, traditional forms of therapy, questions of identity as embodied in song and poetry, initiation into the culture, and funerals (including the treatment of deceased spirits)? Soon such questions have also appeared in matters of a more direct political or economic sort. Should Christians participate in wars of liberation, or in the expropriation of property from colonialists? Can violence be used to resist and overcome recalcitrant wickedness? Sooner or later, clear policies have to be specified, not only on the grounds of orthodoxy but also according to the kinds of *praxis* that are seen to be in accord with the *logos* of God's justice.

In a number of current theories of orthopraxy, it has been argued that precisely these practical questions are the central questions of the faith, and that all questions of orthodoxy and all interpretations of God's justice are to be adjudicated in these terms. And yet, no "churchly," priestly approach — even the sort of approach that most enthusiastically embraces the cultural and societal patterns and dynamics of cultures into which Christianity moves — endorses everything that is engendered in or by a society. Neither the psychosocial structures and dynamics of personal and interpersonal relationships nor the socioeconomic and political movements for justice are beyond evaluation. Indeed, it is necessary to select, modify, and influence that which the faith embraces. The *logos* of God's *praxis* of justice may be in the world, as surely as God's truth may be known in the world, but this truth and justice may not be securely identified simply by appeal to the way things are in the world or to the course of events by which the status quo is changing. Were such appeals all that were needed, there would be no reason to have any religious loyalty to that truth which is beyond the world or to that justice which is not yet actual in human lives or social history.

Thus, even the most "compromising" community of faith maintains some standards distinct from the operating norms, structures, and dynamics of its social-cultural environment. And these standards are necessary for policy. Again, the theological-ethical issue is whether — and if so, how — it can be known with some degree of security where God's *praxis* of justice is present in the midst of sociocultural life. In other words, discerning God's *praxis* of justice requires, from the human standpoint, some defensible criteria, some principles of judgment to guide our policy, and thus our *praxis*. Again, *praxiology* is required.

This is the case because, ultimately, the truth and justice of

God are understood to be one and to be universally valid within and beyond the church. In the end, Christian *praxis* is doing the truth in faith, hope, and love, and Christian orthodoxy involves enacting the *logos* of justice in the public structures of the common life. And this has been done in various degrees by those outside the church as well as by those within it. If enacting in *praxis* something that purports to be orthodox leads to clear injustice, the claim of orthodoxy is falsified. And if commitment to some *praxis* can be shown to be based on some appeal that is demonstrably not true, the regnant *logos* of *praxis* can be judged to be false.

A number of examples from religious history could point to the importance of the mutually implicative character of truth and justice, and to the fact that aspects of both have occurred outside the piety and polity of Christian life. Intense debates have raged, and rage still, over such matters of justice as warfare and self-defense, trade, profit, and private property in economics. Similarly, in terms of pastoral care, very hard questions have been and are still being debated about marriage, homosexuality, divorce, abortion, and the best ways to interpret joy and grief, love and anger, nurture and discipline. These all require a theological praxiology that does not demand a ritual or an ethical orthopraxis, but that nevertheless does and can guide our life policies.

Today the issues involved are perhaps being most sharply posed by contemporary feminist scholars. They and many male sympathizers have come to recognize that the policy of relegating women to secondary status in piety and polity violates fundamental principles of justice, and indicates that a basic mistake of policy may have governed much of church teaching and practice over the centuries.

It is well known that most religions have provided legitimation for the world's societies, which, for most of their histories, have discriminated against women. Women have been treated as property, as slaves, as objects of male gratification, and as less than full participants in social, political, artistic, and economic life. We know that this was the case in varying degrees and forms for much of the history of Israel, in the societies of the Mediterranean wherein Christianity was born, and in most of the societies — East and West, North and South — into which Christianity has moved. We know that Christian authors, leaders, and ordinary followers, including those who have been considered among the most orthodox over the centuries, did not find this treatment of women to be particularly contrary to the fundamental meanings of Christianity. Christian history has, in fact, often endorsed this subordinate condition, taking its very pervasiveness as evidence of the "fact" that it was a law of nature, or possibly a manifestation of the will of God. Further, we know that this perspective has affected the formation of personal self-images and interpersonal roles, and influenced the solidification of discriminatory practices in prayer, worship, polity, and pastoral care, although it violated basic implications of baptism and Eucharist.

In addition, while it may be true to say that Christianity has been more inclusive, or at least less exclusive, of women than a great number of societies, cultures, and religions that could be mentioned, and that the relative justice of Christianity on this point is at least one of the numerous reasons why it has been widely (and sometimes secretly) accepted among oppressed women of the other religions of the world, the demonstrable fact that Christianity has been prejudicially discriminatory in both its piety and its polity means that the faith has been seriously betrayed in the policies the *ecclesia* has taken toward a common social and cultural practice.[9] And it means that while some other societies, cultures, and religions may have been even less in accord with God's justice on this point than Christianity, Christians who say that they know something about the truth and justice of God may be more culpable for their failures in this area in regard to God's *praxis* of justice.

Correction of these failures will demand a broader application of the doctrine of sin and salvation, a new interpretation of the authority of Scripture, a fresh understanding of the relational character of the Trinity, and a nonsexist Christology. In all of these, a quest for a broader and deeper vision of orthodoxy seems to be required, one that takes the foundations of justice seriously. The result would and should become a part of the global mission, to be contextualized everywhere.

4. Program

If what has been suggested thus far is valid, the direct implications for theological education and the indirect implications for the *praxis* of the church in the world are rather striking. At the minimum, it means that each area of theological scholarship and every aspect of preaching, teaching, pastoral care, and social action must subject itself to a constant dual standard: not only must it pursue the truth,

---

9. See Annie Athol, "Christian Social Ethics and the Status of Women in South India," STM thesis, Andover Newton Theological School, 1987.

but it must be preoccupied with questions of justice, recognizing that it is not yet working at a level appropriate to the *logos* of God until the two standards coincide. The usual standards of "academic" and "professional" excellence are thus broadened, and the operating definitions of what is to be contextualized and globalized in mission are revised.

The first thing that would be required is an amplitude of vision. That is, to deprovincialize our own petty perspectives, we must directly encounter those of other peoples, religions, cultures, and societies. This means that we have to continue to promote and augment a familiarity with biblical and church history, especially as these allow students to see how the present pieties, polities, and policies of the churches have been shaped by decisions and developments in times and places that they know not of. It also means, in a cosmopolitan age, that we have to develop, quite intentionally and programmatically, opportunities to become familiar with histories that are not our own. Not only is it important to attend to the histories of minority populations neglected by much of standard history, but some capacity to locate these histories within the religious history of the world must become the nexus of reference. Such a suggestion has direct implications for what ought to be required for admission to seminary if the seminary itself cannot provide such things.

Also implied is a plan that would involve regular and planned exchanges of professors and students in a series of new global partnerships. Personal encounter with international scholars — as we have seen in this study, in which we were aided by such consultants — widens the horizons. Potentially, such a plan would allow us to deprovincialize our students; it also would demand of us and our colleagues familiarity with religions, civilizations, and sociocultural contexts beyond our own. One way of encouraging this familiarity involves making certain that our student body, our scholarship awards, our sabbatical and study-leave policies, and our hiring and promotion practices insure a cosmopolitan diversity and sexual inclusiveness.

More difficult, however, is the question of what will be the central questions of discussion when a cosmopolitan, inclusive body of teachers and students is assembled, and what we will look for when we encounter other histories, religions, and civilizations through study or exchange. The indispensable presence of people from and courses about multiple contexts does not insure that the fundamental questions will be addressed any more than a range of courses in different disciplines insures such. Each can become simply a curiosity unto itself. At the first level of mutual exposure, of course, simply learning that things are believed and done differently in different contexts has its own import. More decisive, however, is the issue of whether or not the beliefs and practices of those from another context are true and just, and whether or not they can offer perspectives on our faith and practices that allow us to assess our own more accurately. In short, the topics for discussion in an ecumenically inclusive dialogue must be *apologia,* orthodoxy, and the topic under focus at this point of our reflections, praxiology.

THREE MARKS OF JUSTICE

One decisive question remains, however. How might we reliably know what an adequate theological praxiology might look like? How, in other words, do we know the just *praxis* of God if and when we encounter it, at home or abroad, in piety, polity, policy, or program? At this point, it is possible to identify three necessary components of a theological praxiology, with the implication that if any of these is absent, some defect in our basic theory of *praxis* is likely to be present.

1. Ethology

In most of what we have already treated in this study is the recognition that intuitions of truth and justice can be found "contextually." Awareness of and sensitivity to how a situation looks and feels from the inside are surely required. If God as Creator made heaven and earth; if, through the Incarnation, God was present in Jesus Christ; and if, in the Holy Spirit, the dynamic presence of God can be experienced by people in their inner lives, in interpersonal relationships, and in the realities of social history, as witnessed by Scripture, tradition, and, indeed, the world's religions and cultures — if these things are true, then it is not nonsense to look in the midst of life for traces of justice directly pertinent to truth. Boonprasat-Lewis, Fontaine, Schreiter, and Farley have already instructed us on this matter.

What is required at the first level of praxiology is the testing of our intuitive sensitivities by recognition of the fact that our intuitions may differ strikingly because they are strongly influenced by the context in which we live. Therefore, careful use of semiotics, phenomenology, and the social and historical sciences is demanded. Through philosophy, psychology, and sociology, if they are at all profound, key issues of anthropology and history can be posed. Yet, insofar as the use of these social and historical sciences has been dominated by those understandings of life that are descriptive only, they are likely to tell us little about the normative questions of God's *praxis,* and whether or not we ought to exercise the will for the sake of justice.

For a theological praxiology, it is indeed necessary to distinguish more clearly than has frequently been the case between those patterns of human consciousness and civilization that are properly to be seen as inevitable products of the natural structures and dynamics of life and thought, and those that are susceptible to alteration, modification, or transformation by nurture. In other words, analysis is required. Of course, most of the important issues in psychological, social, and historical analysis are hotly disputed. Those who follow Freud may disagree with those who follow Jung; those who find Marx convincing may dispute with those who find Weber to be more complete on precisely these points. But that is just the point. It can and should be expected of all students entering seminary that they can recognize the major issues of causation in psyche and society beyond their own intuitions. And if they lack these analytical capacities with regard to the social sciences, supplementary educational requirements can surely be established. Thus, the approach to the first mark of justice involves developing the capacity to analyze the actual conditions in which people live with full awareness of what the basic, alternative hermeneutics of human life and history imply in terms of determinism and freedom, nature and nurture.

But in theological education, we take this one step further. After coming to the point where intuitions are corrected, confirmed, or expanded by analysis, we face the deeper task of trying to discern the spiritual and moral issues that are at stake in every concrete situation where the will can be exercised. This dimension of praxiology can be called human "ethology." It is the attempt to identify which value patterns in a context, whether psychological or social, have become built into the artifactual fabric of everyday life. These patterns often determine how we assess our own worth and that of others; in addition, they frequently dominate structures of power and influence, and they delimit the available possibilities of *praxis.* Here the focus is on those patterns of living, judging, and evaluating that have become "second nature" in a context. We seek, at this point, to understand the *ethos* according to its moral, spiritual, and religious qualities. Of course, those modes of analysis that do not or constitutionally cannot grasp this dimension of reality must be left behind, and the reasons for the intentional neglect articulated.

If it is true that humans have some degree of freedom and can in some measure guide their *praxis*, if it is true that religion is a force in the patterns of thought and the dynamics of will which guide that *praxis*, and if it is true that all of life manifests evidence of sin and salvation, then beyond our empathetic intuitions and beyond even our best analysis, we finally come to the questions of what spiritual and moral patterns are regnant in each *ethos*. This is a dimension of social and historical analysis that is genuinely scientific but that much of modern philosophy and the social sciences neglects.

We can presume to discuss just such matters in cross-religious, cross-cultural, and cross-historical contexts because we presume that every conscious human being and every society manifests some measure of capacity to know the foundations of justice. Theologically, we may prefer to identify that *justitia originalis* in terms of "natural law," or with "general grace," or with that which "has been written on human hearts." The point is much the same: Justice is grounded in something that is not simply a product of upbringing, society, culture, civilizational history, or particular situation. It is, at least in part, rooted in the common human discernment of moral and spiritual qualities that is the decisive first step in a normative discussion, ethology. It is a base point of a theological praxiology.

It is theological precisely because the central content of this common knowledge of justice is this: the law of life is love. Nothing exists without some loving spirituality behind it and within it. Lovelessness and hate destroy, and justice is impossible. Yet without God's *praxis* love is also impossible, and justice becomes simply what the powerful say it is.

On the basis of this kind of discernment, we may not be able to specify what particular acts ought to be undertaken to actualize love. Yet, the beginning of wisdom and the end of *scientia* concerning the justice of God's *praxis* comes just at the point when we recognize that something is spiritually and morally false, that it is unloving and thus unjust, and that something can and ought to be done (or could and ought to have been done) about it.

2. Teleology

But if by "ethology" we come to recognize that something is fundamentally contrary to love, and therefore predisposes an ethos to injustice, it is less clear that any kind of ethological analysis can give us a profound sense of what specific actions ought to be undertaken to secure the relative forms of justice possible within human relationships, human societies, and human history. Those who have attempted to build a whole vision of justice on ethological grounds have often overstated the case to such a degree and made presumptive use of "natural law" to such an extent that their positive prescriptions have been justly ignored. A fuller theological praxiology requires also a positive vision of what ought to be done *beyond* what is already present in the *ethos*. And that positive vision demands a sense of the ultimate good, of the ultimate end of human existence not fully present in the context. What is the purpose of life that humans should attempt to embody in the piety, polities, and policies that guide self, society, and historical existence?

At this point, every theological praxiology must have a teleological element, one centrally governed by a compelling interpretation of what the purpose of life is. With many of the world's religions, Christianity can say that the purpose of life is what God intends. But that only begins the discussion. For the immediate question is whether God intends happiness, *shalom*, life in Paradise, purification, true holiness, nirvana, going to heaven, reconciliation, finding (or founding) the New Jerusalem, or attaining perfection. Each definition of God's ultimate purpose will demand distinctive ways of marking the shape of justice, and thus of guiding *praxis*.

A wide range of highly symbolic terms have been used to identify, so far as humans can reliably know them, the purposes of God for humanity. In Christian thought, many of these symbols are clustered around the vision of "the Kingdom (or reign) of God," a term obviously drawn from the political realm, but applied to interpersonal, social, and cultural patterns of possibility that are not essentially to be gained by coercive power. It is not the function of this study to attempt to sort out all the multiple levels of meaning that have attended uses of this term. But it is proper to suggest that this symbolic phrase would be one of the critical points of departure in any theological dialogue about praxiology. Once a situation is understood to be unloving by ethological analysis and spiritual discernment, it is possible to turn to the second dimension of theological praxiology and inquire about what projects, purposes, and intentional actions humans ought to undertake to live in accord with God's *praxis* of justice in the teleological sense. Insofar as that ultimate *telos* of God is already present amid the aimlessness of human existence, its presence invites, inspires, and empowers hopeful, creative action toward a promising future that transcends the present *ethos*. That action may involve the reform and reordering of piety or of polity, or it may involve new assessments of the location of God's *praxis* of justice in the social and cultural environment, assessments that demand a revolution in public policy. In any case, the teleological element of praxiology opens up an expectation of historical change, one that evokes urgent action in new ventures and projects.

Among the peoples of the world, the idea of change — that things can be different, that it is not necessary to live only by the old and established patterns, that it is possible to become participants in a holy *praxis* of justice for a new future — is a revolutionary one. It is an idea that is found not only in Christianity. It can be seen in Judaism and Islam, which share with Christianity the idea of a God who is active in history and brings novelty. It can also be found in modern secular worldviews, both liberal and Marxist, which have been influenced by theories of historical progress. In all these views, humans live in anticipation, and undertake action toward new goals to be realized at least in part in history.

Christian teleology differs from several of these, however, in that it doubts that the eschatological vision can be fully realized in history. Some clear manifestations of evil can be overcome, and some anticipations of the ultimate future are possible to actualize. Thus, those caught up by the vision of the Kingdom become active transformers of the world, but they remain acutely aware of the limits of what is possible within history. A Christian teleology is always eschatologically modified. Christians, therefore, are unlikely to identify any particular project with the fullness of the Kingdom, and are likely to recognize that while evil may be in part overcome, the full good cannot be made to happen in history. Consequently, praxiology at this level will assess every human project according to its relative capacity to contribute to the possibilities of the Kingdom, and it will be simultaneously suspicious of every project within and beyond Christianity that claims to provide the final answer. It is in part for this reason that Christianity invites initiative, projects, and a reorientation of the will toward actions for the good, but it neither prescribes particular ones nor holds that the ones it does undertake can be final.

Thus, theological education, and the preparing of women and men to be theologians in mission in all the various contexts of the globe, will focus also on the discernment of the *praxis* of God's justice according to whether it empowers people to undertake action for the Kingdom without pretending that the Kingdom can be fully actualized in history and experience. Assessing what does genuinely accord with the most realistic, most universal, and yet most hope-inducing vision of the ultimate future is the second chief topic of conversation when scholars from multiple contexts are mutually engaged in teaching and learning with a concern for justice as well as truth.

3. Deontology

Theological *praxiology* also has a third reference point. This is that aspect of justice which deals most directly with duty and obligation. In spite of the variations of *ethos* and the constantly changing senses of *telos* in human history, Christianity holds, with most of the world's religions, that internal to the *praxis* of God's justice is an eternal moral law. There is a right order of things that stands over and above what is present in the various ethological structures of different contexts and in the dynamic flux of historical change toward an ultimate future that cannot yet be fully actualized. Murder, rape, lying, stealing, oppression, torture, infidelity, greed, and exploitation are always contrary to that order. Any theory that authorizes these, any practice that manifests them, any *praxis* that combines theory and practical experience to legitimate these in a specific context or even toward a desirable end — none of these can be taken as a basic mark of God's justice. Truth-telling, promise-keeping, respect for human rights, protection of the innocent neighbor, and benevolence are always right. No analysis of the *ethos* or spiritual discernment, and no project toward the future, even in the name of the Kingdom of God, which transgresses these principles of righteousness can be taken as an authentic foundation for *praxis*.[10]

But it is not only specific actions that are to be identified as right or wrong. There are also social patterns that are to be assessed according to their relative approximations of right order. A theological praxiology would suggest that there are normative patterns of right order for the human personality, for human relationships, and for social structures. The family, the state, the economic order, the judicial system, the arts, and the institutions of education and medical care all function under the law of God, which serves as the standard for their right ordering. This then becomes another area that must become central to the conversations in theological edu-

---

10. See, for example, Joseph Allen, *Love and Conflict: A Covenantal Model of Christian Ethics* (Nashville: Abingdon Press, 1984); Lewis Smedes, *Mere Morality: What God Expects from Ordinary People* (Grand Rapids: Eerdmans, 1983); and Bernard Gert, *The Moral Rules* (New York: Harper & Row, 1973).

cation when a genuinely cosmopolitan assemblage of people and perspectives is present.

We can now note that one very difficult problem in dealing with justice is that the *logos* of just *praxis* is not simple. Indeed, the bane of much contemporary thinking and teaching about justice and *praxis* is the tendency to oversimplify them. Justice is multidimensional, with each dimension rooted in an aspect of God's *praxis* of justice. Each human attempt to enact just *praxis* demands constant clarification of the possibilities and probabilities that transcend human *praxis*. In other words, the human, historical, contextual, and social understandings of *praxis* demand rootage in and criteria for that which transcends the human, the historical, the contextual, and the social. And each judgment must be defended on the combined grounds that it accords in some substantial measure with God's love, God's purpose, and God's law. These are the unavoidable reference points of a theological praxiology.

But these demand, as can readily be seen, some secure knowledge about what is godly and what is not, some reliable ways of speaking of the *logos* of God in reasonable discourse for teaching and preaching. The vision of justice that can aid us in *praxis* — in piety, polity, policy, and program — is linked to the quest for a truth and an orthodoxy for which an *apologia* is necessary. *Apologia*, then, marked by a quest for orthodoxy and praxiology, must become the core of theological education. These could and should be contextualized around the globe in mission.

CHAPTER 12

Doxology

The vocation of Christian theological education is to prepare women and men to be theologians and ethicists in residence and in mission among the peoples of God in the multiple contexts around the globe. The core of this preparation must be the cosmopolitan quest for the truth and justice of God. In Christian theological education, these will be best treated by careful, critical, and constructive concern for orthodoxy and praxiology, with the constant recognition that an *apologia* is necessary at every juncture.

Much has been neglected in this book. Each one of the topics covered could be expanded and refined. But the purpose of this study has not been to present an exhaustive analysis of each of the multiple issues that have been raised. Rather, the goal has been to present an overview of the issues emerging from a dialogue already underway and to intentionally extend reflection on the most vexing issues. In the process, it seemed necessary to sort out some confusions and to identify some central themes that have been neglected in much contemporary thinking, especially at a time when many are entranced by a variety of notions about contextuality, global encounter, and mission that have very mixed implications when they are thought through, and at a time when the integrity of theological education itself is threatened by perspectives that see all religious questions as secondary in import or that see such religious pluralism in the world that they doubt the possibility of making any normative statements except on a purely confessional basis.

Three remaining major dimensions of such an overview, however, seem to require further and direct attention. They have been implied throughout much of what is already in hand, but they demand more explicit treatment. All three of them are related to the title of this concluding chapter. That is, they have to do with an attempt to identify key characteristics of the spirit necessary for the quest of a justifiable *apologia* for orthodoxy and praxiology, the kind and quality of spirit that virtually sings out with praise to the God who is the source of truth and justice in all the contexts of the globe, the kind and quality of spirit that invites us to mission.

IN PRAISE OF REASON

One dimension has to do with the question of whether we can place any justifiable confidence in reasoned discourse, which this study has suggested is necessary to dialogue, to the analysis of text and context, to education, and to the knowledge of the truth of God in orthodoxy and of the justice of God in praxiology. The second dimension has to do with that kind of humility that the quest for orthodoxy and praxiology seems also to require. And the third sketches some possible implications of this study for the "theological encyclopedia" (as it was called by Edward Farley), or the "system of the theological sciences" (as other scholars call it). Whichever name is used, it is useful to inquire what the special contributions of the various fields of study might be, and what other fields can properly expect of them, as a theological seminary prepares theologians to become apologists for God's truth and justice in a doxological spirit. After all, the *logos* (here as *verbum* and *ratio*) of *doxa* (here as giving or acknowledging glory) is what holds orthodoxy and praxiology together and makes them relevant to all of life.

Many theologians as well as their critics believe that most of what theological education deals with is not rational, and that attempts to deal with it logically are doomed to failure or distortion of its essence. And yet, in this study, in team and faculty discussions, and in theological education as a whole, theological educators make rational, critical evaluations of materials under discussion, of each other's proposals, and of the tasks of the various disciplines within the larger whole. Today some produce the most rational arguments they can muster to show that the decisive questions are beyond rationality.

There is some wisdom in this, for it is surely the case that the full reality of God is veiled in mystery. No one knows it fully; no tradition has exhaustively grasped it; no discipline can finally encompass it. There is also good evidence to suggest that most of the logics by which we daily operate, in life or in scholarship, are quite limited and are frequently distorted by interests, passions, and sociocultural influences that we scarcely understand.

And yet, we do not want to claim that what we hold to be true and just is simply a fabrication of our limitations and distortions with no connection to God's reality. Were that so, there would be no reason for dialogue, for mutual critique, for joining together as a theological faculty, or for developing new interactions with people from other contexts around the globe. We presume, in all that we do and in all that we propose to do, that it is possible to discuss, write about, think about, and teach God's reality in a reasonable fashion. And that presumption surely implies that our reasonable discourse has some connection to the *logos* of God.

It is wise to recognize that the *logos* of God, as present to us in the quest for God's truth and in the attempt to discern God's *praxis* of justice in history, has dimensions that transcend our capacity to grasp logically and rationally. But it is foolish to thus conclude that God is irrational, a-rational, or anti-rational, or that our approaches to the mystery of God are aided by eschewing reasonable discourse and reasoned arguments. Even if it should be claimed — as many have argued by rational proofs from Tertullian through Kierkegaard — that intuitive, spiritual insight grasps far more of the *logos* of God than human logics can imagine, it would not prove that God's *logos* is entirely unreasonable or that human logic can know nothing of it. And even should it be shown that women, minorities, and non-Western cultures know something about the truth or justice of God not known by male groups, dominant groups, and Western cultures — which often pretend to be more logical — it would not prove that the *logos* of God is contrary to reason or that the critique of Western, male, dominant logics is unreasonable. Indeed, such arguments would show two things: that prevailing conceptions of what is reasonable are too small, and that a deeper, broader logic can know something reliable about the *logos* of God. All arguments against the prevailing forms of logic presume a deeper and wider access to a *logos* that can show the distortions and limitations of petty, lopsided, and unreasonable logics.

Theological education rests on the assumption that humans can speak with some measure of reasonable confidence about what is ultimately mysterious, that in some degree it is possible to point to, if not fully grasp, the *logos* of God. In the history of Christianity it has often been pointed out that it is spiritually dangerous to take undue pride in our human rational capacities. But it has also been frequently accented that humans are gifted by God with some abilities to engage in reasonable discourse and to understand that which God has revealed in the form of *logos*.

It is also the case that any mission which attempts to be inclusive of peoples previously excluded, contextually sensitive, and global in reach presumes that the *logos* of God is potentially present and pertinent everywhere and always. If this is so, it simply will not suffice to criticize theological education by saying that it is too male, too right-brained, too Western, or too rationalistic. It may be that much of contemporary theological education (and this report) suffers from all these defects, and insofar as it exhibits these defects it should be subject to sharp criticism as a fabrication of a parochial, male, right-brained, Western rationalism and therefore incapable of representing very much of the full *logos* of God. But the responsible critique will not stop there. It will offer a deeper, broader logic that includes both male and female, that integrates right- and left-brained functions, that comprehends dominant and subcultural logics, that encompasses non-Western and Western logics, and that is more reasonable than rationalism under criticism. And to be accepted by all as genuinely theological, the critique will have to make the case that this broadened view reveals a more reasonable knowledge of the *logos* of God than the constricted definitions present. Otherwise, the critique will be correctly perceived as but an equally lopsided fabrication of some alternative and similarly fragmentary and privileged perspective.

This is not to suggest that the mysterious, the poetic inspiration, the prophetic charisma, the intuitive insight, and the pre-rational leadings of the spirit are irrelevant to theological education. Indeed, quite the opposite. It is to say that precisely these are to be taken with utmost seriousness. These are the sensibilities of much that is religious. These are what often move the souls of people and, if nonmaterialist understandings of societies and cultures are to be trusted, what shape the destiny of civilizations. But it is also to say that investigation of such matters, teaching and preaching about them, organizing our *praxis* on these foundations, and engaging in mission at their prompting demands that we can reasonably talk about them, and have some modest confidence that we are in some positive relationship to the *logos* of God as we do so.

It may be that we should scuttle the notion that what we are about in theological education is non-, a-, ir-, or anti-rational. It is possible that we should instead begin to ask whether it is possible to achieve an "ecstatic reasonability" — an ability to engage in reasonable discourse with each other, with our students, and especially with people from other contexts (of different genders, races, and sociocultural backgrounds) about ultimate questions in a way that pushes, pulls, and hauls us all into a wider framework of meaning. Thereby we might be able to stand outside *(ex + stasis)* the confinements of contextually derived, constricted logics and gain a more reliable and universal vision of the *logos* of God. Then we might be able to identify which aspects of our doctrines and our *praxis* and which particularities of our experience, our contexts, our faith, and our cultures do in fact reveal something of God's truth and justice. Of course, one could argue, as M. M. Thomas has (in Chapter 5), that we can do this best in worshiping together. But as soon as we suggest that, we face the problem of which liturgy we should follow, which hymns we should choose, which texts we should select for our meditation together, how we should interpret the texts, and how we should best understand the context in which our worship occurs and to which it pertains — all of which demand recourse to reasonable discourse, as every chapel committee knows.

Indeed, it could be argued that engaging in reasonable discourse is what we already do in large measure, but that we do it with great ambiguity because we are confused about the nature and character of God's *logos* and our own. Is it not the case that in prayer we give reasonable utterance to the mysteries of both the heart and the communion we feel with God? Is it not true that in pastoral care we aid others in discerning and wrestling with the irrational forces of the psyche so that they may be rightly understood, reordered to gain accord with the deeper logics of spirituality, and deprived thereby of their demonic capacities to induce antirational feelings and behaviors? Is it not among the purposes of teaching the Scriptures, church history, systematics and ethics, preaching, worship, church management, and youth education to identify — within all the chaos of data, event, perspective, and bias — those reasonable patterns of meaning, purpose, and duty that reveal the truth and justice of God? In each case, irrationality is penetrated, sorted, and tested by methodical examination to see whether or not something of the *logos* of God can be discerned and given reasonable articulation. The possibilities of developing an *apologia* for what we do in theological education and for approximating a decent orthodoxy and praxiology pertinent to contextualization, globalization, and mission surely are dependent upon our capacity and willingness to work in new, expanded, dialogical ways on precisely this issue of *logos*. Theological education seems to demand a profound appreciation of reason, and it must offer thanksgiving to God for some modest capacities for reasonable discourse.

A HUMBLE CONFIDENCE

And yet, something of the mystery always remains. We may reasonably doubt that the mystery of God is ultimately irrational or a-rational or anti-rational, but that does not mean that we grasp or have grasped it entirely. We may make modest gains in sorting some previously uncharted area of Scripture or tradition, of piety, polity, or policy — indeed, of psyche, culture, society, or history — where the *logos* of God's truth and justice may be discovered. We may expand our sense of the whole *logos* of God by interaction with peoples, ideas, and cultures that were once beyond our ken, and celebrate these gains as gifts from and gifts to God's truth and justice.

Yet mystery remains. Christians hold that it will always be so until the end of time. We may know something of the *logos* of God, but not everything. That which we can know is the basis for all that we do as educators, as theological educators, and as Christian theological educators. It gives us a warrantable and critical confidence to resist those who would relegate all of theology to secondary or tertiary status, and exclude it from the ranks of that which can be reasonably discussed. It renders a basis for that kind of action for justice which both preserves freedom and guides *praxis* in and beyond the church. It provides, in brief, the prospect of a genuinely public theology.

It may be that, with enlarged visions, we can learn enough to teach what can be trusted by our students and by non-Christians and thus can be carried into the world's contexts with the confidence of ecstatic reasonability. But we must also surely acknowledge that much of what we study, learn, and teach only points to mysteries yet unfathomed. This brings us to the second of the three dimensions that must be mentioned in this concluding chapter.

The awareness of mystery demands a certain attitude in our learning and teaching, one that could be profitably followed both by those secularists who are certain that their rationalities can rid the world of all that "mythical" stuff like religion, God talk, and theology, and by those fundamentalists who are absolutely certain that they know more about the truth, justice, and logic of God than it is ever possible to know with confidence. That certain attitude is humility.

To be sure, humility is out of fashion these days. Indeed, it has seldom been in fashion, although prideful displays of individuals or groups wanting to prove that they are more humble than their neighbors have been frequently in fashion. Yet, humility in the face of the full mystery of God is surely a mark of genuine theological education. It is not opposed to confidence, but it makes arrogance impossible.

Humility means, for one thing, conducting all our learning about, teaching about, and questing for a viable orthodoxy and praxiology in a way that expresses and conveys respect for the mystery that we do not understand as the context of working on that which we might understand, at least in part. Whether or not prayer is offered at the beginning of each class, theological education must be conducted in something of the spirit of the ancient Hebrews, who covered their heads before study of the sacred texts. They bowed their heads before that metaphysical-moral reality which is greater than the object of immediate investigation, and we must do the same.

Humility means, for another thing, showing respect for those forebears in faith who have made it possible for the church to exist, for the Bible to be transmitted and translated, for the great doctrines of the faith to be formed, and for centers of theological education to be founded. On certain issues we may become acutely aware of how frail their efforts were, how laden with racist, sexist, imperialist bias and falsehood, but we have no guarantees that we shall do better. Indeed, we may find that the burden of proof in plumbing the mystery of God and discerning something of God's *logos* rests more on us than on them, even where we know that, for the sake of truth and justice, their work must be corrected.

Such a humility extends to other religious traditions as well. Who is wise enough to decide finally that nothing of the *logos* of God is present in the religious knowledge of the Hindu, the Buddhist, the Muslim, the believer in tribal religion, or the secular humanist, even if it is the case that we can identify some areas where they need something that we know to be true and just to make their faith more complete.

Humility also means subjecting one's faith, one's scholarly work, one's teaching and preaching, one's hermeneutical principles, and one's most precious loyalties to tests that one cannot control — to the judgment and evaluations not only of peers but of peoples who share little or nothing of one's religious commitments, gender, class, race, culture, or civilizational history. Thus, humility does not mean hiding a light under a bushel, speaking only to tiny groups of specialized scholars who all speak the same academic jargon, or forming little enclaves where everyone already agrees. Of course, this does not mean that there is no place for groups where birds of a feather can flock, where scholars can have their work critically examined by those who know most about their field, or where men or women, blacks or whites, young or old, Baptists or Presbyterians or Eastern Orthodox can gather to share their distinctive concerns in ways that everyone present already understands. But it does mean that the issue and substance of such groups must sooner or later take the risks of public discourse. It means publishing the tidings of that which we think we know, and facing the critical responses that will surely follow. It means joining the debates with nonreligious and nontheological historians, philosophers, sociologists, psychologists, and linguists, and expecting that we might learn something as well as teach something. It means preparing ministers who can be theologians among the people who in turn can equip these people to test the theologian's claims with humble confidence in a variety of contexts — in factories and corporation offices, in shops and markets, in political parties and governmental bureaucracies, in hospitals, schools, studios, and laboratories. It means confidently carrying what we do know into the highways and byways of the world without attempting to enforce its reception by coercive means.

In short, humility is inextricably linked to the more profound forms of mission. If, in the past, mission has been seen as a phase of cultural imperialism, let it now be seen as an act of humility. The evangelist or catechist in the local church, the liberationist Christian who engages the dispossessed in the cities and villages and slums of the world, the feminist Christian who struggles with the manifest patriarchy of the tradition, the missionary who enters a foreign culture armed with little but a sense of the *logos* of God's truth and justice — each allows his or her vision of that truth and justice to be put to the apologetic test. Only by the persuasive character and intrinsic worth of the content of what we say and do in such wider contexts — as perceived, often resisted, sometimes appropriated, and nearly always modified, corrected, and revised by those who receive it in their own ways — does some portion of the truth and justice of God, its orthodoxy and praxiology, become contextualized and globalized, and possibly confirmed in life as something more or less in accord with the *logos* of God. Theological education needs to be conducted in such a way that confidence is not shattered by public exposure, dispute, and critique. Confidence tempered with a proper humility guards against humiliation.

But, most important, confidence in the capacity to know

something about the *logos* of God, coupled with a humility in the face of the mystery of God, allows us to joyously study, learn, dialogue, teach, and equip those who are to be the theologians in residence among the peoples and contexts of the world in such a way that they can praise God through their preaching, pastoral care, formation of communities of faith, and *praxis*. Of course, we know that they will experience pain, frustration, and hardship, and that some will betray a serious dedication to orthodoxy and base their work on inadequate orthopraxies. But if they grasp something of the *logos* of God, they will seek God's truth and justice faithfully and diligently, with both confidence and humility. They will take the first principles of orthodoxy and praxiology into the contexts of the world, empowering the people to whom they minister to carry them further into the multiple contexts of numerous societies, cultures, and subcultures. The result will be grace-filled lives and societies that will veritably fill the world with those beliefs, actions, and structures which, in a thousand ways, in idioms we cannot recognize, rightly sing glory to God.

THE FUTURE OF THE FIELDS

Such suggestions surely have implications for how the various fields within the whole of theological education are to define their special tasks. The historical fields, those that focus on biblical studies, world religions, and church history; the normative fields, those that focus on systematics, ethics, and missiology; and the practical fields, those that focus on preaching, education, church management, and psychology and pastoral care — how are they to conduct themselves so that they best contribute to an *apologia* for Christian orthodoxy and praxiology that leads to a worldwide doxology?

Those gifted in and professionally trained for historical analysis must surely continue most of what they do. For the most part, under the influence of modern critical methods of historiography, they work with texts and try to interpret the possible meanings of the texts in their own literary, social, and cultural contexts. But it is seldom the case that the possible meanings of the texts for contexts other than their own are taken into account, or at least taken into account in any systematic or sustained ways. Yet, if theological education is preparing theologians for ministry and mission in contexts other than those in which the texts first appeared and to which they most immediately relate, there is a double peril: the texts are read and used in one of three arbitrary ways. One is fundamentalistic, and recognizes no distinction between contextual observations and normative content in the texts themselves. A second method is the Rorschach approach, perceiving the text as a normless blob, which allows us to project our context-derived confusions into it. And the third approach so accents the strangeness of both texts and contexts that they are only marginally relevant to the wider contexts of the world. If these perils are to be overcome, it may be that three additional accents will have to be made in the historically oriented disciplines.

First, a scholar of the Old Testament, the New Testament, church history, or the history of religions may have to self-consciously attempt postcritical theological reflection about the meaning of a text. It is possible that some aspects of some texts bear within them features that are of universal and perennial import for knowing God's truth and justice. To identify these, of course, close and extended dialogue would have to be undertaken with at least two groups: those who work on systematics and ethics, and those who represent cultures and societies that have not been directly influenced by these texts.

Second, scholars should recognize that other parts of the texts may be pertinent and relevant only to contexts that are structurally, functionally, and semiotically similar to the contexts in which these texts appeared and to which they speak. To identify these, of course, requires greater familiarity with comparative studies of societies and cultures than scholars frequently possess. Here, it would at least be instructive for biblical scholars to be in close conversation with church historians and missiologists to explore how a text, taken as authoritative, functions in various periods and places. But also necessary would be greater familiarity with the tools of social, economic, political, and cultural analysis by which the contexts of human life can be shown to be more or less similar or different.

And third, scholars should recognize that some aspects of the texts appear to be pertinent only to the contexts in which they first appeared. This feature of sacred texts is most clearly accented by many contemporary historical-critical studies. But at this point too the biblical scholar and the church historian may want to risk asking what that phenomenon reveals about contemporary spiritualities, doctrines, preachings, and teachings that may be of quite ephemeral import, and to point out the dangers of taking everything purportedly sacred as valuable.

Both in their use of historical-critical methods and in their increased use of these postcritical discernments, the historically oriented scholars must make the case for the import of what they do and the material they treat for contexts around the globe. These are new challenges, and what they seek to prove cannot simply be presumed. Already, much of what historically oriented scholars do is ignored by the wider world, by social and cultural contexts outside those that already presume the authority of Scripture, and even by the theologians working among the people or in other disciplines on the same faculty. The contribution that historical scholars can make to *apologia,* to orthodoxy and praxiology, involves testing the adequacy of what they do, in confidence and humility, by showing how it aids in clarifying God's truth and justice in new and wider contexts. If these studies fail the test, they will properly be relegated to antiquarian hobbies. If they pass the test, they will allow those who study their findings to sing them out doxologically.

Those engaged in the normative disciplines — systematics, ethics, and missiology — must surely have as their primary concerns the clarification of the means by which metaphysical principles of truth and moral principles of justice can be known with relative reliability. These individuals bear the heaviest burdens for *apologia* in an age of epistemological suspicion. Not only must they face the issues posed by contemporary anti-religious and anti-theological modes of thinking, but they must encounter the great world religions and the problems of pluralism in a new way. A Christian systematician, ethicist, or missiologist who knows only his or her own tradition or church context is incompetent in the face of the modern needs for *apologia.* Even more, the systematician must investigate both ancient and modern forms of philosophical reasoning, from the Greeks to phenomenology, much as the ethicist must work with those forms of social theory — material, functional, structural, cultural, and semiotic — to try to understand what forms a viable *ethos,* and how a careful ethology ought to be related to teleology and deontology. And the missiologist must take account of the spiritual movements that sweep through or come to dominate various peoples and groups, and determine how these movements are to be assessed.

In each case, the scholars in these disciplines must attend to the normative questions: what is true, what is just, what is of God, what is in accord with the *logos* of God, how do we know, and how ought we to know?

On the far side of these investigations, the systematician, the ethicist, and the missiologist must be willing to take risks. Proposing a normative answer to any of the questions just listed is more difficult than posing the question. Those in historical and practical fields will always be ready to treat such proposals as unhistorical or impractical. And, if these charges prove correct, those in normative fields of study will find the principle of humility necessary in theological education is well exercised. But, because those in the normative disciplines live by and for the confidence that we can know something reliable about the truth and justice of God, they will present models of orthodoxy and praxiology and defend them in the face of both the cultured despisers of religion and the plethora of alternative religious commitments. If what they propose contains obviously unreasonable patterns of thought, they will get little hearing. Indeed, the proposal will scarcely be understood. If they present matters that are only ephemeral or pertinent to a highly particular context, they will have their moment and pass into oblivion. But if their ideas are found to be reasonable cross-culturally and cross-historically in some enduring or episodic way that accords with the *logos* of God and is pertinent to multiple contexts of the world, they will contribute to the singing of the doxology at home and abroad.

Those involved in the practical fields are, in some senses, at the mercy of the historical and the normative thinkers, for they inevitably rely on understandings of the past and on proposals about what is true and just in what they do. But in other ways, the practical fields are the adjudicators of the adequacy of what the others offer. The preachers, the teachers, the administrators, the evangelists, the counselors — they bear the heaviest burden of contextualization. They are the closest to those theologians in residence among the people, and the most directly responsible for sensitizing the people to all those dynamics of pretheological reality that inhibit, limit, and distort the quests for God's truth and justice. If they are alert to the contexts in which people live, they are able to recognize the psychological disabilities, the power plays and hidden interests, the structural constrictions, and the stinginess and meanness that preoccupies much of life in every context. In short, those in the practical fields encounter sin, and the need for salvation, firsthand. And it is in the face of the realities which they force theologians to confront that they identify the strategic openings to, the optimal modes of presentation of, and the nurture necessary for the contextualization of that which the historical and normative thinkers develop. Further, these practitioners cultivate at the local levels the pieties, the polities, the policies, and the programs that practically test all that is rendered by historically and normatively oriented colleagues. They test it in the formation of ongoing tradition and in *praxis,* although they find themselves dependent also on some fundamental definitions of orthodoxy and praxiology, which means that they must be in constant dialogue with their colleagues.

Today, the boundaries of the practical fields must be widened. The local contexts must become increasingly alert to the broader and more diverse contexts in which people live. The testing of what biblical scholars tell us about God's truth and justice as they study it by sustained, scholarly encounter with Scripture, with the long traditions that church historians study, and with modern constructive proposals advanced by systematicians and ethicists demands the recognition of horizons of sin and salvation scarcely yet recognized in most locales. Yet, if the practical fields grasp and help implement the wider, deeper, and more global perspectives on truth and justice, they too will enable generations to sing the doxology.

At the end of Chapter 9, we suggested that theological education had been indelibly stamped by two great moments of *apologia* in its history (the development of warranted wisdom and the development of a critical *scientia*), both of which have been sharply challenged by post-Enlightenment developments in thought and society. Then we posed the question of whether or not we are now in a new age requiring a fresh wrestling with the problems of *apologia*, an age that must take account of a much broader and deeper set of contextual and global factors. This question was posed after we noted that leading ecumenical voices are calling for a new spiritual awareness and a new active engagement on a global scale, that major voices in liberation thought and political theology are calling for a new *orthopraxis*, that cultural-linguistic scholars of Christian doctrine are calling for the new construction of local theologies and a new confessionalism, and that major philosophical theologians are calling for a reappropriation of sapiential knowledge by phenomenological means. And we were disposed to evaluate these calls on the basis of insights derived from episodic dialogues in a theological school among faculty and with international consultants. We are now prepared to answer this question. The answer is yes.

But it is not an unqualified yes. It is a yes that accents continuity with the great moments in which warranted wisdom and a critical *scientia* were formed, and continuity with classical debates about "nominalism" and "realism," text and context, and indigenization and translation. It is a yes that also demands awareness of discontinuities in thought posed by the rise of the social sciences in particular, and by the massive technologization, urbanization, and cosmopolitanization of the world that forces us to encounter powerful civilization-forming religions with at least as much subtlety and history, complexity and influence as Christianity has ever had. Indeed, it is precisely these factors that drive us into a new quest for a broad-gauged orthodoxy and an ample praxiology. That quest will demand the most rigorous intellectual *apologia* that theology has ever mounted.

This study did not provide that, but it may well have identified some of the key components of what would be required in such an *apologia*. If the collegium of theological educators is able to meet the demands of our now-global context and the demands of that truth and justice which we serve, it is possible that it would lead to a new doxology, contextualized among all peoples. That is our mission; that is the implicit covenant of all our dialogues; that is the vocation of theological education. May it be extended, corrected, and refined in further dialogue. As Reinhold Niebuhr wrote,

> Nothing that is worth doing can be achieved in a life-time; therefore we must be saved by hope. Nothing which is true or beautiful or good makes complete sense in any immediate context of history; therefore we must be saved by faith. Nothing we do, however virtuous, can be accomplished alone. Therefore we are saved by love.

APPENDIX 1

A Response to Apologia, *with Special Reference to Problems of Text and Context*

Ilse von Loewenclau, German Democratic Republic*

Coming from the G.D.R. as a visiting professor and being in the United States at the time this study was being discussed and completed helped me to understand the problems of theological education in this country. Over the years, I have been on a number of committees reflecting on theological education at Das Sprachenkonvikt in East Berlin. It was especially interesting to compare the problems of theological education in that setting with those of this one.

In Das Sprachenkonvikt we tend to have a more introverted discussion. That is, our discussion centers more on problems in teaching the classical languages (Hebrew, Greek, and Latin are all required) and on the number and length of papers students have to hand in during their five years of study (two papers for Old Testament, two for New Testament, one paper each for systematics and church history, one sermon, one lesson for youngsters). Another important issue remains the *Gemeindepraktikum,* or practical work in the congregation. Students are required to put in six weeks of activity in a parish during the holidays. This requirement

---

*Ilse von Loewenclau is presently a visiting professor at Bangor Theological Seminary. Her most recently published work is "Kohelet und Sokrates — Versuch eines Vergleiches," *Zeitschrift für die alttestamentliche Wissenschaft,* vol. 89, no. 3 (1986), pp. 327-38.

signals changes that have taken place since the 1950s and 1960s. During those days, students applying to Das Sprachenkonvikt were very much involved in their own parishes, often working with youth groups or Sunday schools. Today, students often come from atheistic or agnostic families. Frequently they are recently baptized and without previous experience of church life. Knowledge of the Bible has declined in general, including among those students who come from clergy families. Therefore, basic information about the contents of the Bible has to be taught in special courses that end with an examination.

In general, theological education at Das Sprachenkonvikt (and perhaps in most Eastern European institutions) is more or less focused on the traditional fields of theology, and heavily academic in its style. A major change has been the introduction of *koine* Greek instead of the classical Greek required earlier (although the latter is still a requirement in the theological faculties in the universities). Except for the *Gemeindepraktikum,* and an additional period of required work in a church-related nursing home *(Diakonisches Praktikum),* classes in practical theology are very few. For the most part, problems of ministry are taken up only after the student has taken the theological exam and has worked as a vicar in a parish.

The broader educational context of the G.D.R. influences theological education (and the church in general) to a significant degree. High-school education, with a few exceptions, concentrates on mathematics, the natural sciences, and technology, and places much less emphasis on languages and the humanities. Thus, students are not very well prepared for the academic study of theological subjects. In addition, there is a shrinking pool of academic theologians from which to draw our teachers, and relatively few who are able to introduce creative new ways of teaching for ministry. Where creativity is absent, we tend to continue to do things like they have always been done even if the presuppositions of the structures of former times have faded away.

Naturally, the developments I have mentioned have something to do with the Marxist character of the society in which our ministry and teaching takes place. Such a society is, in many ways, very exclusive. The government does not allow its people to be inspired by seeing different societies and cultures other than the country's most immediate eastern neighbors. Only a few individuals have chances to meet people from non-Marxist parts of the world and hear about their issues. Thus, it is a very special occasion when guests from other countries visit a parish or seminary or college in the G.D.R. or when professors who have traveled abroad return home. Such occasions generally attract many parishioners (especially young people) who are eager to learn how Christians live, teach, and carry out ministry and mission beyond the borders of the G.D.R. and its close allies. Although in recent years many ecumenical contacts have been established between the churches of the G.D.R. and the churches of other lands, most of these relationships are conducted at the higher levels of church organization, and things have hardly changed on the lower levels. Consequently, knowledge of how Christian churches encounter world religions is not widespread. The issue of "globalization" and the new definitions and directions in missiology would seem quite strange to most of our students.

We have, however, much experience with the problem of "contextualization," in part because the churches of the G.D.R. often speak of being the *Kirche im Sozialismus* (that is, the "Church in Socialism," and specifically not the "Church for Socialism" or the "Church against Socialism"). Such a stance involves a particular confinement, one in accordance with the confinement of our citizens to socialism as it is interpreted in the G.D.R. and protected by its borders and its army. The peril of this stance is that it could result in the church's becoming an enclave within the larger nation, something G. Gauss describes as a *Nischengesellschaft* ("niche-society"), wherein everyone tries to procure some privacy for his or her own options when they differ from the public ones required by the government. A Marxist state will be quite willing to accept a religious community concerned only about its own options (and for that reason the more sectarian churches have always had better relations with the state).

But this is not what the *Kirche im Sozialismus* is intended to mean. It wants to address the "new society" that socialism is building, confronting it with the Word of the gospel — hence its involvement in peace activities (watched critically by the state) as well as its services to the elderly and handicapped in church-directed centers of care (much appreciated by the state). In this view, *socializmus* is to be taken not as a confinement only but as *a context that needs the address of the gospel as much as any other context in this world.* All the same, the danger remains that Christians in socialist countries might lose sight of this meaning, so that a minister might settle comfortably into his or her parish, enjoying a certain freedom granted to the church, and turning the little enclave into a very special "niche-society."

It is possible that *this* danger is not confined to socialistic nations. Means must be found to counteract this peril—at the very least there must be sustained, effective consideration of the situation of world Christianity in theological education. A broad introduction to the problems of globalization and missiology is surely required.

With these brief introductory remarks about my own context as a Christian minister and theological teacher in mind, I want to take up the question of "text and context" as it appears in this book, specifically in discussions of "the problem of the biblical fields." I think the whole problem is deficiently handled, probably because of certain views that are represented in the discussions.

Having first studied classics before I became a theological student of the Scriptures, I am well aware of all the difficulties that arise when we try to perceive the meanings of ancient texts. I can easily understand why people would rather avoid the issue and bypass the difficulties that we must encounter in considering ancient texts. Indeed, I can understand the fundamentalists who want to avoid these difficulties by taking the Bible in a literal sense and proclaiming it to be free from error. But it is a matter of fact that Scripture is not error-free. Some passages that seem most important for a Christian understanding of God's will and way have been passed on in a very bad textual state (e.g., Ps. 22; Job 19; Isa. 53). Such vitiations occur in all ancient texts; they are never without errors. Further, as anyone who has studied any ancient texts—whether Homer or the Bible—will recognize, basic contradictions occur (consider, for example, Gen. 1:27ff.; Adam could not have been alone as Gen. 2:18 requires). *The Bible demands at least the same efforts to understand it as any other text from ancient times. However, unlike any such other text, it is a document of faith in a God whom Christ addresses as his Father.* Therefore, it is "scientific" to read it as a document of faith, to read it theologically as a textbook witnessing to and praising God, expressing God's actions and expectations. (Gerhard von Rad's conception of Old Testament theology ought to have taught us this much at least.) As God becomes visible for Christian faith in Christ, it can only be Christ who gives us the key for understanding also the Old Testament. (This distinguishes Christian understanding from Jewish interpretations, although they should not be ignored.)

The Bible has accompanied the church through the ages, always read, explained, preached, and often misunderstood and therefore also subject to misuses. Misuse can be avoided in some measure if the "translation" truly renders its text, the basic requirements being that the text itself is comprehended as far as possible in its original meaning. The latter is the task of exegesis, whereas the translation into our contexts is a matter of hermeneutics. It could be said, therefore, that we always have to deal with the text in terms of *both* its "contextuality" and its "contextualization," in terms of both exegesis and hermeneutics.

To cite an example, it may be interesting to note that Jeremiah 21:11-12 originally appears in the context of an address to the king of Judah. The same verses appear later (22:1-5) in a new context. Here the context is one of exile. This version speaks to the people in general; it extends the former expectations and reflects on future kings, thereby expressing implicitly that no king is in Judah anymore. Or we might take the New Testament passage of Matthew 8:23-27, where Jesus calms the storm. The focus is on the disciples following Jesus into the boat and being caught in a storm. But at Matthew's hand, this story seems clearly to be retold as a judgment against the wider circles of followers who are of "little faith," with the boat symbolizing the church in stormy times. To understand such texts, we need both to rely on exegesis, which helps us see the contextuality of the text, *and* to recognize the fact that the Scriptures themselves are engaged in hermeneutics, or contextualization of the text and its meanings within the Gospel tradition.

A different kind of interplay of text, context, and contextualization may be caused by the encounter with other peoples and their religions. When the tribes of later Israel moved into Canaan, they adopted aspects of Canaanite religious belief. Among these were the myths of creation (Ps. 74:13-14; Gen. 14:18-19, with Melchizedek probably being a priest-king worshiping). Such interpenetrations of faith partly enriched the faith of Israel and partly endangered it. Elijah and Hosea fought against Baalism while at the same time assigning some of Baal's deeds (fertility and so forth) to YHWH. The Deuteronomic tradition considered Baalism to be the sin above all sins (e.g., 2 Kings 17:7ff.), provoking YHWH's wrath in a way that led to destruction and exile. Many, even today's theologians, read our Old Testament through Deuteronomic eyes, and will not acknowledge any positive meaning of the encounter and interrelationship of Yahwism and Baalism. Sometimes they are tempted to solve all problems by introducing the term "revelation" to describe one, and denouncing the other as "mere natural religion." In other words, they deny the possibility of any "natural revelation" or "common grace" that could be inferred from a number of texts, including Romans 1:18ff., in which Paul seems to know that Gentiles may have written on their hearts what the law requires, that human conscience bears witness to what is truly of

God. In the Old Testament, too, many references to Adam seem to refer to all of humanity and not to a specific religious group (be it Israel or the church). Acts 17:16ff. seems to show undeniably how the altar to an unknown god can become a point of contact for the missionary. In short, it is essential to recognize the globalizing elements of contextuality and contextualization when reflecting on ministry and mission.

Finally, let me turn to the leitmotif of this study, *apologia*, in view of these reflections on my own context, and in view of these observations about text, contextuality, and contextualization in the biblical record. What does this term stand for?

In common Greek, *apologia* refers to the speech that an accused person delivered in court, rejecting the charges filed against him or her. The apologists of the second century chose this term because they wanted to show that the charges filed against Christians were unjustified and that the truths of their faith could be described and defended. An *apologia* was dedicated to the Roman emperor, who certainly never read it. Today the church and its message are challenged by many in whose context the gospel is being preached (I think of my own country). It would seem appropriate to consider the eternal truth embedded in its message, a truth that this study finds in the terms *theos* and *logos*, as the subject of theology. I think it would be desirable to express this truth in a manner acceptable to all ages and contexts. And, although certain key affirmations of the classical traditions of Christianity can be stated in clear form, I do not believe that we can grasp the eternal truth of God and the Logos in a fully appropriate manner. (This reminds me of a picture book I read recently. A child asks his father, "Did God make questions?" The father responds, "Yes, son. Mostly questions.")

I am deeply convinced of the provisionality inherent in all *logoi* endeavoring to express the greatest subjects of human thought and questioning (see Plato, *Phaedo*, 107.A,B and 85.C,D). This does not mean that we can or should despise *logoi* altogether (*Phaedo*, 89.Cff.). Life is a constant search for the truth that in its depths means God as the *agathon* giving essence to every being. Socrates accounts for his search in an *apologia* (as written by Plato) that seems to refute the charges filed against him. The refutation of those charges really does give an account of his call to philosophy, described as a service to God *(tou theou latreia)*. This service is delivered by testing human knowledge in dialogues with various groups who claim to have it and by proving how inferior the value of their knowledge is, thus honoring God, who alone is *sophos*, and thus implicitly identifying philosophy and theology.

It seems to me that Paul expresses a similar view in 1 Corinthians 13:12 regarding Christian theological knowledge: "For now we see in a mirror dimly, but then face to face. Now I know in part; then I shall understand fully, even as I have been fully understood." Making such statements certainly does not prevent Paul from striving to understand God and his will among us. Moreover, every part of Scripture strives to do so, reflecting at the same time its own context and the problems arising within it. Therefore, the New Testament (like the Old) has different theologies. But they do not fall apart; they are all focused on the old creed-formula of Philippians 2:11, and at the same time include the problems of Christology and theology because Isaiah 45:23, quoted in the verse, refers to YHWH. I venture to say that within Christian theology, this creed formula corresponds to the position of the *agathon* within Platonic philosophy. It is therefore Philippians 2:11 that must be explained in every new context (around the globe — the verse refers to "every tongue") and with full recognition of who it is, in each context, that is claiming to be "Lord." That, for any German, was the problem of Barmen.

In sum, an *apologia* is justified if it is considered not as something final, but as something having to occur anew at all times in fresh form, according to changing contexts. It is only in this sense perennial. It is thus very like the relationship of text to its context of origin and its context of interpretation — to its exegesis and its hermeneutics. An *apologia* is justified if founded in Scripture, in the sense that it not only speaks of the meaning of the God of the Hebrews in a tribal sense, but recognizes this God as the God of all humanity (Adam), the God who connects the Israelite experience of liberation with the belief in God's covenant of society and creation, and sees all of this to be interpreted by the Logos (John 1:18).

APPENDIX 2

A Response to Apologia, with Special Reference to the Seminary as a Faith Community

Robert W. Pazmiño*

Apologia represents a bold attempt to provide a unifying vision to guide the efforts of theological education in a global context characterized by pluralism and relativism. This work contributes to the ongoing discussion regarding the training of individuals for ministry in seminaries located throughout the world. It directly addresses two questions: Is there a common or shared vision for ecumenically oriented seminaries at this point in the twentieth century? If so, what is that vision?

The history of higher education in the United States since the late nineteenth century reveals that various institutions, including seminaries, have often accommodated competing visions within their structures and among faculty and administrators.[1] This accommodation can mean that participants in such education develop a fragmented or at least multifaceted vision for life and ministry. Viewed from this perspective, the perennial problem for ecumenical efforts in seminaries has been the fostering of some integrated

---

*Robert Pazmiño recently joined the Andover Newton faculty. He is the author of *Foundational Issues in Christian Education: An Evangelical Perspective* (Grand Rapids: Baker Book House, 1988).

1. For a full discussion of this history, see the work of Laurence R. Veysey in *The Emergence of the American University* (Chicago: University of Chicago Press, 1965).

230

understanding of the Christian faith and ministry in the minds of both professors and students. Without such an understanding, it is questionable how significant an impact the efforts of seminary training have upon the church and the world.

"Part I: A Dialogue" reports a series of attempts by an ecumenical seminary faculty, working with international consultants, to engage the global responsibilities of theological seminaries. One wonders if what is attempted is an impossible task in a postmodern context typified by an alarming diversity of understandings and concerns. But this research team contends that an integrated view is absolutely essential if Christianity is to be a viable intellectual option in our time. If the challenge is not addressed, Christian theology is reduced to fantasy and ideology. Such an effort grapples seriously with the exhortation Paul shared with the church at Philippi: "Whatever is true, whatever is noble, whatever is right, whatever is pure, whatever is lovely, whatever is admirable — if anything is excellent or praiseworthy — think about such things. Whatever you have learned or received or heard from me, or seen in me — put it into practice. And the God of peace will be with you" (Phil. 4:8-9, NIV). We need to think deeply and seriously about the nature and purpose of theological education in terms of its major thrust — that of being education, of being an intellectual process.

Similar questions have been explored in general education in terms of the analytic parts of the learning process. Different approaches will differently accent cognitive content, person, and social context. Twentieth-century developments have accented the fact that schools teach content to individuals in the context of their society, but that the cognitive content does not always touch the individuals or the contexts directly. Thus many have opted for educational models that center on personal formation or contextual awareness. The report of the ANTS team can be viewed in part as a reaction to current approaches in theological education that have attempted to give greater attention to both personal and societal factors to the relative exclusion of important dimensions of the Christian content to which seminaries must attend. God has created humankind with minds; therefore, the ideas and texts of the Christian faith are important and must be understood. The claim of Christian orthodoxy is that the texts of Scripture provide context-transcending truths that must be shared while appropriately interpreted and contextualized globally. Such emphases can be affirmed in this work. Christians are called to draw upon biblical, theological, and philosophical foundations to identify norms for faith and morals in a global village experiencing rapid change. The search for a *nomos* that can be intellectually and existentially both satisfying and unsettling to Christian individuals and communities is a necessity in the current historical situation.

It is likely that some readers of *Apologia* will question whether adequate consideration is given to both personal and societal factors in the effort to restore consideration of Christian content. Some will suspect that this study presents a vision that is so focused on cognitive content that it excludes Christian individuals with distinct experiential, cultural, or gender orientations. In fact, this study poses a crucial question related to precisely this issue: Which dimensions of personal, cultural, and gender orientations are able to reflect, sustain, and make concrete the context-transcending truths of Christianity, and what is the basis for such judgments? An additional question to raise is, Who is making such judgments?

From my understanding and perspective as a Hispanic evangelical, I offer the following response. When a distinction is drawn between the particular calling of formal theological education and that of the church, one basis for fellowship in the seminary is not adequately emphasized. While the seminary is a community of scholars, it is also an arm of the church, and its participants have personal and corporate relationships with Jesus Christ and the Christian church. Consideration of both relationships and partnerships on this basis may provide a ground less exclusive than the vision presented in this text. The Christian faith is exclusive and inclusive in terms of a response to the person and work of Jesus Christ. This response results in a vision that is not only cognitive and normative but also transformative—indeed, transformative of the academic task itself. Christians recognize the limitations of their best-conceived proposals in the light of God's hidden nature and agenda along with that which has been revealed. The problem is complex; cognitive formulations alone can exclude the recognition of mystery and God's supernatural working in community. Yet, without intellectual clarity, every passing spiritual fad can be identified with the Holy Spirit. An appreciation of both of these dimensions must also be a concern in seminary education as it bears upon the spiritual formation of individuals for ministry. This study may neglect those aspects of teaching and learning that are formative for individuals in favor of a relentless pursuit of the cognitive content around which they are formed.

Having raised these objections, I also applaud the effort to incorporate a variety of voices in the vision proposed and to grapple with perspectives from other cultures beyond Western contexts. The challenge in theological education is to balance both content and experience, with experience including both personal and societal factors. As Lois LeBar has aptly observed, "Content without experience is empty, and experience without content is blind."[2]

In Part II of this work, entitled "Wider Discussions," the authors who are represented call for integrity and responsibility in the areas of Christian theorizing, imagining, and living. They warn against the danger of reductionism in perspectives that exclusively center on *praxis* and *poesis* at the expense of *theoria*. But equal danger exists in a rationalistic approach devoid of adequate consideration of *praxis* and *poesis*. Today, in protest against previous rationalistic approaches to *theoria*, the emphasis is on *praxis* and *poesis*, and major current alternatives are at one in holding that a rationalistic approach fails to adequately consider the place of the passional, intentional, experiential, personal, and communal dynamics of the Christian faith. The dialogical critique of *praxis* and *poesis* in this study emphasizes the place of reason in the search for a normative core to guide *praxis* and *poesis*.

One of the key debates about this part of the study will be whether it redresses the current imbalance or succumbs to the older peril of rationalism. The first of the two great commandments, as shared by the author and perfecter of the Christian faith, is "Love the Lord your God with all your heart and with all your soul and with all your strength and with all your mind" (Luke 10:27, NIV). The use of reason in theological education is responsive to loving God with the mind, but cannot exclude that love of the heart, soul, and strength. The analysis does not exclude these dimensions when it deals with *praxis* and *poesis*, but it will be perceived by many as little more than a return to old-fashioned rationalism. This is a danger of which the authors are aware and an emphasis that they do not intend.

The authors represented in Part II do insist upon a coherent philosophical theology even when theology turns to *praxis* and *poesis*. Theological knowledge and *theoria* must be considered in terms of the possible human motives of control, curiosity, and compassion or love.[3] Though we recognize mixed motives in all human endeavors, we must ask ourselves in our *theoria* and intellectual dialogues, Which motives have priority? At points, *Apologia* reveals a struggle

---

2. LeBar, "Curriculum," in *An Introduction to Evangelical Christian Education*, ed. J. Edward Hakes (Chicago: Moody Press, 1964), p. 89.

3. Parker Palmer provides a helpful discussion of these motives in *To Know As We Are Known: A Spirituality of Education* (San Francisco: Harper & Row, 1983), pp. 1-16.

presently going on in regard to the guiding vision for theological education. Hard questions must be asked: What options are there for those who do not share or appropriate the vision shared by those who give priority to *praxis, poesis,* or *theoria?* Does a critical analysis of other options dismiss their viability? Are those who are not convinced subject to a marginal position in the theological education enterprise? I trust not, and just as Jesus trusted in the power of the truth to convince his hearers, this effort trusts in the power of careful debate about God's truth and justice to convince those with alternative visions to at least dialogue on these essential questions. The whole format of this work witnesses to an openness to dialogue and a willingness to grapple intellectually with a vision and a mission for seminaries today.

Part III of this work, "A Proposal," essentially represents Stackhouse's effort to offer a constructive direction in the light of the preceding discussions. The quest is for "warranted wisdom and grounded *scientia,"* which at their best are "linked with profound piety, sensitive to contextual realities, and dedicated to a mission of global reach" (p. 159). This proposal is a cognitively oriented attempt to provide a necessary vision that combines intellectual discipline, Christian piety, and orthodox belief. It calls for an encounter with world religions and advocates a specific role for clergy as "theologians and ethicists in residence and in mission among the peoples of God in the multiple contexts around the globe" (p. 209). It is well done and comprehensive, but Stackhouse sets it forth with such intensity that he fails to recognize that seminaries always have to accommodate alternative visions and ideals in their efforts. Other individuals with distinct senses of ministry have been formed and informed by study and research experiences that move in different directions, and their contributions must be honored. Thus this proposal necessitates further efforts directed toward the formation of a consensus not yet realized.

Given the need for consensus and my personal commitments to seminary education and intellectual endeavors, I am committed to the dialogue necessary to explore this proposal. Adequate time is needed for the thorough discussion of this work and the appropriation of this vision or an alternative one that incorporates various concerns. Other ideals and visions shared by those from feminist or minority perspectives deserve equal consideration, but require equal rigor and elaboration. Still, Stackhouse has demonstrated, at least for me, that there can be an orthodoxy and a praxiology that is not the imposition of the peculiarities of the Western tradition but the manifestation of warranted wisdom and critical *scientia* that can be somewhat known and justified by an *apologia* that is, in principle, universal in import.

How far has Stackhouse advanced the continuing discussion of theological contextualization? It is helpful to evaluate this effort in relation to the way this concept is used in *Ministry in Context: The Third Mandate Programme of the Theological Education Fund* (1972), a study not adequately considered in *Apologia*. This report outlined four areas of contextualization and linked each with a question:

1. *Missiological contextualization:* Is the seminary seeking to develop a style of training which focuses upon the urgent issues of renewal and reform in the churches, and upon vital issues of human development and justice in its particular situation?
2. *Structural contextualization:* Is the school seeking to develop a form and structure appropriate to the specific needs of its culture in its peculiar social, economic, and political situation?
3. *Theological contextualization:* Is the seminary seeking to do theology in a way appropriate and authentic to its situation? Does it offer an approach to theological training that seeks to relate the gospel more directly to urgent issues of ministry and service in the world? Does it move out of its own milieu in its expression of the gospel?
4. *Pedagogical contextualization:* Is the seminary a school seeking to develop a type of theological training which in its approach attempts to understand the educational process as a liberating and creative effort? Does it attempt to overcome the besetting dangers of elitism and authoritarianism in both the methods and the goals of its program to release the potential of a servant ministry? Is it sensitive to the widespread gap between the academic and the practical?[4]

In terms of missiological contextualization, Stackhouse's proposal does offer distinctions between contextuality, contextualization, and contextualism, but it may not be sensitive to the various dimensions of teaching and learning styles. These styles affect the openness to address issues in the churches and those of human development and justice. A highly cognitive and academic style may preclude extensive dialogue with many in the churches and

---

4. TEF staff, *Ministry in Context: The Third Mandate Programme of the Theological Education Fund (1970-77)* (Bromley, Kent, England: Theological Education Fund, 1972), p. 31.

those struggling with human development and issues of oppression at points where the immediate crises of life demand suspension of reflective leisure.

In terms of structural contextualization, this proposal is quite radical, but in another sense it may not be sufficiently radical to realize a necessary transformation in forms and structures. It emphasizes the radical importance of theological education and the impact of religion on society. Yet in this proposal the prime vehicle for the radical transformation of life is the theological school. Stackhouse has opted for a schooling model with resulting commitments to the academies of theological education. What may be needed are closer linkages with the churches and other organizations, institutions, and groups in the wider society. The investment of Western society in schooling (which includes education at seminaries) must be recognized, but the insights of "deschoolers" such as Ivan Illich must be considered in exploring alternative networks and linkages for theological education. These networks and linkages demand more creative forms and structures than those that currently exist. In particular, networks must include local churches and denominations. This point is made in the discussion of Chapter 11 but not adequately developed.

In relation to theological contextualization, this proposal represents a genuine and masterful effort to do theology in a way that is appropriate and authentic to the context of an ecumenical Protestant seminary. It seeks to relate the gospel to urgent issues of ministry and service to the world and to address current concerns regarding contextualization, globalization, and mission. But, while it grapples with insights from a variety of individuals, it needs to further relate these insights to personal and corporate commitments in the church. Feminist and minority contributors must share alternative visions that are similarly integrative.

In consideration of the fourth and final category of pedagogical contextualization, Stackhouse's work can be judged as contributing to liberation and creativity through the careful articulation of an alternative and comprehensive vision. There is some justification for the opinion that this vision calls for elitism, because behind this study stands a very high doctrine of the responsibility and authority of the clergy and a view that theology (or theological ethics) remains the queen of the sciences. Nevertheless, from my perspective, this study has sought to be faithful to Christian foundations and to bridge the perceived gap between the academic and the practical.

As might be anticipated from my evangelical heritage, I am both critical and supportive of Stackhouse's emphasis. His delineation of Christian orthodoxy is perhaps too broad, yet it recognizes the potential of both decontextualization and contextualization. Contextualization can be defined as the continual process by which God's truth and justice are applied to and emerge in concrete historical situations. Decontextualization can be defined as the judgment of the Word of God that transforms personal, social, cultural, political, and economic spheres of life.[5] The first process is contextualization, which necessitates a dialogue between the Christian individual or community and the context of ministry. In this first process a hermeneutic of the world in its social and cultural particularity is required. The second process is decontextualization, which necessitates dialogue between the Christian individual or community and the transcendent text of the Scriptures. In this second process a hermeneutic of the Word is required. Both processes complement one another and are necessary for a faithful response to the gospel demand of being in but not of the world. Stackhouse is sensitive to both of these processes in his proposal and must be commended for his work.

In sum, this work represents a formative effort to develop a comprehensive vision for theological education that merits the careful consideration of all those called to this ministry. It deserves serious reading and discussion by a wide variety of individuals at all levels of the Christian global community.

---

5. See Harvie M. Conn, "Contextualization: Where Do We Begin?" in *Evangelicals and Liberation*, ed. Carl E. Armerding (Nutley, N.J.: Presbyterian and Reformed Publishing Co., 1977), p. 104.

www.ingramcontent.com/pod-product-compliance
Lightning Source LLC
Chambersburg PA
CBHW020646230426
43665CB00008B/335